Changing Patterns
of Voting in the
Northern United States

Robert W. Speel

Changing Patterns of Voting in the Northern United States

Electoral Realignment
1952–1996

The Pennsylvania State University Press
University Park, Pennsylvania

Library of Congress Cataloging-in-Publication Data

Speel, Robert W.
    Changing patterns of voting in the Northern United States :
electoral realignment 1952–1996 / Robert W. Speel.

        p.   cm.
    Includes bibliographical references and index.
    ISBN 0-271-01784-8 (alk. paper)
    1. Voting—New England—History—20th century.   2. Voting
—Snowbelt States—History—20th century.   3. Party affiliation—New
England—History—20th century.   4. Party affiliation—Snowbelt
States—History—20th century.   5. Republican Party (U.S. : 1854–   )
—History—20th century.   I. Title.
JK2295.N53S65   1998
324.974'044—DC21   98-17050
                                                                          CIP

It is the policy of The Pennsylvania State University Press to use acid-free paper for the
first printing of all clothbound books. Publications on uncoated stock satisfy the mini-
mum requirements of American National Standard for Information Sciences—Permanence
of Paper for Printed Library Materials, ANSI Z39.48–1992.

Contents

———⟶●⟵———

List of Tables

———►◄———

Preface

—————

When independent presidential candidate John Anderson managed to win only about 7 percent of the vote in November 1980, his candidacy and his cause seemed to become something of a national joke, and his run for the presidency was forgotten by most people soon after the election. When Democratic presidential candidate Michael Dukakis lost the 1988 election, he became a national joke soon afterward, even though his performance was the best of any Northern Democratic presidential candidate since 1960, and the second best since 1948.

While much of the country rejected these two candidates and their beliefs, each of the two doomed presidential bids had strong pockets of support in parts of the Northern United States. Anderson and Dukakis, the governor of Massachusetts, did particularly well in New England.

As a native New Englander, raised amid the often colorful politics of the state of Rhode Island, I wondered if my home region, with its long-declining share of the national population, still played any significant role in national political trends. Or, alternatively, did the recent patterns of voting behavior found in New England represent merely an eccentric opposition to the type of political leaders favored elsewhere in the United States?

This book began with a desire to understand recent New England politics and how the politics of that region fit into other recent political trends found in the United States. The chapters that follow document that recent politics in New England are not isolated from political trends found in the rest of the United States, and that they have in fact represented the strongest examples of trends found throughout much of the northern tier of the nation, trends that have led to victories by the Democrats in the last two presidential elections.

While the book argues that a clear electoral realignment has occurred in the Northern United States since 1950, it does not examine realignment in the way traditionally found in other studies. Rather than focus on critical elections, I argue that the North has realigned more gradually; instead of using public opinion surveys for data, I rely on voting statistics;

and rather than argue that split-ticket voting reflects a dealignment of voters, I incorporate such voting behavior into a new form of realignment.

I wish to thank many people for their assistance in preparing this book and for influencing my thoughts. Lee Benson at the University of Pennsylvania first introduced me to the concept of realignment in a freshman history seminar, and his teaching influenced me more than I ever let him know. In my graduate studies at Cornell University, Martin Shefter was of immeasurable help with his suggestions and comments about my research on electoral behavior. He is also responsible for putting me in contact with Penn State Press to publish this work, for which I will always be grateful.

Also at Cornell, Ted Lowi introduced me to many of the wonderful past studies of individual state politics. Milton Esman helped to expand my knowledge of ethnic politics, which is so important to understanding political trends in the United States. Ben Ginsberg, now at Johns Hopkins University, gave me a great understanding of practical politics and the hidden motives and strategies politicians have that can be instrumental in causing realignments. Sheila Jasanoff and Sidney Tarrow were also of great help in reading some of my early research efforts. Two friends I made at Cornell, David Patton and David Reynolds, have also kindly listened to me go on and on about my research over the years, and have commented in response.

At my current position at Penn State Erie, I wish to thank Roberta Salper for reading my original manuscript and making comments, and also to thank Gwen Pellam, Samuel Epps, and Michael Woycheck for their research assistance on aspects of the book. My students in all my courses have always provided a chance to test and reevaluate my ideas, and I thank them for that.

At Penn State Press, Director Sanford Thatcher has been a great help in advising me how to get my manuscript to market, and I am grateful that he found it worthy of publication. Copy Editor Peggy Hoover amazed me with the diligence and care she took while going through my manuscript, which allowed me to communicate my ideas better than I could on my own.

My father, Rodney Speel, and mother, Roberta Ward, deserve thanks for introducing me to an interest in politics at an early age, as do my paternal grandparents, J. Kenton and Dorothy Speel, for maintaining my political interest as I grew up in Rhode Island. My maternal grandmother,

Celia Weinstein, has been a great support to me through the years, for which I can never thank her enough.

Finally, I wish to thank Sheba and Renard, two very patient dogs, who sat quietly at the door looking at me on countless occasions, while I asked them to please wait until I finished the next page.

Chapter One

Realignment in Historical Perspective

In 1896, William McKinley, the Republican candidate for president of the United States, won an easy electoral college victory, sweeping the states of the Northeast, the Pacific Coast states of California and Oregon, and all the Midwestern states except for Missouri and some states in the Great Plains (South Dakota, Nebraska, Kansas). Populist Democratic candidate William Jennings Bryan lost the election but captured all the states of the South and the Rocky Mountain West, as well as Missouri and the three Great Plains states McKinley lost. Political scientists studying American elections have traditionally labeled the presidential election of 1896 as a classic realignment, where the partisan voting patterns of large numbers of Americans are disrupted and permanent partisan preferences change.[1]

Exactly one hundred years later, in 1996, Democratic presidential candidate Bill Clinton won his electoral college victory by sweeping all the states of the Northeast, the Pacific Coast states of California, Oregon, and Washington, and all the Midwestern states except Indiana (home to the Republican vice presidential candidate) and the Great Plains states of North Dakota, South Dakota, Nebraska, and Kansas. Republican presidential candidate Bob Dole's best election performances came in the South, where he won a majority of that region's electoral votes, in the Great Plains, and in the Rocky Mountain West, where he won more

1. For examples, see Walter Dean Burnham, *Critical Elections and the Mainsprings of American Politics* (New York: W. W. Norton & Company, 1970); James L. Sundquist, *Dynamics of the Party System* (Washington, D.C.: The Brookings Institution, 1983); and E. E. Schattschneider, *The Semi-Sovereign People* (New York: Holt, Rinehart & Winston, 1960).

than half the states in the region. Clinton's Democratic victory in 1996 duplicated almost exactly the Republican victory of 1896 in every region of the nation. Clinton also won almost exactly the same set of states in 1992. While some ventured to call the 1994 congressional elections in favor of the Republicans a national realignment, few political scientists seem to want to point to the presidential election results of the 1990s as another indicator of realignment.

On its own, the 1996 presidential election cannot yet be labeled as a permanent realignment. The analysis that led political scientists to conclude that the 1896 election signified major political changes among the American electorate occurred dozens of years after that election, and any lasting impacts of the 1996 election will not be known for certain until many years have passed. However, when the 1996 election is examined as one of a series of presidential elections over the previous fifty years, a clear realigning pattern emerges. The pattern does not necessarily match up with any from the nineteenth century, nor does it fit exactly with the patterns political scientists have devised to describe elections of the past. Using these electoral patterns of the past, political scientists have been reluctant to label political trends since the 1950s as a realignment, because no election of a so-called "critical" nature has occurred, nor have voting trends been consistent at all office levels. In addition, public opinion polls have shown an increase in voters who are unwilling to describe themselves as attached to any political party.

Yet since 1952, much of the northern tier of the United States has grown more Democratic in presidential elections, almost the entire South has become more Republican, and these changes have been occurring on a persistently increasing basis with each election. Attempts to analyze the 1952–1996 period solely through a framework created to study political patterns before 1940 will undoubtedly show that the later patterns do not fit the earlier patterns. Voters in the 1990s are better educated than those in earlier decades, and they are exposed to a mass media that could not even be imagined in the nineteenth century.

The realignment pattern of 1952–1996, which became most apparent when the Democratic presidential election victories of 1992 and 1996 mirrored the Republican presidential election victory of 1896, has not clearly replicated the realignment patterns of the past. But if the recent realignment is understood to have been gradual, rather than critical, in nature, and if actual voting behavior in the American states is studied, rather than national public opinion polls, and if a concept of "federalized realignment" is recognized, in which partisan voting patterns may consistently and rationally differ by office level, then the political changes in the American electorate since 1952 can be recognized as a realignment every bit as significant and as strong as those of the past.

The political scientist who first made popular the concept of realignment to describe partisan changes among the electorate was V. O. Key. Key, studying the voting patterns of two Massachusetts communities in the 1920s, published "A Theory of Critical Elections" in 1955.[2] Key found that 1928 was a critical election in Massachusetts in establishing Democratic dominance in an urban, Catholic, low-income community and strong Republican dominance in a Protestant rural community. In the 1916 and 1920 presidential elections, both towns had leaned toward the Republicans in similar proportions. Although the charts Key presented in his 1955 article showed that a realignment process had clearly begun throughout New England by 1924, he focused mostly on the 1928 election as the critical realignment—a point that will be addressed further in the next few pages.

Since 1955, several other authors have used Key's concept of realignment in their own studies. In *The American Voter*, Angus Campbell, Philip Converse, Warren Miller, and Donald Stokes, near the conclusion of their book on electoral behavior, discussed a classification of presidential elections: "maintaining" elections, in which partisan attachments remain stable; "deviating" elections, in which voters temporarily switch parties based on candidate or short-term issue appeal; and "realigning" elections, in which large groups of voters shift party loyalties on a more permanent basis.[3]

Walter Dean Burnham's *Critical Elections and the Mainsprings of American Politics* perhaps brought critical realignment theory to its full fruition.[4] Burnham defined critical realignments as characterized by short-lived intense disruptions of traditional voting patterns, high political intensity, and reorganization of party coalitions and policy choices. He did look at how such realignments play out at the state level, and he did discuss possible realignments over the issues of the 1960s, but he did not seem to consider state-level or gradual realignments as being significant like national critical realignments.

2. V. O. Key Jr., "A Theory of Critical Elections," *Journal of Politics* 17 (1955), 3–18.

3. Angus Campbell, Philip E. Converse, Warren E. Miller, and Donald E. Stokes, *The American Voter* (New York: John Wiley & Sons, 1960), 531–538.

4. Burnham, *Critical Elections*.

James L. Sundquist also described the major critical realignments in American history in *Dynamics of the Party System*, but he classified gradual and regional realignments as "minor."[5] In 1983 he wrote that the New Deal party system remained dominant in American politics. A few remnants of the New Deal system do remain in contemporary American politics, but it is almost certain that a political scientist in 1940 could not have predicted accurately the 1996 electoral returns in various states and among various groups based on the politics of the Roosevelt era.

In 1959, Key published an article titled "Secular Realignment and the Party System,"[6] offering a concept that might be much more significant in American politics but that is cited less often than his "Theory of Critical Elections." In the 1959 article, Key ignored his data on critical elections and instead showed the gradual shifts in partisan support in differing types of towns in Northern New England from the 1910s to the 1940s. Key noted that what he called secular partisan change in the United States may be significant because the slow movement allowed preparation time for accommodation both to new groups coming to power and to old groups that were shrinking in size or importance.[7] Such secular realignments probably played a larger role in New England politics of the 1920s than Key seemed to realize in his "Critical Elections" article.

An update of Key's 1955 "Critical Elections" demonstrates this well. Key chose the Massachusetts towns of Somerville and Ashfield to make his argument—Somerville being a low-income, Catholic city near Boston, and Ashfield being a rural, agricultural, Protestant village in the western part of the state.[8] The characters of these two communities remain basically the same in the 1990s. A third Massachusetts community—the Boston suburb of Quincy—was not included in Key's study, but it makes a useful comparison to the first two. Quincy, predominantly Catholic, is "filled with the grandsons and granddaughters of Irish, Italian, and Jewish immigrants"[9] but is somewhat more middle-class than Somerville.

---

5. Sundquist, *Dynamics of the Party System*.

6. V. O. Key Jr., "Secular Realignment and the Party System," *Journal of Politics* 21 (1959), 198–210.

7. Ibid., 209.

8. Key, "Critical Elections," 5.

9. Michael Barone and Grant Ujifusa, *The Almanac of American Politics 1988* (Washington, D.C.: National Journal, 1987), 571.

Table 1.1 shows the Democratic percentage of the major-party vote for president for each community between 1944 and 1992. Somerville became even more Democratic in presidential elections than when Key's article appeared. Quincy also became more Democratic, although Democratic strength declined after hitting a peak in the 1960s. But Ashfield, where the Democratic share of the presidential vote hovered around 10 to 15 percent from 1924 to 1956, showed the sharpest Democratic gains of the three towns in the last forty years. In 1984, Protestant Ashfield surpassed, for the first time since the New Deal, Catholic Quincy in support for a Democratic presidential candidate, and in 1988, for the first time in the twentieth century, Ashfield gave a majority of its votes to a Democrat for president. The town has gained some population, which possibly includes many of the new Democratic voters, but Republican vote totals actually decreased while the population grew. In 1956, Republican Dwight Eisenhower received 467 votes for president in Ashfield; in 1976, Republican Gerald Ford received 415 votes; in 1984, Republican Ronald Reagan received 414 votes; in 1988, Republican George Bush received only 366 votes and in 1992 managed only 216 votes. The total vote in the town grew from 530 to 990 over the period.[10]

The partisan changes in Ashfield's presidential voting occurred gradually. During the period, there was no great political crisis or overriding political issue of the sort that many political scientists have searched for to label an election as the key to a critical realignment. But in towns like Ashfield and states of the Northern United States, dramatic changes have nevertheless occurred since the 1930s—changes that have occurred gradually, have differed by state, and have not always been consistent across presidential, congressional, and state office elections. The South is no longer safely Democratic; in fact, it is actually one of the safest Republican areas in presidential elections. The isolationist states of the Midwest are not all among the most Republican in the nation. Iowa gave Democratic presidential candidate Michael Dukakis his second-best state-winning percentage in 1988. These are not "maintaining" or temporary "deviating" processes, as described in *The American Voter*. They indicate realignment, one that may not occur quickly or nationally but one that is significant to politics at both the state and the federal level.

Part of the reason many political scientists have been reluctant to label recent electoral changes as realignment has to do with different concepts

---

10. *Manual for the General Court of Massachusetts* (Boston: Causeway Print, several editions).

Table 1.1. Democratic percentage of major party (Democratic, Republican) vote in presidential elections in three Massachusetts towns, 1944–1992

Town	1944	1948	1952	1956	1960	1964	1968	1972	1976	1980*	1984	1988	1992*
Ashfield	16	13	10	11	21	50	26	41	41	42	50	59	71
Quincy	42	48	39	36	60	76	68	57	58	50	49	53	61
Somerville	54	67	55	49	75	87	81	67	72	64	65	71	77

SOURCES: For 1944–88, Manual for the General Court of Massachusetts (Boston: Causeway Print, several editions). For 1992, Office of the Secretary cf State of Massachusetts.

of the term "realignment." Political theorists of the phenomenon have often looked for creation of a new national majority party, overriding political issues that change political cleavages during a short period, and the infusion of large new groups of voters into the electorate. None of these events has been apparent in the last fifty years. Yet such a limited view of electoral change has often been shaped by spotlighting three or four points in American history and trying to find factors that these few have in common. What this view misses is the more continuous change through American history of the social forces that make up each political party.

Key addressed these gradual processes in his article "Secular Realignment." And John Petrocik has also argued in favor of a social-group coalition approach to electoral change, including change gradual in nature, stating that "almost any other model of the party-voter alignment ignores politics in the ordinary sense of the word and deals too lightly with the persistent and substantively significant sociodemographic differences between supporters of the Republican and Democratic parties."[11] Petrocik added that changes in the social base of a party will obviously be reflected in the party's stands on the issues. However, it is also important to note that changes in a party's stands on the issues are a major component in actually changing the party's social base.

In recent years, Gary Jacobson and Morris Fiorina have written about how members of Congress use their positions to take stands and perform activities in an effort to aid their own reelection rather than make good policy or strengthen their party.[12] Some political scientists, such as Everett Carll Ladd, have concluded that the party dealigning process of the 1960s and 1970s allowed "political individualism [to triumph] over institutional and collective requirements."[13]

Yet an emphasis on individual candidates in modern political campaigns need not rule out the importance of party labels in those same

11. John R. Petrocik, *Party Coalitions* (Chicago: University of Chicago Press, 1981), 19. Petrocik notes in the book the decline in support for Republicans in the North. However, his use of surveys of partisan preferences rather than election statistics seems to underestimate the trend toward the Democrats in the region.

12. Morris P. Fiorina, *Congress: Keystone of the Washington Establishment* (New Haven: Yale University Press, 1989); Gary C. Jacobson, *The Politics of Congressional Elections* (Boston: Little, Brown & Company, 1987).

13. Everett Carll Ladd, "The Shifting Party Coalitions, from the 1930s to the 1970s," in Seymour Martin Lipset, ed., *Party Coalitions in the 1980s* (San Francisco: Institute for Contemporary Studies, 1981), 148.

campaigns. Many candidates from one party usually adopt similar messages in their candidacies, and even if the efforts are not directly tied together, a persistent type of appeal coming from one party is often remembered by voters. In addition, national party strategies have continued in the era of individual candidates, and these strategies have frequently found success in recent years.

Several authors have written about coalition-building strategies that parties have used to attract groups of voters in the last few decades. Frances Fox Piven and Richard Cloward cited Democratic support for the 1960s civil rights movement as arising from a necessity for votes in the South: "The Southern blacks represented a huge untapped pool of potential Democratic voters; their numbers could affect Southern white defections."[14] In the 1980s, authors such as Seymour Martin Lipset, Benjamin Ginsberg, and Martin Shefter described a New Politics movement of feminists, environmentalists, and other liberal middle-class forces, which increased its influence within the Democratic party, while Ronald Reagan and his supporters used issues such as tax cuts, defense spending, and school prayer to attract a majority of voters to the Republican party in presidential elections and in some elections at lower levels.[15]

While political appeals to groups of voters may cause partisan realignments, a political appeal by itself is not sufficient. Campaigning on abortion rights is probably not a winning strategy in Utah. A movement to teach creation science in high schools is unlikely to realign Massachusetts. It is only when such issues tap into a set of views that are generally supportive of the values or ideas behind the issue that political appeals can cause large voter shifts. For this reason, national Democratic support for socially liberal policies has lost the party many supporters in the South and among certain ethnic groups. Meanwhile, national Republican conservative policies have gained support among these groups. What has been less noticed is that such conservative policy stands may have lost the Republicans support in some of the party's historically stronger areas outside the South.

14. Frances Fox Piven and Richard A. Cloward, *Poor People's Movements* (New York: Vintage Books, 1979), 231.

15. Benjamin Ginsberg and Martin Shefter, "A Critical Realignment? The New Politics, the Reconstituted Right, and the 1984 Election," in Michael Nelson, ed., *The Elections of 1984* (Washington, D.C.: Congressional Quarterly, 1985), 1–25; Seymour Martin Lipset, "Party Coalitions and the 1980 Election," in Lipset, ed., *Party Coalitions in the 1980s*, 15–46.

Relatively few authors have examined deeply enough this important connection between political appeals and the political culture or the political environment of an area in realignments. Two who have include historian Lee Benson and political scientist Martin Shefter. Benson, in *The Concept of Jacksonian Democracy*, found that the national party platforms of the 1820s and 1830s, a period of shifting party loyalties, contributed to the realignment of various ethnic groups in national politics. As one example, he shows a mostly Dutch county in New York becoming solidly Democratic in the 1826–1832 period, while an upstate English Yankee county with a large population turnover became solidly Whig. The state as a whole remained fairly evenly divided between the two parties.[16]

Shefter, in an article on the Progressive era (1900–1920), wrote that the Progressive movement had more success in realigning parties of Western states, such as California, because the national parties of the time stressed issues that were of minimal interest in the region, and therefore local party organizations had been weak. In Eastern states, such as New York, strong party machines had developed to attract supporters for the national parties and their policies, and these machines were able to maintain their coalitions after the initial appeal of the Progressives had passed.[17]

The Benson and Shefter works both show how political appeals can affect political environments differently and how the right combination of a political appeal to a political environment can cause a realignment of voters. Benson looked at the ethnic and religious aspects of political culture that became key in a critical realignment, while Shefter focused on the historical development of two state political environments and the varying impact of an independent movement on partisan politics in the two states.

Shefter and Benson also demonstrated the importance of examining partisan voting behavior at the state level. Many political scientists conclude that between the large realignments of the 1890s and 1930s, no other realignments occurred of the same magnitude, but this is true only for the nation as a whole. Burnham, for example, found major electoral

16. Lee Benson, *The Concept of Jacksonian Democracy* (Princeton: Princeton University Press, 1961), 293–317.
17. Martin Shefter, "Regional Receptivity to Reform: The Legacy of the Progressive Era," *Political Science Quarterly* 98 (1983), 459–483.

shifts in individual states within the period, but declined to label these as realignments.[18]

Studies of individual state politics seem to have become less popular since the 1950s and 1960s, when books such as Duane Lockard's *New England State Politics*, John Fenton's *Midwest Politics*, and V. O. Key's classic *Southern Politics* each took state-by-state looks at local political values, attitudes, and practices.[19] These books examined the many political themes and leaders of each state in a designated region of the nation and used voting statistics to analyze how political themes affected differing areas of political culture within each state. V. O. Key, in *American State Politics*, noted: "In the organization and spirit of their politics, the states vary markedly. Their oddities and variations may be accounted for in part by the fact that they are members of a federal system. The impact of national policies and parties powerfully influences the form and behavior of state political systems. The manner in which that impact strikes different states differently constituted and situated contributes to the variation in organization and conduct of state politics."[20]

A few political scientists, realizing the significance of the separate political arenas that make up the United States, have studied the secular realignments at the state level that have clearly occurred since World War II. Harold Lamis's *The Two-Party South* is a good update of Key's *Southern Politics*. Like Key, Lamis examined each state individually to discover the differing state factors that all led in one direction—the strengthening of the Republican party throughout the region.[21] A volume edited by Peter Galderisi, Michael Lyons, Randy Simmons, and John Francis noted similar trends in the Rocky Mountain States, previously a Democratic stronghold along with the South and now containing the most Republican states in the nation.[22]

18. Burnham, *Critical Elections*, 22–23. Burnham does seem to show that no realignment occurred in six states around the 1912 Progressive presidential candidacy of Theodore Roosevelt, but for two of the six states shown, his statistical table for the period indicates changes in party strength between 1900 and 1925 as large as those in the 1890s and 1930s.

19. V. O. Key Jr., *Southern Politics* (New York: Alfred A. Knopf, 1949); Duane Lockard, *New England State Politics* (Princeton: Princeton University Press, 1959); John H. Fenton, *Midwest Politics* (New York: Holt, Rinehart & Winston, 1966).

20. V. O. Key Jr., *American State Politics: An Introduction* (New York: Alfred A. Knopf, 1956), 19–20.

21. Alexander P. Lamis, *The Two-Party South* (New York: Oxford University Press, 1984).

22. Peter F. Galderisi, Michael S. Lyons, Randy T. Simmons, and John G. Francis, *The Politics of Realignment: Party Change in the Mountain West* (Boulder, Colo.: Westview Press, 1987).

The best-known literature on realignment, though, tends to ignore or dismiss the types of data presented earlier, with a claim that realignment is not occurring; instead a process of dealignment or weakening party attachment has permeated American electoral politics. Much of the evidence for dealignment theory has come from public opinion surveys that found that fewer and fewer voters identify themselves with a political party. According to dealignment theory, voter preferences depend on passing valence issues and individual candidate appeal, with residual party loyalties remaining weak from election to election.[23]

However, the arguments that just dealignment and not realignment has occurred in recent years are valid only if one recognizes realignments as occurring over brief periods and necessarily creating a new dominant party over all election levels. Maybe voters no longer go to polling places and pull straight party levers without knowing for whom they are voting or why, most of the time, but they still retain general ideological and value preferences from election to election. If one party consistently appeals to these preferences over a period of time, that party is likely to gain voter support at the expense of an opposing party that is less openly supportive of the preferences. Because of the American system of federalism, it is possible for a national party to emphasize one group of issues while its affiliated state party emphasizes different issues altogether. Therefore, if one recognizes that realignments can occur gradually and can differ by political office levels, then the political realignments that have occurred in much of the Northern United States in recent years become obvious.

Standard critical realignment and dealignment theory has missed the significance of recent electoral trends in three ways by focusing too much on critical elections, national voter surveys, and the need for united party government, and by focusing too little on gradual electoral trends, state and regional voting data, and the possibility of rational and consistent voter behavior behind split-ticket voting. First, by looking for realignment over a brief one or two presidential election period, critical realignment theorists miss the gradual electoral shifts that can cause political and policy changes after a thirty-year period, which are just as significant as those caused after an eight-year period. Key himself, in his "Secular Realignment" article, alluded to this significance.

---

23. Everett Carll Ladd Jr. and Charles D. Hadley, *Transformations of the American Party System* (New York: W. W. Norton & Company, 1978), 320–333.

In addition, the role of critical elections in the great policy changes in the past may have been overstated.[24] As Key showed in his "Secular Realignment" article, towns all over Northern New England changed gradually in partisan preferences during the 1910–1940 period, of which the 1928–1936 "critical" period was only a part. If the partisan preferences of an area have shifted in one direction for thirty years, spotlighting a briefer period in which this trend has a greater magnitude may be interesting but can lead to ignoring some of the factors that played a role in the realignment. Again, Key seemed to make such an omission himself in his article "Critical Elections," in which he downplayed the 1924 election, which his own charts showed was the beginning of divergence between Catholic and Protestant voting.

A second problem in much of the writing on critical realignment and dealignment is the tendency for writers to look solely at national data encompassing large demographic and socioeconomic groups when examining causes of partisan shifts (Burnham and Sundquist are notable exceptions here). Such studies often depend on national surveys of voters who are asked their party identification.[25] Besides the problems inherent in survey research, including the ambiguity of asking people with which party they identify, such a broad statistical overview can also obscure realigning forces occurring at the state level.

24. Joel Silbey has recently questioned the assertion that the United States has undergone four critical realignments in its history. He claims that studies of elections instead show periods of increasing partisan alignment up until the 1890s, and a pattern of declining partisan alignment ever since. However, Silbey's framework apparently does not recognize the consistent gradual shifts of many areas toward or away from one party in the last forty years as realignments. Joel H. Silbey, "Beyond Realignment and Realignment Theory: American Political Eras, 1789–1989," in Byron E. Shafer, ed., *The End of Realignment?* (Madison: University of Wisconsin Press, 1991), 3–23.

25. For example, see Paul A. Abramson, John H. Aldrich, and David W. Rohde, *Change and Continuity in the 1988 Elections* (Washington, D.C.: Congressional Quarterly, 1991); and Norman H. Nie, Sidney Verba, and John R. Petrocik, *The Changing American Voter* (Cambridge, Mass.: Harvard University Press, 1979). The authors of *The Changing American Voter* do spot clear regional realignments, including a trend among Northern Protestants toward Democratic presidential candidates in the 1952–1972 period. The book also states: "A party realignment is a substantial change in the support that various social groups give to the political parties. If a group shifts its support from one party to the other or if a group that had no particular partisan bias comes to support one of the parties, there has been an important change in the party/vote alignment. . . . But a movement of social groups from one party to the other does not necessarily imply a net change in the relative strength of the two parties" (213). Yet the book, in its conclusion, discounts these earlier assertions and focuses instead on the decline of party identification and the decline of party consistency when voting, both measured through national survey data, to argue that some form of dealignment or "party decomposition" is occurring.

The secular realignment of the American electorate since 1950 is easily detectable only by breaking down the national data among the states and looking at actual voting results rather than surveys. Looking at broad national socioeconomic groups in surveys often reveals important political changes, such as the gender gap and racial attitudes, but can actually miss much of the diversity of the states and their electoral patterns. Examining the political attitudes of Americans of African ancestry is essential to understanding national politics, but such attitudes explain nothing about the politics of Northern New England, where blacks make up a minuscule proportion of the population. Similarly, examining the attitudes of people of Norwegian ancestry may provide clues into Minnesota's politics but provides very little to explain trends in Louisiana. By focusing almost exclusively on national survey data to analyze modern realignment, some political scientists have completely missed either the existence or the best explanation of realignments in many of the states.[26]

A third and final problem with current conventional wisdom among those who study American elections is the growing popularity of the theory that dealignment, but not realignment, is occurring. Proponents of the theory of dealignment usually point to differing partisan results in presidential, congressional, and state-office elections as evidence of the decline in consistent voter preferences.[27] If dealignment is understood solely as an increase in split-ticket voting, then it is an accurate description. However, few supporters of dealignment theory stop with that simple assertion; instead, they go on to attribute the phenomenon of increased split-ticket voting to a decline in any party attachments (as measured by surveys asking for party identification) and to the growth of candidate-centered campaigns.

26. Many historical studies have studied realignment in the states, but it is rare for the current period. Relevant works of history include Joel H. Silbey and Samuel T. McSeveney, eds., *Voters, Parties, and Elections* (Lexington, Mass.: Xerox College Publishing, 1972); and Joel H. Silbey, Allan G. Bogue, and William H. Flanigan, eds., *The History of American Electoral Behavior* (Princeton: Princeton University Press, 1978).

27. Sundquist argues that voters cannot realign until they choose to switch to their new party for all offices. "Divergence between national and state-local political behavior is inherently unstable. A voter who identifies with one party nationally and another locally enters into such a contradiction with reluctance in the first place; once in it, he normally feels some degree of pressure to resolve it. . . . The realignment of that individual voter cannot be considered to have occurred until the reidentification is completed, for until that time the possibility exists that the conflict may be resolved the other way and the voter may turn out to have been only a deviant. As long as the conflict is unresolved—and that may last many years, even a lifetime—the realignment is only in process; it has not yet happened" (*Dynamics of the Party System*, 228–229).

Critical election theorists have generally believed that declines in party attachments following the critical period were temporary in the past and set the stage for a new critical realignment. However, many of these theorists now believe that the declines are more permanent and imply that partisan voting now is more random, with candidate personalities and transient issues overcoming the importance of partisan attachments in voting. Rarely considered is the possibility that voters may actually have strategic reasons for choosing a Republican for one office and a Democrat for another office, reasons other than either a preference for divided party government or differing expectations of institutions. If the national Republican party stresses lots of defense spending and prayer in the schools, while the state Republican party emphasizes cuts in government spending and environmental regulation, any voter could easily and rationally vote against a Republican presidential candidate and for a Republican gubernatorial candidate. And in addition, if the national Democratic party opposes school prayer and favors cuts in defense spending, while the state Democratic party takes the opposite stands, any voter could rationally vote for different parties at different office levels. Any voter choosing among the parties in such a way would have a difficult time answering standard party identification questions on a survey, and interpreting such a survey's results as clearly indicating a decline in the consistent use of parties as a cue in voting would be an error.

Because of our system of representation, in which national party leaders have no control over whom the state parties decide to support, differences in issues stressed by presidential candidates and state office candidates of the same party have existed since the beginning of the American republic. Such differences existed during the 1930s critical realignment when Northern and Southern Democrats used very different appeals in their respective regions to gain votes. For a brief period in the 1930s and early 1940s, the differing strategies taken by the national and state Democratic parties managed to increase or maintain support for the national party in both the North and the South. But the later outcome of the same strategies, in which partisan competition at the presidential level differed from partisan competition in state elections in many areas, should be seen as an obvious alternative to the outcome on which realignment theorists usually focus—that in which one party dominates at all levels. This recent variant of electoral change, which separates presidential partisan voting from partisan voting in state elections, can accurately be described as "federalized realignment."

Individual elections continue to contain various economic issues or foreign policy crisis issues, which can swing less attached voters between parties from election to election. But many, and probably most, voters retain ideological and value preferences that make their partisan voting relatively consistent over election periods. These preferences may cause voters to support a different party in state office elections than in presidential elections. And these preferences may cause voters to vote against their usual party choice when the party presents an occasional candidate of differing views and ideology, an event that has repeated itself hundreds of times in the nineteenth and twentieth centuries both. Overall, though, voter consistency probably remains as strong as it was during the years of sometimes mythical partisan voting consistency, even if the consistency now revolves more around issue and value preferences than supporting one party for all offices.

If voters in an area consistently vote for candidates that express a similar set of values and views, and do not support those with opposite values and views, it seems highly inaccurate to label these voters as ideologically adrift in a sea of candidate personalities and transient issues. And if parties at the state level relatively consistently nominate candidates with similar values and views, even if these differ from the values and views of the national party's candidates, and if voters of the state respond by generally favoring one party for state elections, even if the same group of voters favor a different party in presidential elections, it seems highly inaccurate to label such a pattern only with the somewhat negatively tainted term of "dealignment" without also acknowledging some of the consistency and rationality of the state's voter behavior. Instead the voters could be more accurately labeled as undergoing a federalized realignment.

Table 1.1, which gives recent presidential election data for three Massachusetts towns, also demonstrates well the gradual, federalized, and local or regional nature of recent realignment in the United States. In Ashfield, there has been a clear gradual upward trend in support for the Democrats since 1960 (the 1964 landslide briefly exaggerates the trend). Quincy and Somerville possibly exhibit instead a classical "critical" realignment in the 1960–1964 period, with dramatic increases in support for the Democrats, followed by a slow and gradual drop-off, but still at levels of support higher than before 1960. But the two towns also indicate the need to look for regional and state realignments that may be lost in national survey data. The voting trends of Quincy and Somerville are common to heavily Catholic areas of the Northeast and the Midwest but are not found elsewhere, a phenomenon that will be discussed in later chapters. The purported gains of Republicans among Catholics during the 1970s and 1980s seemed mainly to be a rebound following the temporarily very high popularity of Democrats in the 1960s. Democratic presidential candidates still did better in Catholic, middle-class Quincy in the 1980s than they did when the New Deal coalition was stronger, in the 1940s and 1950s.

Besides demonstrating the gradual and regional realignments of Massachusetts, Table 1.1 also partly helps to show how realignment can vary among different office levels. Throughout the 1950s, 1960s, and 1970s, the Republican percentage of Ashfield's presidential vote had been dropping, from a high of 90 percent in 1952 to 59 percent in 1972 and 1976. In 1980, Reagan received 58 percent of the major party vote but only 44 percent overall (Independent candidate John Anderson received 21 percent of Ashfield's votes), and in 1984 and 1988, Republican presidential candidates received only 50 percent and 41 percent, respectively, of the town's major party votes. All through the 1980s, the Massachusetts Republican party made the apparent mistake of nominating Reagan-style conservatives for statewide office, all of whom lost by large margins. Ashfield voted for Democratic statewide candidates in the 1980s, but its voting record in 1978, a time when the town was clearly turning against Republican presidential candidates, is indicative of the town's true preferences.

In 1978, liberal Republican Francis Hatch faced conservative Democrat Ed King in the state governor's race, while liberal Republican Edward Brooke ran for reelection to the U.S. Senate against liberal Democrat Paul Tsongas. Before 1980, Massachusetts Republicans had been nominating moderates and liberals for dozens of years, candidates that usually received much support in Ashfield. In 1978, Hatch received an overwhelming 80 percent of Ashfield's votes, while Brooke won 63 percent of the vote in the town.[28] Meanwhile the rest of the state elected the two Democrats, King and Tsongas, to their respective offices. Ashfield's voters clearly preferred the traditional type of Massachusetts moderate Republicanism to Reagan's style of conservative Republicanism, and were willing to vote for Republicans at the state level while increasingly rejecting them at the presidential level.

28. *Manual for the General Court of Massachusetts*, 1979–80.

In 1990, the Massachusetts Republican party returned to its moderate roots and nominated William Weld for governor over the opposition of more-conservative party leaders. Weld, a more traditional Massachusetts Republican than those nominated by the party in the 1980s, advocated cuts in government spending and services but also supported gay rights, choice in abortions, and environmental protection.[29] The strategy was successful statewide, where Weld was the first Republican governor elected since 1970, and it also succeeded in rural Ashfield, where voters once again found the type of moderate Republican politician they preferred. While majorities of voters in Quincy and Somerville supported the Democratic candidate in the 1990 gubernatorial race, 64 percent of Ashfield's voters went for Weld.[30] Ashfield's voters in the 1990s retain a preference for moderate to liberal Republican politicians but find none available in presidential elections. Voting for two different parties at two different office levels does not, therefore, seem well described under the label of dealignment.

The trends and voting patterns for the three Massachusetts towns, as well as for most of the United States, show clearly that areas of party strength have shifted greatly since the 1950s. These shifts in party strength, when the importance of gradualism, the states, and the federalized nature of elections are understood, can be considered evidence of realignment. And once the existence of realignment has been clearly demonstrated in many case studies to follow, it will be possible to begin to explain why certain areas have been trending Democratic during the last forty years.

The proper identification of recent political trends as realignment will also contribute further understanding to the phenomenon of partisan change and coalition-building. As many political scientists have noted about past realignments, third parties have played an important role for voters who have been in the process of switching major parties during the last thirty years. But one inevitable change that occurs during realignments has not received as much focused attention by students of Ameri-

29. Michael Barone and Grant Ujifusa, *The Almanac of American Politics 1992* (Washington, D.C.: National Journal, 1991), 566.

30. Office of the Secretary of State of Massachusetts. In 1994, Weld won easily everywhere in Massachusetts while getting reelected as governor. In 1997, he resigned the governor's office to work full-time, he said, toward gaining confirmation for his appointment by President Clinton to be ambassador to Mexico. Conservative Republican North Carolina Senator Jesse Helms, chair of the Foreign Relations Committee, blocked confirmation hearings over alleged ideological intraparty disputes with Weld, and Weld eventually withdrew his nomination.

can elections: when a party attempts to expand its base with new groups of voters, it inevitably loses voters from its old base. That the North and the South voted along opposite partisan lines in the presidential elections of 1860, 1896, and 1996 is not merely a coincidence. Rather, historical attempts by parties to form coalitions of Northerners and Southern whites under one party label have inevitably failed to last.

The Whigs as a national party disintegrated over the issue of slavery in the 1850s. The Democratic merger of Southern whites and Western populists in the 1890s scared away many of the party's Northeastern voters, who switched to the Republicans for a generation. And Franklin Roosevelt's attempt in the 1930s to tie together the interests of Southern whites and Northern liberals and blacks disintegrated soon after his death over the issue of civil rights. When Republicans in the 1960s, 1970s, and 1980s again attempted to resurrect a North-South coalition, their efforts may have met the same fate. This is the subject of the next chapter, which discusses the Northern realignment away from the Republican party since 1952.

Chapter Two

―━━＞●◀━━

Vermont, the North, and Realignment

In 1888, the American contest for president between Democrat Grover Cleveland and Republican Benjamin Harrison promised to be close. At that time, the state of Maine had the peculiar practice of holding its state elections several weeks before the national elections, so many around the nation waited with anticipation for any trends that could be found in Maine's results. When Maine voted solidly Republican, and the whole nation followed by giving Harrison an electoral college majority in November, the saying "As Maine goes, so goes the nation" was coined.[1] Of course, Maine voted for the losing Republican candidates in the presidential elections of 1884 and 1892, as it did in almost every election in which a Democrat won between 1856 and 1960,[2] but Maine's spotty prediction record did not seem to matter to those who liked catchy slogans.

In 1936, Democratic President Franklin Roosevelt won reelection with 61 percent of the national vote and the electoral votes of every state but two. He got only 43 percent of Vermont's votes and 42 percent of Maine's votes, leading Roosevelt's campaign manager, James Farley, to invent the

1. Henry F. Woods, *American Sayings* (New York: Essential Books, 1945), 109. Woods lists the phrase as "As Maine goes, so goes the country." Bartlett's *Familiar Quotations* and *The Home Book of American Quotations* list the phrase as the better known "As Maine goes, so goes the nation." John Bartlett, *Familiar Quotations*, ed. Emily Morison Beck (Boston: Little, Brown & Company, 1980), 923. See also Bruce Bohle, *The Home Book of American Quotations* (New York: Dodd, Mead & Company, 1967), 316. Bohle adds that the originator of the phrase is unknown.

2. Between 1856 and 1960, Maine voted for a Democrat for president just once: in 1912, Woodrow Wilson won Maine's electoral votes with only 39 percent of the state's popular vote.

new saying "As Maine goes, so goes Vermont."[3] Although Roosevelt had reached the zenith of his popularity in 1936, by forging a strong Democratic coalition of support and staging a major electoral realignment away from the Republicans, Vermont's and Maine's voters were clearly unimpressed and retained their strong preference for the Republican party.

In 1988, Republican George Bush, who had been born and raised in New England, received only 51 percent of Vermont's vote, which was below his 53 percent national average. The year 1988 almost became only the second election year that Vermont had voted for a Democratic presidential candidate in its history, the first being the 1964 Lyndon Johnson landslide. Democrat Michael Dukakis received 48 percent of the state's vote, besting Roosevelt's best performance in Vermont (1940) by 3 percent. The state elected its first Democratic governor since the Civil War in 1962, and its first Democratic U.S. Senator in 1974, and it elected a socialist to the House of Representatives in 1990. By 1992 and 1996, Republican presidential candidates George Bush and Bob Dole received only 30 percent and 31 percent, respectively, of Vermont's vote. In both elections, Vermont was among the five states in the nation with the lowest Republican vote percentages. Vermont's partisan preferences have obviously changed since the 1930s.

In his 1936 landslide, Democrat Roosevelt won 42 percent of Maine's votes, 54 percent of Iowa's votes, 53 percent of Rhode Island's votes, and 51 percent of Massachusetts' votes. In 1988, Democratic losing candidate Dukakis won 44 percent of Maine's votes, 55 percent of Iowa's votes, 56 percent of Rhode Island's votes, and 53 percent of his home state Massachusetts' votes. In 1944, with the Democratic New Deal coalition still at full strength, Roosevelt was reelected with 53 percent of the national vote and 432 electoral votes over his Republican opponent Thomas Dewey, who received 46 percent of the national vote and 99 electoral votes. The 1988 presidential election had almost directly opposite results: Republican Bush, with 53 percent of the vote and 426 electoral votes; and Democrat Dukakis, with 46 percent of the vote and 111 electoral votes.[4] Yet Dukakis in 1988 did better than Roosevelt had done in 1944 in seven states (Vermont, Massachusetts, Wisconsin, Minnesota, Iowa, South Dakota, and Kansas).

3. Woods, *American Sayings*, 109.
4. Dukakis was supposed to receive 112 electoral votes, but one of his electors from West Virginia voted for Lloyd Bentsen for president instead.

The partisan shift toward the Republican party in the South since the 1940s is well documented and well known, but a simultaneous decrease in popularity for Republicans in many of their old Northern and Midwestern strongholds has been much less publicized. Table 2.1 shows each state's Republican vote, arranged regionally, relative to the national vote in presidential elections between 1940 and 1996.

Just from looking at these figures, nine states seemed to have clearly changed from generally supporting Republicans in the 1940s and 1950s to generally supporting Democrats relative to the nation in the 1980s and 1990s: Maine, Vermont, Connecticut, Maryland, New York, Illinois, Wisconsin, Iowa, and Oregon. While looking at trends of each state relative to other states does show the changing bases each party must seek in order to capture a majority of the electoral vote in presidential elections, it does not necessarily show well any realignments toward the Democrats, because of the possibility of Southern and Rocky Mountain states becoming much more Republican, and other states staying stable in their party balance.

Luckily, a statistical fluke in presidential elections can help to clarify which states are clearly realigning toward the Democrats. In the 1950s, most political scientists believe, the New Deal party system still dominated electoral politics.[5] Vermont, for instance, was Republican Dwight Eisenhower's best state in both 1952 and 1956. In 1952, Eisenhower got 55 percent (rounded off to the nearest whole number) of the national vote; in 1956 he got 57 percent, for an average of 56 percent. In 1984, Republican Ronald Reagan received 59 percent of the national vote, and in 1988, Republican George Bush received 53 percent, for an average Republican share of 56 in the last two elections. Third parties received no more than 1 percent of the vote in any of the four elections, and Table 2.1 amply shows that none of the elections was a major statistical fluke in state voting patterns relative to other states. Because the average from the 1950s equals that from the last two elections of the 1980s, the two pairs present a good opportunity to compare changes in Republican support among the states.

The 1992 and 1996 elections, while still providing ample evidence of realignment, are less easily compared state by state with the elections of

5. Everett Ladd and Charles Hadley, for example, in their *Transformations of the American Party System*, call the 1940s–1950s period one of "extension" for the New Deal party system before the upheavals of the 1960s and 1970s (88–89). Sundquist, *Dynamics of the Party System*, agrees with Ladd and Hadley.

Table 2.1. State Republican vote percentage relative to national Republican vote in presidential elections, 1940–1996

State	1940	1944	1948	1952	1956	1960	1964	1968	1972	1976	1980	1984	1988	1992	1996
Maine	+6	+6	+12	+11	+14	+7	-8	0	+1	+1	-5	+2	+2	-7	-10
New Hampshire	+2	+2	+7	+6	+9	+3	-3	+9	+3	+7	+7	+10	+10	+1	-2
Vermont	+10	+11	+17	+16	+15	+9	-5	+10	+2	+6	-7	-1	-2	-7	-10
Massachusetts	+1	+1	-2	-1	+2	-10	-16	-10	-16	-8	-9	-8	-8	-8	-13
Rhode Island	-2	-5	-4	-4	+1	-14	-20	-11	-8	-4	-14	-7	-9	-8	-14
Connecticut	+1	+1	+5	+1	+7	-4	-7	+1	-2	+4	-3	+2	-1	-1	-6
New York	+3	+1	+1	+1	+4	-3	-8	+1	-2	0	-4	-5	-5	-3	-10
New Jersey	+3	+3	+5	+2	+8	-1	-5	+3	+1	+2	+1	+1	+3	+4	-4
Pennsylvania	+1	+2	+6	-2	0	-1	-4	+1	-2	0	-1	-6	-2	-1	-1
Delaware	0	-1	+5	-3	-2	-1	0	+2	-1	-1	-4	+1	+3	-2	-4
Maryland	-4	+2	+4	0	+3	-4	-4	-1	0	-1	-7	-6	-2	-1	-3
West Virginia	-2	-1	-3	-7	-3	-3	-7	-2	+3	-6	-6	-4	-5	-2	-4
Ohio	+3	+4	+4	+2	+4	+3	-2	+2	-1	+1	+1	0	+2	+1	0
Michigan	+5	+3	+4	0	-1	-1	-6	-1	-5	+4	-2	0	+1	-1	-2
Indiana	+6	+6	+5	+3	+3	+5	+5	+7	+5	+5	+5	+3	+7	+6	+6
Illinois	+4	+2	+4	0	+3	0	+2	+4	-2	+2	-1	-3	-2	-3	-4
Wisconsin	+3	+4	+1	+6	+5	+2	-1	+5	-8	0	-3	-5	-5	0	-2
Minnesota	+3	+1	-5	0	-4	-1	-3	-1	-9	-6	-8	-9	-7	-5	-6
Iowa	+7	+6	+3	+9	+2	+7	-1	+10	-3	+2	0	-6	-8	0	-1
Missouri	+3	+2	-3	-4	-7	0	-3	+2	+1	0	0	+1	-1	-3	0
North Dakota	+10	+8	+7	+16	+5	+5	+3	+13	+1	+4	+13	+6	+3	+7	+6
South Dakota	+12	+12	+7	+14	+1	+8	+5	+10	-7	+2	+10	+4	0	+4	+6
Nebraska	+12	+13	+9	+14	+9	+12	+8	+17	+10	+11	+15	+12	+7	+10	+13
Kansas	+12	+14	+9	+14	+8	+10	+6	+12	+7	+5	+7	+7	+3	+2	+13
Alaska						+1	-5	+2	-3	+10	+3	+8	+7	+3	+10
Washington	-4	-4	-2	-1	-3	+1	-2	+2	-4	+2	-1	-3	-4	-5	-4

Oregon	+1	+1	+5	+6	−2	+3	−3	+7	−9	0	−3	−3	−6	−4	−2
California	−4	−3	+2	+1	−2	0	+2	+5	−6	+1	+2	−1	−2	−4	−3
Hawaii						0	−18	−4	+2	0	−8	−4	−8	0	−9
Montana	−5	−1	−2	+4	0	+1	+2	+8	−3	+5	+6	+2	−1	−2	+3
Idaho	0	+2	+2	+10	+4	+4	+10	+14	+3	+11	+16	+13	+9	+5	+11
Wyoming	+2	+5	+2	+8	+3	+5	+4	+13	+8	+11	+12	+12	+8	+3	+9
Colorado	+6	+7	+2	+5	+3	+5	−1	+8	+2	+6	+4	+4	0	−1	+5
Utah	−7	−7	0	+4	+8	+5	+6	+14	+7	+4	+22	+16	+13	+6	+13
Nevada	−5	−1	+2	+7	+1	−1	+2	+5	+3	+2	+12	+7	+6	−2	+2
Arizona	−9	−5	−1	+3	+4	+6	+11	+12	+4	+8	+10	+7	+7	+2	+3
New Mexico	−2	0	−2	+1	+1	−1	+1	+9	0	+3	+4	+1	−1	0	+1
Virginia	−13	−9	−4	+1	−2	+2	+7	0	+7	+1	+2	+3	+7	+8	+6
North Carolina	−19	−13	−12	−9	−8	−2	+5	−3	+9	−4	−2	+3	+5	+6	+8
South Carolina	−41	−41	−41	−6	−32	−1	+20	−5	+10	−5	−2	+5	+9	+11	+9
Georgia	−30	−29	−27	−25	−24	−13	+15	−13	+14	−15	−10	+1	+7	+6	+6
Florida	−19	−16	−11	0	0	+2	+10	−2	+11	−1	+5	+6	+8	+4	+1
Kentucky	−3	−1	−3	−5	−3	+4	−3	+1	+2	−2	−2	+1	+3	+4	+4
Tennessee	−13	−7	−8	−5	−8	+3	+6	−5	+7	−5	−2	−1	+5	+5	+5
Alabama	−31	−28	−26	−20	−18	−8	+31	−29	+11	−5	−2	+2	+6	+11	+9
Mississippi	−41	−40	−42	−15	−32	−25	+48	−29	+17	−1	−2	+3	+7	+13	+8
Arkansas	−24	−16	−24	−11	−11	−7	+4	−12	+8	−13	−3	+2	+3	−1	−4
Louisiana	−31	−27	−27	−8	−4	−21	+18	−19	+4	−2	0	+2	+1	+4	−1
Oklahoma	−3	−2	−9	0	−2	+9	+5	+5	+13	+2	+10	+10	+5	+6	+7
Texas	−26	−29	−20	−2	−2	−1	−2	−3	+5	0	+4	+5	+3	+4	+8

SOURCES: 1940–1952 elections from *Congressional Quarterly's Guide to U.S. Elections* (Washington, D.C.: Congressional Quarterly, 1985); 1956–1992 elections from *America Votes*, vols. 2–18 (Washington, D.C.: Congressional Quarterly Elections Research Center, 1956–1988); 1996 election from *Congressional Quarterly Weekly Report*, January 18, 1997, 188.

NOTE: Plus sign (+) indicates state more Republican than national average; minus sign (−) indicates state less Republican and than national average.

the 1950s because of the presence of Ross Perot's independent presidential candidacies in the campaigns. His role, and the differing impact he had on party strength in different regions will be examined further in Chapter 8.

Table 2.2 presents the presidential election result averages from the 1950s and the 1980s, and the differences between the two averages. Four states that gave solid majorities of their vote to Eisenhower in the 1950s—Massachusetts, Rhode Island, Minnesota, and Iowa—actually gave a majority of their vote to the two losing Democrats of the last two elections in the 1980s. Nine other states shifted toward the Democratic candidates by more than 5 percent between the two periods—Vermont, Maine, New York, Maryland, Wisconsin, North Dakota, South Dakota, Kansas, and Oregon. Eleven states also show slight shifts away from the Republicans, for a total of 24 (half the 48 states from the 1950s) moving toward the Democrats and away from the Republicans in presidential elections between the 1950s and 1980s.

If 1960's election is substituted for 1952, in order to lessen any impact of Eisenhower's personal popularity, the average Republican share of the national presidential vote would be 53.5 percent in 1956–1960, compared with 56 percent in 1984–1988. Despite the national Republican increase, twelve states (Maine, Vermont, Massachusetts, New York, Pennsylvania, Maryland, Illinois, Wisconsin, Minnesota, Iowa, Kansas, and Oregon) still have the GOP performing worse in the 1980s, with three other states (Ohio, South Dakota, Washington) showing equal averages for the two periods.

A 1989 *Congressional Quarterly Weekly Report* documented at the county level the trend of some areas toward the Democrats in the 1988 presidential election.[6] Some 64 counties in 17 states voted for the Democrat for president in 1988, despite his losing national effort, for the first time since the landslide of 1964. These Dukakis counties included several in upstate New York and northern Illinois outside the Chicago area, 29 counties in Iowa, and 1 to 4 counties each in Massachusetts, Pennsylvania, Vermont, Michigan, Minnesota, Nebraska, South Dakota, Wisconsin, northern California, Colorado, Idaho, Montana, Oregon, and Washington.

Several types of variables suggest themselves as possible explanations

6. Rhodes Cook, "Democrats Search for Clues to Regain White House," *Congressional Quarterly Weekly Report*, February 18, 1989, 347.

Table 2.2. Average Republican vote by state in presidential elections of 1952–1956 and 1984–1988 (percentage)

State	1952–56	1984–88	Increase or Decrease in Republican Average
Vermont	72.0	54.5	− 17.5
Iowa	61.5	49.0	− 12.5
Maine	68.5	58.0	− 10.5
Wisconsin	61.5	51.0	− 10.5
Massachusetts	56.5	48.0	− 8.5
New York	58.5	51.0	− 7.5
Rhode Island	54.5	48.0	− 6.5
Minnesota	54.5	48.0	− 6.5
Oregon	58.0	51.5	− 6.5
Kansas	67.0	61.0	− 6.0
North Dakota	66.5	60.5	− 6.0
South Dakota	63.5	58.0	− 5.5
Maryland	57.5	52.0	− 5.5
Illinois	57.5	53.5	− 4.0
Connecticut	60.0	57.0	− 3.0
Pennsylvania	55.0	52.0	− 3.0
New Jersey	61.0	58.0	− 3.0
Colorado	60.0	58.0	− 2.0
Ohio	59.0	57.0	− 2.0
Nebraska	67.5	65.5	− 2.0
Montana	58.0	56.5	− 1.5
Washington	54.0	52.5	− 1.5
California	55.5	54.5	− 1.0
New Mexico	57.0	56.0	− 1.0
West Virginia	51.0	51.5	+ 0.5
Michigan	55.5	56.5	+ 1.0
Indiana	59.0	61.0	+ 2.0
Nevada	60.0	62.5	+ 2.5
New Hampshire	63.5	66.0	+ 2.5
Arizona	59.5	63.0	+ 3.5
Idaho	63.0	67.0	+ 4.0
Wyoming	61.5	66.0	+ 4.5
Delaware	53.5	58.0	+ 4.5
Missouri	50.5	56.0	+ 5.5
Virginia	55.5	61.0	+ 5.5
Kentucky	52.0	58.0	+ 6.0
Texas	54.0	60.0	+ 6.0
Florida	56.0	63.0	+ 7.0
Louisiana	50.0	57.5	+ 7.5
Tennessee	49.5	58.0	+ 8.5
Oklahoma	55.0	63.5	+ 8.5
Utah	62.0	70.5	+ 8.5

Table 2.2. (Continued)

State	1952–56	1984–88	Increase or Decrease in Republican Average
North Carolina	47.5	60.0	+12.5
Arkansas	45.0	58.5	+13.5
Alabama	37.0	60.0	+23.0
South Carolina	37.0	63.0	+26.0
Georgia	31.5	60.0	+28.5
Mississippi	32.5	61.0	+28.5

SOURCES: See source note for Table 2.1.

NOTES: Election-year data are rounded to the nearest whole number. Averages are shown in either whole or half numbers. National average = 56% in each pair of elections.

for the Democratic trends of the North, including cultural factors (ethnic ancestry, religious affiliation, areas of New England Yankee settlement), educational factors (high school or college graduation levels), economic factors (income and poverty levels, labor force categorizations), and in some areas migratory factors (percentage of native-born, recent arrivals). Most of these variables, as well as others of possible relevance (population density or median age, for example), are available in the U.S. Census. In addition, certain voting statistics, such as support for liberal Republicans in primaries or support for John Anderson and opposition to George Wallace in presidential elections, can supplement or strengthen the above demographic data, as well as demonstrate ideological consistency in voting patterns that may not show up in the traditional analysis of two-party voting. Political scientists have widely used each of the above categories of variables to explain past realignments, and, more important for this book, some have speculated that current political trends relate to the above variables as well.

Cultural variables have a long history as probably the most commonly used explanation for electoral shifts in American history,[7] and those who have noted recent electoral shifts have also partially used ethnic or religious explanations.[8] The authors of *The Changing American Voter* found a

7. Many explanations of historical realignments have relied on ethnic and religious factors. For examples, see Benson, *The Concept of Jacksonian Democracy*, and Sundquist, *Dynamics of the Party System*.

8. Such cultural factors could also include racial classifications, but nonwhite racial minorities tend to make up tiny proportions of the population in most of the areas this book will be examining. Chapter 7 will include a discussion of trends in predominantly Hispanic, Native American, and African American areas. Most of these areas have shifted heavily toward the Democrats in the last forty years, but this discovery is probably much less surprising than the similar heavy shifts to the Democrats in some Northern mostly white areas.

decline in support for Republican presidential candidates among Northern white Protestants from 1952 to 1972.[9] James L. Sundquist also noted
a trend among young, suburban, middle-class, college-educated Northeastern Protestants away from Republican voter registration toward independent status.[10] But most of the writers on modern political trends do
not seem to distinguish among Protestant ethnic groups. In this book, it
will become clear that some Protestant groups are becoming more Democratic while others remain steadfastly Republican.

One other cultural factor of particular relevance to studying political
trends in Northern Protestant areas is the pattern of New England Yankee settlement in the nineteenth century. Burnham noted the importance of the residual effects of New England ancestry in both the 1860s
and 1890s realignments.[11] And a couple of authors writing on recent
history believe Yankee culture remains politically salient to this day. William Schneider, for example, believes that a national political realignment based on social and cultural issues started in the 1960s, and noted
that liberal ideology is strongest in New England, the Middle Atlantic
States, the Northern Midwest, and the Pacific Coast States. He added:

> What these areas have in common is a particular cultural heritage:
> they are the areas of Yankee settlement and influence which are
> the peculiarly moralistic political heritage of New England Protes-
> tantism. . . . It is precisely these Yankee areas that have trended
> liberal in their voting behavior in the last fifteen years. . . . It
> is not unfair to characterize Yankee culture as profoundly anti-
> Southern in the Civil War period, and their anti-Southern bias
> was revived in the recent era of civil rights. This bias is one of the
> unifying features of "the Yankee environment" along with cold
> and wet weather, a scarcity of white Southerners and blacks, and
> a history of Yankee/Catholic antagonism.[12]

Conservative Republican strategist Kevin Phillips recognized and predicted a Yankee realignment in his well-known 1969 book, *The Emerging
Republican Majority*. He saw the dwindling Yankee base in the Republican

---

9. Nie, Verba, and Petrocik, *The Changing American Voter*, 223–226.
10. Sundquist, *Dynamics of the Party System*, 407.
11. Burnham, *Critical Elections*, 36–49.
12. William Schneider, "Democrats and Republicans, Liberals and Conservatives," in Lipset, ed., *Party Coalitions in the 1980s*, 211–212.

party as a favorable trend for the GOP, because it allowed the party to devote more attention to gaining support in the growing South and West—rather than the more liberal Northern states, which have been losing electoral votes and congressional seats.[13] He even distinguished between rural Yankees and rural non-Yankee Protestants in the Northeast, finding the former group becoming more Democratic and the latter group more Republican since the 1940s.[14] If Phillips and Schneider were right, then areas with large numbers of New England migrants in the 1800s should be shifting to the Democrats now, independent of other factors.[15]

13. Kevin P. Phillips, *The Emerging Republican Majority* (New Rochelle, N.Y.: Arlington House, 1969), 93–105. Note that Phillips and many current political analysts and journalists exaggerate somewhat in describing the bounty of electoral votes Republicans collect from the shift in population to the South and the West. Most of the gains in the South come from two states—Texas and Florida—with only a few other states in the region gaining one electoral vote in the 1990s. (One Southern state, Louisiana, actually lost an electoral vote and a seat in Congress.) And the description of the West as a solidly Republican area in presidential elections is somewhat false. In 1988, Bush lost three Western states (Washington, Oregon, and Hawaii) with 21 electoral votes. He won California's 47 electoral votes with only 51 percent of the popular vote, and he did worse than his 53.4 percent national vote in three other states of the region (Colorado, Montana, and New Mexico), with 17 electoral votes. This left just Idaho, Utah, Wyoming, Arizona, Nevada, and Alaska, with their 26 electoral votes, as "solid" Republican states in the 1988 election—less than half the number of electoral votes held just by California has after the 1990s reapportionment. Bush won five of the six "solid" Republican states in 1992, losing all the other Western states to Clinton—including Nevada, where Independent Ross Perot played a big role. In 1996, Clinton again won most of the West's electoral votes—including Arizona, which voted Democrat in a presidential election for the first time since 1948.

14. Phillips, *Emerging Republican Majority*, 123–140.

15. Phillips, in his later writings, largely abandoned his earlier predictions. In *Mediacracy*, he argued that rural Yankee voters are likely to stick with the Republican party, having more in common with conservative coalition voters than with the residents of "fashionable areas" leading the Democratic trend. Kevin P. Phillips, *Mediacracy* (Garden City, N.Y.: Doubleday & Company, 1975), 90. In *Post-Conservative America* (New York: Random House, 1982), 228–232, Phillips asserted that the Watergate scandal scuttled his predicted realignment, that Sun Belt states were unlikely to continue to support conservative economic policies, that third parties were likely to increase their influence in American politics, and that a process of dealignment was occurring. His emphasis in this book was on postindustrial society and global realignment. In two more recent books, Phillips continued in the direction his previous books had been taking by emphasizing the importance of domestic and international economic factors in American political change. See Kevin Phillips, *The Politics of Rich and Poor* (New York: Random House, 1990); and *Boiling Point* (New York: Random House, 1993). Phillips's analysis of partisan realignment was quite accurate in his first book, *The Emerging Republican Majority*, although even there his analysis of individual states was sometimes off the mark. (Minnesota was labeled a "battleground" state likely to stay with Republican presidential candidates, while New Hampshire was identified as a lost cause for the Republicans, 472–473.)

Another variable that writers have used to explain recent electoral trends is level of education. Almost thirty years ago, both Phillips and Burnham noted the shift of certain university communities and graduates toward the Democrats. Burnham focused on seven Northeastern university towns shifting heavily between 1948 and 1968 toward the Democrats in presidential elections,[16] while Phillips expanded the assertion to cover "the high-education belt of the Yankee Northeast and kindred areas of the upper Midwest and Pacific Coast" in his 1975 follow-up to *The Emerging Republican Majority*.[17] In this second book, *Mediacracy* (a play on the words "media" and "mediocre"), Phillips focused in part on the elite forces, people who had advanced degrees or undergraduate New England college degrees, that had taken over the Democratic party in 1972.[18] But neither Phillips nor Burnham examined the possibility that education had played a role in realignment beyond the small minority who had attended college in the Northeast or who had earned advanced degrees. In many parts of the nation, areas with less nationally prominent universities or with relatively high numbers of high school graduates but not high numbers of college graduates are also becoming Democratic, requiring a reexamination of the role of education in modern electoral shifts.

Variables measuring income level or poverty level are often linked to educational level variables, because in the general population high educational achievement and high income are strongly related. One might expect, therefore, that if high educational levels relate to a Democratic shift, high income levels would too. Indeed, Phillips, when writing on "post-industrial society," considered the educated elite a wealthy elite.[19] And Seymour Martin Lipset has said that the new postmaterialist portion of the Democratic party derives from "affluent segments of the well educated."[20]

However, as the following chapters show, in most parts of the nation that are becoming more Democratic, educational factors appear to be related more significantly than several types of economic factors to recent changes in voting patterns, and it is possible that the appeal of tax cuts blunted the appeal of environmental regulation to some wealthy or mid-

16. Burnham, *Critical Elections*, 159–160.
17. Phillips, *Mediacracy*, 122.
18. Ibid., 122–123.
19. Ibid., 36.
20. Lipset, "Party Coalitions and the 1980 Election," 24.

dle-class voters in the 1980s, especially those with lower educational levels.[21]

In addition to the previously listed cultural, educational, and economic factors, a fourth set of variables that some have used to explain recent electoral shifts in certain areas involves changes in state populations caused by newcomers from other states. Many observers of Vermont's politics have concluded that the influx of Democratic migrants, mainly from Massachusetts and New York, have been responsible for changing the partisan balance of the state. "The real arrival of two-party politics came in the 60s as new voters migrated into Vermont from elsewhere," said Neal Peirce and Jerry Hagstrom in *The Book of America*.[22] University of Vermont political scientist Garrison Nelson has attributed the state's Democratic shift to outsiders who "learned to be Democrats in other states."[23] And a *Congressional Quarterly Weekly Report* in 1987 claimed that the increase in Democratic support in Vermont resulted from "urban refugees" coming from other states in the Northeast.[24] Oddly, it is difficult to find sources that make similar comments about Oregon's large shift to the Democrats in the last forty years. Oregon, once called the "Vermont of the West" for its staunch Republicanism,[25] has seen an influx of newcomers escaping the cities of California, yet few seem as willing to speculate, as they do with Vermont, that out-of-staters have caused Oregon's political changes.

While many political scientists studying realignment have been guilty of ignoring state data in favor of national data, many political observers of Vermont may be guilty of the opposite. Newcomers to Vermont have likely affected the extent of the Democratic shift, but they cannot be the sole cause of the shift. Otherwise, why would Iowa, which lost population in the 1980s, be so heavily trending Democratic? And why would New Hampshire, with numbers of new arrivals similar to Vermont's, be so heavily trending Republican? Obviously, factors other than just the arrival of people from out of state are having an effect on Vermont and Oregon, and statistical analysis will show this.

---

21. See Ginsberg and Shefter, "A Critical Realignment?" for discussion of such a possibility.

22. Neal R. Peirce and Jerry Hagstrom, *The Book of America* (New York: W. W. Norton & Company, 1983), 199.

23. Tom Slayton, "Vermont's Voting Patterns Blurring," *Barre Times-Argus*, October 16, 1983.

24. *Congressional Quarterly Weekly Report*, August 29, 1987, 2008.

25. Peirce and Hagstrom, *Book of America*, 825.

Finally, certain voting statistics can serve as additional explanations or as supplements to demographic variables in examining Democratic party trends. Phillips noted back in 1969 that Republican appeals to Southern, Western, and Catholic voters may cause the party to lose support among its more liberal members in Yankee, Scandinavian, and educated elite areas.[26] And as Phillips predicted, many areas that tended to support liberal Republicans against conservatives in primaries between the 1940s and 1970s have trended Democratic in recent years.

In addition, many political scientists studying historical realignments have noted the importance of third parties in the process. Sundquist, among others, has documented the role of the Populist party in the 1890s realignment.[27] Burnham has labeled third-party movements as "protorealignment phenomena."[28] Writing in 1970, Burnham believed that the 1968 presidential candidacy of George Wallace had the potential for influencing a realignment, but ultimately would not, due to dealignment and the lack of a crisis necessary for a critical election to occur.[29] Any role John Anderson's 1980 presidential candidacy may have played in a realignment seems to have been largely forgotten or ignored by many within a few years after that election.[30] Yet high numbers of John Anderson votes and low numbers of George Wallace votes usually relate positively to a shift toward the Democrats over the last forty years, so it is likely that these third-party movements have played a role in the gradual realignment of the period.

The chapters to follow will in part be organized on a regional basis and will use demographic and political data and multiple regression methodology to show which factors provide the best explanations for Democratic trends and which become insignificant when other variables are taken into account. The next chapter will focus on the state with the highest shift to the Democrats in presidential elections of any state in the nation between the 1950s and the 1980s—Vermont—and will examine the causes of Northern realignment. Chapters 4 and 5, on New Hampshire

26. Phillips, *Emerging Republican Majority*, 464–465.

27. Sundquist, *Dynamics of the Party System*, 106–169.

28. Burnham, *Critical Elections*, 27.

29. Ibid., 170–171.

30. For example, Gerald Pomper's volume on the 1988 election makes no mention of Anderson in its seven articles. The book obviously focuses on the 1988 election, but does include discussions of political trends and does mention past losing Democratic presidential candidates Jimmy Carter, Walter Mondale, and George McGovern several times each. Gerald M. Pomper, ed., *The Election of 1988* (Chatham, N.J.: Chatham House Publishers, 1989).

and Rhode Island, demonstrate the importance of individual state voting data analysis and the phenomenon of federalized, or split-level, realignment. Chapter 6 examines realignment patterns in three other Northern states, and Chapter 7 provides an overview of realignment in other parts of the nation.[31]

Each chapter will include a brief political history of the states under examination and a statistical analysis of voting trends in recent years. Each analysis will determine which variables seem most responsible for the Democratic shift and provide an argument as to why areas with certain characteristics are the most likely to be bucking the supposed national trend toward the Republicans. The analysis will also include tables of state trends to indicate how gradual or sudden the electoral shifts have been and comparative discussions of voting in presidential elections and voting for state offices to demonstrate the logic that may exist behind divergent trends within a state. Explanations for realignment will vary somewhat between regions and will sometimes differ even in neighboring states, lending credibility to the argument that states must be examined separately for a fuller understanding of recent electoral trends. Discussions of how national Republican party strategies in recent years have lost some of the party's traditional base will also appear in several of the chapters.

Chapter 8 will go beyond the period under study (1952–1988) in much of this book to study the results of the 1992 and 1996 presidential elections, when the Northern realignment toward the Democrats over the previous forty years became most apparent. While some might attribute

31. Most writers on state electoral politics automatically use entire states as units of analysis, while including intrastate political differences within discussions for each state. Although choosing states as units for analysis of political environments is convenient and usually sensible (see Key, *American State Politics*, 19–20, for support), in some parts of the nation, a different type of unit of analysis is often useful or logical. For instance, New York City and Upstate New York have historically had very different and even opposing political cultures. Because the focus of much of this book will be on traditionally Republican areas becoming more Democratic, traditionally Republican Upstate New York will be discussed separately from traditionally Democratic New York City and from suburban counties near New York City, which are quite different politically from both the city and upstate. Such a pattern is also relevant for Chicago and Illinois, and for other areas as well. In addition, some states in a region have historically been considered quite similar in political environment. For that reason, studying Maine, New Hampshire, and Vermont as a group can add to the analysis of each individual state by providing a more comparative perspective, which will bring together similar patterns in the three states and help answer the question of why New Hampshire has been shifting in the opposite partisan direction from its Northern New England neighbors.

Democrat Bill Clinton's sweep of the Northeast, the Pacific Coast states, and most of the Midwest in 1992 to short-term economic factors, Bush's unpopularity, and the independent candidacy of Ross Perot, and Clinton's 1996 reelection, with the same regional support, to economic prosperity, evidence throughout this book will indicate that the Clinton electoral college victories also resulted from long-term changes in partisan voting behavior that will persist beyond the temporary factors present in the 1992 and 1996 elections. A discussion of 1992's and 1996's results will also necessarily include an analysis of voters for Perot and how Perot's candidacy cut into support for both the major parties.

Since 1952 there has been a clear regional political trend sweeping across the northern tier of the United States in opposition to the trend sweeping the South. The gains for each major party in one region have inevitably accompanied losses in the other region, just as with previous realignments. Long ago, Maine lost whatever value it had in predicting national elections, but its 1936 companion state of Vermont has been quietly leading the way as the most extreme example of Northern election trends toward the Democrats in presidential elections from the 1950s into the 1990s.

Chapter Three

———◦◦◦———

Who Are Vermont's New Democrats?

In the 1950s and 1960s, it seemed obvious to label Vermont as a one-party Republican state. Many political scientists considered the state a unique opposite to the one-party Democratic systems of the South. Duane Lockard, in his study of New England politics, wrote in 1959 that categorizing Vermont "as one-party requires no feat of analysis or re-search" and that "although the Democratic party musters a larger vote in Vermont than does the Republican party in most Southern states, this fact does not really mean much, for up to the present at least the Demo-crats in Vermont are more notable for their persistence than for their ultimate political significance."[1] Several other political scientists in the 1950s and 1960s, while ranking party competitiveness in the states, ranked Vermont among the lowest and chose it as the most completely Republican in the nation.[2]

While the state's shift toward the Democrats in presidential elections since the 1950s has already been documented in Chapter 2, the Demo-crats have actually made even larger gains in elections for certain other statewide offices. Table 3.1 gives the percentage of the vote received by the Republican candidate in all general elections for president, governor, and Congress since 1920. The final section of the table provides decade averages for the Republican candidates. As the table shows, Democrats were sometimes competitive in statewide elections during the depths of

1. Lockard, *New England State Politics*, 13.
2. Frank M. Bryan reviews the various rankings in *Yankee Politics in Rural Vermont* (Hanover, N.H.: University Press of New England, 1974), 69–71.

Table 3.1. Vermont Republican vote for president, governor, U.S. senator, and U.S. representative, 1920–1994 (percentage of vote for Republican party, including Republican decade averages)

	President	Governor	U.S. Senator	U.S. Representative
1920	76 (+16)	78	78	76
1922		75	68	65
1924	78 (+24)*	79	66 (special 1923)	79
1926		61	73	76
1928	67 (+9)	74	72	71
1930		71	64 (special 1931)	67
1932	58 (+18)	62	55	64
1934		57	51	57
1936	56 (+19)	61	58 (special 1934)	59
1938		67	66	64
1940	55 (+10)	64	67	64
1942		78	62 (special 1940)	70
1944	57 (+11)	66	66	62
1946		80	75	64
1948	62 (+17)	72		61
1950		75	78	73
1962	72 (+17)	52	72	72
1954		52		61
1956	72 (+15)	58	66	67
1958		50	52	49
1960	59 (+9)	56		57
1962		49	67	57
1964	34 (−5)	35	54	58
1966		42		66
1968	53 (+9)*	56	100 (unopposed)	61
1970		57	59	68
1972	63 (+2)	44	64 (special 1972)	65
1974		38	46	53
1976	54 (+6)	53	50	67
1978		63		75
1980	44 (−7)*	59	49	79
1982		55	50	69
1984	58 (−1)	49		65
1986		38	35	89 (no Dem. in race)
1988	51 (−2)	43	70	41*
1990		52		40*
1992	30 (−8)*	23	43	31*
1994		19	50	47*

Table 3.1. (Continued)

| | | Republican Decade Averages | |
	President	Governor	U.S. Senator	U.S. Representative
1920s	74 (+16)	73	71	73
1930s	57 (+19)	64	59	62
1940s	58 (+13)	72	68	64
1950s	72 (+16)	57	67	64
1960s	49 (+5)	48	74 (61)**	60
1970s	59 (+4)	51	55	66
1980s	51 (−4)	49	51	69

SOURCES: 1920–1952 vote for president and 1920–1944 vote for governor and senator from *Congressional Quarterly's Guide to U.S. Elections* (Washington, D.C.: Congressional Quarterly, 1985); 1956–1992 vote for president, 1946–1994 vote for governor and senator, and 1972–1980 vote for U.S. representative from *America Votes*, vols. 1–17 (Washington, D.C.: Congressional Quarterly Elections Research Center, 1954–1986); 1920–1970 vote for U.S. representative from Edward Franklin Cox, *State + National Voting in Federal Elections 1910–1970* (Hamden, Conn.: Archon Books, 1972); 1982–1994 vote for U.S. representative from *The Almanac of American Politics* (Washington, D.C.: National Journal, 1984–1992).

NOTES: Figures are rounded to the nearest whole number. Figures in parentheses indicate the difference between Vermont's vote and the national vote for Republican presidential candidates. + = Vermont more Republican, − = Vermont less Republican. Special U.S. Senate elections are listed as close to the year in which they took place as possible.

*Large third-party presidential votes: in 1924, LaFollette received 6% in Vermont, 17% nationally; in 1968, Wallace received 3% in Vermont, 14% nationally; in 1980, Anderson received 15% in Vermont, 7% nationally; in 1992, Perot received 23% in Vermont, 19% nationally. Independent socialist Bernard Sanders won 36% of the vote to finish second in the U.S. representative race in 1988 and won with 56% in 1990, 58% in 1992, and 50% in 1994.
**61% if unopposed 1968 election not included.

the Great Depression in the 1930s. By 1938, however, the Republican party had reasserted its overwhelming dominance of statewide elections.

The first permanent breakthrough for the Democrats did not come until the 1952–1954 period. In 1952, the Republican party had a bitter gubernatorial primary, which resulted in the losing candidate running as an independent in the general election, helping the Democrats to hold the Republican nominee to only 52 percent of the vote that November. In 1954, the Republican party had a new nominee for governor, but the fallout from the previous election apparently helped the Democrats gain 48 percent of the vote, with the Republican candidate finishing again at 52 percent. Since then, the Democratic party has been very competitive with the Republican party in gubernatorial elections, finally winning the office in 1962. In addition, the Democratic party has gradually been becoming more competitive in U.S. Senate elections since the 1950s. Republicans remained dominant in elections for the U.S. House until 1986 but have lost all elections for Vermont's one House seat since 1990.

Table 3.1 also casts doubt on the widespread belief discussed in Chapter 2 that Vermont's shift to the Democrats has resulted from newcomers moving into the state. The shift to the Democrats in statewide elections began in the 1950s, a period of minimal population growth in Vermont. Frank Bryan notes: "The Democratic breakthrough in Vermont during the 50s appears to have been an indigenous one. The state experienced no sharp influx of people to form the base of a new party alignment."[3]

This chapter will attempt to explain the indigenous realignment of Vermont politics and why standard critical election theory has not provided an adequate framework to explain it. And the chapter will first turn to an examination of the reasons for Vermont's dramatic shift to the Democrats since the 1950s, the largest of any state in the nation in presidential elections. Using a statistic explained in the second chapter—the average Republican vote in the 1952 and 1956 presidential elections, minus the average Republican vote in the 1984 and 1988 presidential elections—several variables will be tested to see which provide the best explanations for the Democratic shift.

In the tables to follow, the shift away from (and occasionally toward) the Republicans in presidential elections has been calculated for 245 of Vermont's towns and cities.[4] These shifts range from 53.5 percent toward the Democrats in the southern Vermont college town of Marlboro, to 25 percent toward the Republicans in the Canadian border town of Jay. In Marlboro, Dwight Eisenhower got 115 votes for president in 1952, while George Bush got 111 votes in 1988. Meanwhile, Adlai Stevenson received a total of 24 votes in Marlboro in 1952, while Michael Dukakis received 292 in 1988.

To test the effect of cultural background on the electoral shift, 1980 U.S. Census results from questions asking about ancestry are available for each town.[5] In Vermont, people claiming English, French (mostly French

3. Ibid., 104.
4. The only town not included is Sunderland, in Bennington County, for which data was missing. Also not included are the various small geographical units in Vermont, with names like Avery's Gore or Buel's Gore, which had either no official population or a miniscule (5–15 people) population in the 1980 U.S. Census.
5. The census did not ask about religious affiliation; therefore, the best statistics on religion are compiled in other sources by church membership in each county in the nation. Determining church membership in townships would likely be a fruitless exercise, because many people

Canadian), or Irish ancestry make up the three largest ancestral groups in all fourteen of the state's counties, with other groups accounting for much smaller percentages, so only the three groups mentioned will be included here.[6] The Census allowed people to identify either single ancestries or multiple ancestries; only the numbers of people claiming single ancestries will be used here, since they are most likely to retain any cultural traits that exist in a group. (Use of the numbers of people claiming at least partial ancestry in each group actually turns out to have only minor effects on the tables below for Vermont.)

As stated earlier, many observers of Vermont politics have claimed that the state's Democratic shift has resulted mainly from the large numbers of people moving into the state from elsewhere. The Census also provides numbers for the percentage of town residents born in Vermont, and the percentage of town residents who moved to Vermont between 1975 and 1980, so this theory of Vermont politics can be easily tested.

Other variables to be tested against the Democratic shift include town size, per capita income, median age, and the percentage of town residents who have graduated from high school.[7] These will help evaluate the impact of economic, educational, and other demographic factors on Vermont's partisan politics.

Table 3.2 indicates that towns with high numbers of people of English ancestry are becoming more Democratic, while towns with a high percentage of French ancestry are either becoming increasingly Republican or are not part of the statewide trend toward the Democrats. The table also indicates that smaller towns, towns with higher incomes and educational levels, and towns with fewer people born or raised in Vermont are having a stronger influence on the state trend toward the Democrats than towns on the opposite end of each scale.

However, many of these demographic variables are themselves correlated. For example, towns with higher high school graduation levels also tend to have higher incomes, and fewer native Vermonters and French

---

probably commute to nearby towns to attend church. Statistics on church membership by county will be used in tables in later chapters.

6. All racial minorities combined made up only about 1 percent of Vermont's population in 1980 and therefore are unable to have a significant effect on state elections.

7. Percentages of college graduates will be used when examining county data later in this book. In some states, college graduation levels make high school graduation levels insignificant in accounting for electoral trends, but in other states, high school graduation levels make college graduation levels an insignificant variable.

Table 3.2. Relationship of nine variables to Democratic gains in presidential elections in 245 Vermont towns and cities, 1950s–1980s

Variable	Correlation Coefficient
% English ancestry	.17**
% French ancestry	− .58**
% Irish ancestry	− .03
Town population	− .14*
% High school grad	.47**
Per capita income	.12*
% Born in Vermont	− .23**
% Moved to Vermont 1975–80	.27**
Median age	.04

SOURCES: Town electoral data from *Primary and General Elections: Vermont* (Montpelier: Office of the Secretary of State of Vermont, 1974–1988), and *Vermont Legislative Directory and State Manual* (Montpelier: Office of the Secretary of State of Vermont, 1950–1972) (data before 1980 are given in raw numbers, and percentages are calculated by the author of this book); Ancestries and percentage born in Vermont from *1980 Census of Population and Housing for Vermont: Summary Tape Files* (Washington, D.C.: U.S. Department of Commerce, Bureau of the Census) with the Tape Files printed and prepared by Vermont State Data Center, Center for Rural Studies, University of Vermont, Burlington, Vermont (data are given in raw numbers, and percentages are calculated by the author of this book); Town population, % high school grads, % new to Vermont, median age, and income data are from *1980 Census of Population and Housing: Summary Characteristics for Governmental Units and Standard Metropolitan Statistical Areas* (Washington, D.C.: U.S. Department of Commerce, Bureau of the Census, 1982).

*Significant at the .05 level.
**Significant at the .01 level.

residents, than towns with lower high school graduation levels. To determine which of these variables are the most important factors in explaining a Democratic shift, multiple regression is required.

Table 3.3, with its multiple regressions, presents a different explanation of Vermont's shift to the Democrats. While towns with higher-than-average numbers of high school graduates remain likely to be trending Democratic, and towns of higher-than-average French ancestry remain unlikely to be part of that trend, towns of high Irish ancestry also now appear to be less likely than the average town to be becoming more Democratic. In

Table 3.3. Multiple regression of selected variables to Democratic gains in presidential elections for 245 Vermont towns and cities (only variables that contribute to the overall model are listed), 1952–1956 to 1984–1988

R^2 = 42.6% R^2 (adjusted) = 41.6%
s = 9.728 with 245 − 5 = 240 degrees of freedom

Source	Sum of Squares	df	Mean Square	F-ratio
Regression	16832.2	4	4208	44.5
Residual	22714.2	240	94.6423	

Variable	Coefficient	s.e. of Coeff	t-ratio
Constant	5.40002	5.723	0.944
French	− 0.792460	0.1004	− 7.90**
High school grad	0.546025	0.0950	5.75**
Irish	− 0.599334	0.3047	− 1.97*
Income	− 0.002214	0.0007	− 3.36**

SOURCES: See source note for Table 3.2.

*Significant at the .05 level.
**Significant at the .01 level.

addition, once these other variables are taken into account, towns with lower incomes rather than higher ones become more likely to be trending Democratic.

But Tables 3.2 and 3.3, while useful in offering some explanations, still do not present a full picture of the statewide electoral trends for two reasons. First, some of the correlations between Democratic shifts and demographic variables have strong outliers in the data, most coming from a three-county area of Vermont sometimes called the "Northeast Kingdom," where Democratic trends are weaker than variables would predict in other parts of the state. Second, larger towns and cities have a much greater influence on statewide results than Vermont's many small and tiny towns. Table 3.4 attempts to solve these two problems.

Dubbed the "Northeast Kingdom" by former Vermont Governor and U.S. Senator George Aiken in the 1930s,[8] Caledonia, Essex, and Orleans counties (and especially the towns within these counties that border on New Hampshire or Quebec) have in recent years had voting patterns more similar to those of neighboring New Hampshire than to the rest of Vermont, a phenomenon that will be discussed more later in the chapter.

8. Neal R. Peirce, *The New England States* (New York: W. W. Norton & Company, 1976), 237.

Table 3.4. Relationship of nine variables to Democratic gains in presidential elections in three categories of Vermont towns and cities, 1952–1956 to 1984–1988

A = All Vermont towns in all 14 counties (taken from Table 2.2), N = 245.
B = All Vermont towns and cities in 11 counties (excludes Caledonia, Essex, and Orleans counties, the "Northeast Kingdom"), N = 199.
C = All Vermont towns and cities over 2,500 in population, N = 52.

	Correlation Coefficient		
Variable	A	B	C
% English ancestry	.17**	.38**	.45**
% French ancestry	−.58**	−.56**	−.77**
% Irish ancestry	−.03	−.05	.17
Town population	−.14*	−.24**	−.07
% High school grad	.47**	.41**	.32*
Per capita income	.12*	.08	−.01
% Born in Vermont	−.23**	−.44**	−.48**
% Moved to Vermont 1975–80	.27**	.39**	.35**
Median age	.04	.09	.16

Mutiple regression of nine variables on the Democratic shift in presidential elections for select Vermont towns and cities. Only variables that contribute to the overall model are listed.

Eleven Counties (B)

R^2 = 50.0% R^2 (adjusted) = 48.5%
s = 8.377 with 197 − 7 = 190 degrees of freedom

Source	Sum of Squares	df	Mean Square	F-ratio
Regression	13352.5	6	2225	31.7
Residual	13331.5	190	70.1660	

Variable	Coefficient	s.e. of Coeff	t-ratio
Constant	−2.72352	5.818	−0.468
English	0.536662	0.1242	4.32**
French	−0.548876	0.1069	−5.13**
High school grad	0.478387	0.0960	4.98**
Population	−0.000431	0.0002	−2.57**
Income	−0.002698	0.0006	−4.16**
New to Vermont	0.315854	0.1060	2.98**

Towns of More Than 2,500 People (C)

R^2 = 68.1% R^2 (adjusted) = 66.1%
s = 6.188 with 52 − 4 = 48 degrees of freedom

Table 3.4. (Continued)

Source	Sum of Squares	df	Mean Square	F-ratio
Regression	3915.54	3	1305	34.1
Residual	1838.17	48	38.2952	

Variable	Coefficient	s.e. of Coeff	t-ratio
Constant	28.6648	6.479	4.42
English	0.668125	0.2037	3.28**
French	− 1.16954	0.1384	− 8.45**
Income	− 0.001574	0.0008	− 1.97*

SOURCES: See source note for Table 3.2.

*Significant at the .05 level.
**Significant at the .01 level.

For now, it should be noted that, while the three counties combined are more rural, more French, less educated, and poorer than the state as a whole, other Vermont counties having some or all of these same characteristics do not diverge from correlation patterns to anywhere near the same extent.

Table 3.4 indicates that once the three Northeast Kingdom counties are removed from Vermont's data, high English ancestry and high numbers of non-native Vermonters become much more closely related in a positive direction to the trend toward the Democrats. Multiple regression shows that these factors remain very significant, even when low numbers of French ancestry, low incomes, and high educational levels are taken into account.

Towns and cities of more than 2,500 people have more impact on statewide elections than smaller towns, simply because of their size. In Vermont, only 21 percent of the 246 towns and cities contain more than 2,500 people, but that percentage contains 65 percent of the people. Therefore, separating these larger towns out of the state data provides information essential for explaining the statewide Democratic trend.

In Vermont's larger towns, according to Table 3.4, ancestry (high numbers of English, low numbers of French) seems by far to be the best predictor of a town's shift toward the Democrats. Even high school graduation levels seem to be insignificant once ancestry is taken into account.

As discussed in Chapter 2, cultural, educational, economic, and migratory factors have all been used by political scientists and observers to explain recent Democratic gains in Vermont and in the North, and according to the above tables, all these factors do play some role, although not always to the extent that some authors claim. For instance, as *New York Times* reporter Fox Butterfield asserted in 1986, "most scholars and politicians trace the political change [of increase in support for Democrats] to the influx of newcomers to Vermont in the late 1960s and 1970s, many of them young people from New York and Massachusetts."[9] While the tables above do indicate a significant positive relationship between non-natives in a town and a shift toward the Democrats, this relationship remains significant in only one of the three multiple regression models, which take other factors into account.

It is likely that non-natives have increased the magnitude of Vermont's shift toward the Democrats, but migratory factors cannot explain the similar Democratic trends of many other Northern states, nor the initial Democratic gains in Vermont gubernatorial elections, which occurred before the arrival of large numbers of non-natives. And the implication of many writers that the non-natives by themselves are responsible for the Democratic shift in Vermont seems clearly inaccurate from the tables above. Vermont political scientist Frank Bryan and Vermont state senator John McLaughry have written:

> There is a subtle intellectual snobbery among those who claim that it took outsiders to change Vermont politics. It is the kind of sniff rural people are used to from those who always have a better way and believe they have been ordained to bring enlightenment to the boondocks. Fox Butterfield, writing for *The New York Times* in 1986, came to Vermont, arched his eyebrows, and decided that without the influx of outsiders, Vermont would still be conservative and Republican. Many newcomers themselves are only too happy to claim credit for Vermont's renaissance in partisan politics. Even close observers take the easy way out, accept the linkage between correlation and causation, and simply assert that political change was not indigenous to Vermont but was brought to the state by outsiders.[10]

9. Fox Butterfield, "Vermont Shifting to Left in a Flow of Newcomers," *New York Times,* January 31, 1986, A13.

10. Frank Bryan and John McClaughry, *The Vermont Papers* (Post Mills, Vt.: Chelsea Green Publishing, 1989), 280.

Clearly other factors that are at least as important in the shift are also relevant in states without large numbers of people from New York and Massachusetts.

Two such factors are education and income. As discussed in the last chapter, Phillips and Burnham both found that people associated with prestigious Northeastern universities were trending strongly toward the Democrats.[11] The strong association between high school graduation levels and Democratic shifts in Vermont towns does not contradict that finding. However, Phillips and Burnham were too conservative in their arguments. In Vermont and in most Northern states, not only are the communities of prestigious universities strongly trending Democratic, but so are some towns of small colleges little known outside their home states. Marlboro, Vermont, home to Marlboro College, a small quality private liberal arts college that does not have the national prominence of the schools Burnham or Phillips consider, has had the highest shift of any of Vermont's 246 towns and cities toward the Democrats in presidential elections over the last forty years.

High levels of education are clearly related to the Democratic shift in Vermont. Because educational level and income level are so closely related, it might be assumed that higher income people must be trending Democratic as well, an assumption that authors such as Phillips and Lipset do not contradict when writing about how wealthy educated elites have switched to the Democratic party.[12] However, while there is a significant positive correlation between town income level and town Democratic shift when all Vermont towns are included, the relationship becomes strongly negative in all three multiple regression models once other factors are taken into account.

Many years ago, well-educated, well-off people tended to vote Republican, and there seemed to be no contradiction between their educational level and economic status in their voting. Yet now in Vermont, it appears that towns with well-educated but relatively low-income voters are shifting to the Democrats. The solution to this puzzle may lie in an examination of national party images. A better-educated, lower-income person is more likely than average to benefit from government spending programs, for which the Democrats are usually seen as better advocates than Republicans. Low or moderate income allows one to qualify for many programs,

11. See Burnham, *Critical Elections*, 159–160; and Phillips, *Mediacracy*, 122–123.
12. See Phillips, *Mediacracy*, 36; and Lipset, *Party Coalitions in the 1980s*, 24.

and a good education not only provides a better understanding of how to receive benefits but also expands the number of benefits for which one is eligible, such as assistance with college loans or local development projects or even employment with government agencies. The corresponding Republican appeal of tax cuts is less likely to have any impact on non-wealthy voters. In addition, well-educated people of any income level are likely to be more interested in such issues as environmental and consumer regulation, which tends to help the national Democrats, than in issues like school prayer, which tends to help the national Republicans and which may interest less-educated, low-income voters.

Ethnic ancestry, the most consistently strong predictor of a Democratic trend in Vermont among the four types of factors under discussion, may also be the most difficult to explain. Neal Peirce has suggested that French Canadian immigrants to New England were "instinctively conservative."[13] And historian Charles Morrissey has noted that French Canadian support for the Democratic party created "a seeming anomaly, which permits some lifelong Vermont Democrats to win by big margins in legislative races in Burlington but speak like conservative Republicans when they get to Montpelier."[14] Some electoral data may help to confirm, at least partly, the conservative nature of French Canadian voters in Vermont.

Table 3.5 provides a comparison of the Democratic vote for president during the 1968–1976 period for the five towns in Vermont with the highest French ancestry and the five towns with the highest English ancestry, excluding all towns in the three Northeast Kingdom counties. In 1968 and 1976, the Democrats nominated presidential candidates considered to be in the mainstream of their parties, but in 1972 they chose George McGovern, whom some considered far too liberal for many traditional Democratic voters.

As Table 3.5 demonstrates, French Canadian towns were not enthralled with McGovern's liberal politics, but they seemed mostly willing to return to the Democratic party once it nominated someone more moderate. By the 1980s, however, as the national Democratic party began to be perceived as consistently liberal, and the national Republican party came to be seen as consistently conservative, many of the French Canadian towns had a more permanent increase in support for the Republi-

---

13. Peirce, *The New England States*, 289.
14. Charles T. Morrissey, *Vermont* (New York: W. W. Norton & Company, 1981), 116.

Table 3.5. Democratic presidential vote in Vermont's most French and English towns (excluding towns in Caledonia, Essex, and Orleans counties), 1968–1976 (percentage)

	1968	1972	1976
French Towns:			
Sheldon	50	37	49
Winooski	79	54	59
Highgate	61	38	59
Berkshire	43	41	47
St. Albans Town	50	29	46
English Towns:			
Turnbridge	27	28	33
Baltimore	14	16	42
Landgrove	24	42	31
Brookfield	24	29	31
Chelsea	15	22	31

SOURCES: *Primary and General Elections: Vermont, 1976,* and *Vermont Legislative Directory aned State Manual, 1968–1972* (data are given in raw numbers; percentages are calculated by the author of this book).

cans. All five English towns, on the other hand, liked McGovern even better than 1968 Democratic candidate Hubert Humphrey and continued a gradual trend toward the Democrats.

Political analysts have been less likely to label New England Yankees as liberal than they have been to label French Canadian descendants as conservative. Actually, many of the stereotypical traits associated with New England Yankees seem quite conservative. Historian Ralph Nading Hill calls the "legendary" Vermont Yankee "independent, frugal, laconic, somewhat austere."[15] Of course, New England Yankees also gained a deserved reputation in the 1930s as adamant opponents of Franklin Roosevelt and New Deal policies, a stand that certainly does not suggest liberal tendencies.

By the 1970s, however, some political analysts began to observe that the political leanings of Yankee voters were changing, although the reasons for this apparent ideological shift are not altogether clear. Kevin Phillips noted that Yankees have had "a historic penchant for government social planning and moral proselytizing," although he added that

15. Ralph Nading Hill, *Yankee Kingdom: Vermont and New Hampshire* (New York: Harper & Row, 1973), 6.

before the 1960s such preferences did not get expressed in federal elections.[16] Phillips believed that the emerging conflict within the Republican party, between Goldwater conservatives of the South and West and Rockefeller liberals of the Northeast, pushed Yankee politicians to side with the Rockefeller wing of the party, which was linked to liberal causes.[17]

William Schneider later expanded on Phillips's arguments about Yankee voters and politicians. To repeat part of a quotation in Chapter 2, Schneider stated that: "It is not unfair to characterize Yankee culture as profoundly anti-Southern in the Civil War period, and their anti-Southern bias was revived in the recent era of civil rights. This bias is one of the unifying features of 'the Yankee environment' along with cold and wet weather, a scarcity of white Southerners and blacks, and a history of Yankee/Catholic antagonism."[18]

In the 1930s, Franklin Roosevelt's New Deal policies and Democratic party strategies were aimed in part at attracting support among Southerners and Northern Catholics, the two traditional political opponents of Northern Yankees, so perhaps it was natural to find that Vermont's Yankees were not supportive of Roosevelt's presidential candidacies. However, beginning in the 1960s, and gaining strength in the 1980s, was a new national Republican party strategy of gaining support among Catholics and Southerners through such policies as favoring school prayer and patriotic rituals and opposing abortion and affirmative action.[19]

Such a Republican strategy seemed doomed to lose support for the national party in Vermont. First, on the issues listed above, most English Yankee voters tend either to have views opposite those of the national Republican party, or at least much less interest in the issues than Catholics or Southerners. Second, one reason for Vermont's relative support for or disinterest in issues like affirmative action, which the Republican party has used so effectively in the South, is the minuscule proportion of minorities in the state, whose population was 0.2 percent African American in 1980. And finally, the Republican party was targeting for support precisely those groups, especially in the South, that have been in political

16. Phillips, *Emerging Republican Majority,* 101.
17. Ibid., 101–102.
18. Schneider, "Democrats and Republicans, Liberals and Conservatives," 211–212.
19. For an excellent discussion of how Republicans used such issues to capture white Southern voters, see Earl Black and Merle Black, *The Vital South* (Cambridge, Mass.: Harvard University Press, 1992).

opposition with Northern Yankees for well over a hundred years.[20] As Robert Kelley has stated, "When their common enemy, England, was removed [after the American Revolution], Yankees and Southerners would take each other as their principal antagonists. . . . This bipolar conflict between two American ethnic communities, alive and full of tension, would determine much of later American history."[21]

It is possible that Republican appeals to Catholic voters turned off some traditional Yankee supporters of the party, but even more likely is the possibility that Yankee voters have perceived many national Republican candidates as catering to Southern values and attitudes. Southern voters in some states often seem perfectly willing to confirm Northern Yankee stereotypes of the South by frequently electing or nominating politicians like Republicans Jesse Helms and David Duke or Democrat George Wallace for high offices. Despite the claims of some in 1991 that former Ku Klux Klan and Nazi Party leader David Duke (running for governor of Louisiana) was part of a national phenomenon present beyond Louisiana or the South,[22] it is doubtful that Duke or Helms would be considered serious candidates in any statewide Vermont election or in most areas outside the South.

This may be overstating the influence of regional animosities on modern electoral realignments, but cultural stereotyping does remain in American society and does continue to play a role in voting decisions. Numerous cases of black-white tensions playing a role in elections, for

20. David Hackett Fischer extensively traced the emergence of various regional antagonisms back to the founding of colonial political cultures, which he believes derived from the different British regions of origin from which the settlers in each section of colonial America came. He believes that these early patterns of settlement have affected regional political cultures and differing regional political attitudes to the present day, but he states that explanations for such regional cultural persistence, such as socialization, institutional structures, or local ways of bargaining, have been generally neglected by social scientists. David Hackett Fischer, *Albion's Seed* (Oxford, Eng.: Oxford University Press, 1989).

21. Robert Kelley, *The Cultural Pattern in American Politics: The First Century* (Washington, D.C.: University Press of America, 1979), 97–98. Among others who have studied and written on the history of North-South cultural differences and opposition in American politics persisting into modern times are two books by Kevin Phillips, *The Emerging Republican Majority* and *Mediacracy*; Daniel J. Elazar, *American Federalism: A View from the States* (New York: Harper & Row, 1984); and Raymond D. Gastil, *Cultural Regions of the United States* (Seattle: University of Washington Press, 1975).

22. Anthony Lewis, "It Can Happen Here," *New York Times*, November 11, 1991, A15; C. Vann Woodward, "Pests of the Lower South," *New York Times*, November 15, 1991, A31; Richard Morin, "Bringing Out the Alienated Voter," *Washington Post National Weekly Edition*, November 4–10, 1991, 38.

example, are well known (David Duke's many campaigns for office in Louisiana are among the most recent), but the partial persistence of Northern Yankee aversion to perceived Southern values and attitudes, which is usually much more subtle than racial prejudice in the United States, is often overlooked. The insistence on large numbers of comedians in portraying Bill Clinton—a Rhodes Scholar and a Yale Law School graduate—as a Southern hillbilly is only one example of such stereotyping.

Sociologist John Shelton Reed, one of the few to study this phenomenon thoroughly in recent years, noted that "since sectional ill will has played such a prominent part in the history of the United States (even in eras of good feeling it seems merely to have been dormant), one might expect it to have been tagged as a fundamental 'social indicator' and monitored from time to time. One would be mistaken."[23] Southern white antagonism toward the North became apparent in the civil rights era and through political movements like George Wallace's candidacy for president in 1968.[24] Reed's studies made clear, however, that negative perceptions of Northerners by Southerners not only persisted in the 1960s and 1970s but were matched or exceeded by negative perceptions of Southerners among Northerners.[25]

The differing electoral patterns that appear in Vermont when national Republican strategies are not in use may also help bolster the argument that loss of Republican support in the state has resulted partially from the national party's Southern strategy. First, the factors causing the increase

23. John Shelton Reed, *The Enduring South* (Chapel Hill: University of North Carolina Press, 1986), 21.

24. See Black and Black, *The Vital South*, for evidence of anti-Northern rhetoric in the Wallace campaign.

25. See John Shelton Reed's books *The Enduring South* and *Southerners* (Chapel Hill: University of North Carolina Press, 1983). Reed's studies relied mostly on his own surveys of Southerners and on national data indicating regional differences in factors like religious beliefs and gun ownership. Therefore the data on Northern attitudes toward Southerners is limited. Reed cited a 1957 Gallup Poll in which 23 percent of non-Southerners expressed an unfavorable opinion of Southerners (45 percent claimed to hold a favorable opinion, and 17 percent of Southerners viewed Northerners unfavorably). See Reed, *The Enduring South*, 22. He also discussed the perception among Southerners that Northerners viewed them unfavorably—half the Southerners surveyed believed that Northerners looked down on them (*Southerners*, 73). Again, as Reed has stated, data directly measuring regional perceptions toward other regions in the United States is scarce, and it is doubtful that any recent survey asking Northerners "Do you hold an unfavorable opinion of Southerners?" would get an accurate response rate, especially because any such opinions, even if they subtly affect voting behavior, may not have been given much thought previously.

Table 3.6. Relationship of nine variables to Democratic gains in Vermont presidential elections; to the vote for John Anderson for president in 1980 (general election); and to the vote for Bernard Sanders for U.S. representative in 1988 (data for 245 Vermont towns and cities included)

	Correlation Coefficient		
Variable	Democratic Shift	Anderson	Sanders
% English ancestry	.17**	.00	−.17**
% French ancestry	−.58**	−.36**	.21**
% Irish ancestry	−.03	−.05	−.07
Town population	−.14*	.10	.05
% High school grad	.47**	.58**	.04
Per capita income	.12*	.46**	−.14*
% Born in Vermont	−.23**	−.36**	.43**
% Moved to Vermont 1975–80	.27**	.28**	−.23**
Median age	.04	.00	−.39**
1980 Anderson vote	.58**	XXX	.16**
1988 Sanders vote	.21**	.16**	XXX

SOURCES: See source note for Table 3.2.

NOTE: XXX = perfect correlation.

*Significant at the .05 level.
**Significant at the .01 level.

in support for Democratic presidential candidates in Vermont can be compared with support for the two strongest third-party candidates in the state in the 1980s: John Anderson and Bernard Sanders. Second, a statewide campaign by a Republican emphasizing his ties to the national Republican party can be compared to a statewide campaign where the Republican candidate distanced himself from national party policies.

Table 3.6 suggests that the strongest support for John Anderson's 1980 independent presidential candidacy came from the same towns that have shifted most heavily to the Democrats, while support for Bernard Sanders's 1988 independent candidacy for the U.S. House is also significantly related to the Democratic shift, although to a lesser extent. However, while the influence of the nine variables being tested seems similar for the Democratic shift and the Anderson candidacy, many of the variables have an opposite relationship with the Sanders candidacy.

According to Table 3.6, high-income towns were more important in John Anderson's support than in the Democratic shift, and English-ancestry towns showed no special relationship to the Anderson candidacy, but other variables had similar relationships with both the Democratic shift and the Anderson vote. The Sanders vote, however, seemed to come largely from towns with characteristics that were directly opposite to those trending Democratic, with Sanders doing well in French towns and poorly in English towns and towns with lots of non-native Vermonters.

However, comparing the Anderson and Sanders vote results for all Vermont towns does not provide the most accurate picture of Vermont voting patterns. Anderson's vote, like the Democratic shift, tends not to follow its statewide patterns in the three Northeast Kingdom counties, while Sanders's vote may have been heavily affected by the "friends and neighbors" phenomenon. V. O. Key, among others, has described this phenomenon as one in which statewide candidates receive exceptionally strong support from the towns or counties in which they live and have served in office.[26] Sanders's strongest areas of support were all in northern Vermont, including Burlington, where he served as mayor for eight years.

It may seem odd for Sanders, a New York City native, to benefit from a friends-and-neighbors phenomenon in Vermont, but most voters in northern Vermont rely on the Burlington media for local news (Burlington has the only television stations in the area, and the newspaper with the largest circulation[27]), news in which Sanders, as mayor of the state's largest city, no doubt got a lot of attention. And Sanders's mayoral tenure, as a proclaimed socialist, during a period of economic growth was generally considered a success by national observers. In 1987, Sanders was chosen as one of the nation's top twenty mayors by *U.S. News and World Report*, and in 1988 the U.S. Conference of Mayors named Burlington as the "most livable city" of under 100,000 people in the nation.[28] Even the *Burlington Free Press*, which had long opposed Sanders, endorsed him and praised his tenure as mayor during his final candidacy for the office in 1987.[29] And Sanders was happy to remind voters of this record during his 1988 campaign,[30] which likely made more of an impression on voters who had been hearing about it for years than on the voters of southern Vermont, who usually rely on non-Burlington print media and who receive television stations from New Hampshire, Massachusetts, or New York.

26. See Key, *Southern Politics*, 37–41, for a discussion of this phenomenon in Alabama.
27. *Editor and Publisher International Year Book 1991* (New York: Editor & Publisher Company, 1991).
28. Ellen J. Bartlett, "A Socialist in City Hall," *Boston Globe*, August 4, 1988.
29. Ibid.
30. Dan Billin, "Wild Cards," *White River Junction (Vt.) Valley News*, September 30, 1988.

To better assess the bases of support for Anderson and Sanders, while removing the factors of Northeast Kingdom aberrations and friends and neighbors support, Table 3.7 shows the relationship of several variables to the voting patterns of five counties of eastern and southern Vermont. Of Vermont's fourteen counties, three make up the Northeast Kingdom; one, Chittenden County, includes Sanders's home base of Burlington; and five more border on Chittenden County, leaving just five in neither area.

In these five counties, the similarities between the factors behind the Anderson vote and the factors behind the Democratic shift are even more similar than in the state as a whole. English ancestry becomes an important variable in both phenomena, and the two differ greatly only on income levels, lower-income towns being part of the Democratic shift when other factors are taken into account, but not being a significant part of the support for Anderson. The bases of the Sanders vote, however, remain very different, even when the friends and neighbors factor is removed. Sanders, like Anderson and the Democrats, did well in towns with higher educational levels, but Sanders, the New Yorker, seemed to have a large base of support in towns with a lot of Vermont natives—totally opposite the pattern found in towns trending Democratic and towns that supported Anderson in high numbers. In addition, Sanders did better in French towns than in English towns, and he also did well in towns with younger populations, unlike the results found for Anderson and the Democratic shift.

Sanders's national reputation would likely lead observers to believe that his strongest support comes from the non-native Vermonters, who came to the state in the 1960s and 1970s, having formed liberal or leftist views in Massachusetts and New York, and who maintain counterculture lifestyles or started businesses with a "social conscience," like Ben and Jerry of ice cream fame. Yet while many activists who have worked for Sanders campaigns have probably fit that profile, much of his statewide success, at least in the 1980s, was due to his ability to capture some of the old state Democratic constituency, the descendants of the Vermont minority that supported the New Deal. Vermont's New Deal Democrats tended to be largely of French Canadian ancestry, socially conservative, and supportive of social welfare programs that benefited the working class, although still somewhat antagonistic toward the taxes that paid for these programs.

Sanders, the "independent" socialist mayor of Burlington for most of

Table 3.7. Relationship of nine variables to Democratic gains in Vermont presidential elections; to the 1980 Anderson candidacy; and to the 1988 Sanders candidacy, in 106 towns and cities in five Vermont counties (Bennington, Orange, Rutland, Windham, and Windsor) in southern and eastern Vermont

	Correlation coefficient		
Variable	Democratic Shift	Anderson	Sanders
% English ancestry	.38**	.35**	.00
% French ancestry	−.22*	−.18	.26**
% Irish ancestry	−.11	−.15	.01
Town population	−.14	.00	.10
% High school grad	.48**	.50**	.11
Per capita income	.14	.32**	−.18
% Born in Vermont	−.44*	−.48**	.33**
% Moved to Vermont 1975–80	.44**	.35**	−.02
Median age	−.08	.00	−.35**
1980 Anderson vote	.60**	XXX	.07
1988 Sanders vote	.21*	.07	XXX

Multiple regression of nine variables on each of the following voting results for 106 Vermont towns and cities. Only variables that contribute to the overall model are listed.

Democratic Shift

$R^2 = 41.9\%$ R^2 (adjusted) = 39.6%.
s = 7.717 with 106 − 5 = 101 degrees of freedom.

Source	Sum of Squares	df	Mean Square	F-ratio
Regression	4328.85	4	1082	18.2
Residual	6014.17	101	59.5462	

Variable	Coefficient	s.e. of Coeff	t-ratio
Constant	− 17.399400	6.5640	− 2.65
English	0.497285	0.1399	3.55**
High school grad	0.492805	0.1276	3.86**
Income	− 0.001569	0.0007	− 2.20*
New to Vermont	0.484181	0.1288	3.76**

Anderson 1980

$R^2 = 35.2\%$ R^2 (adjusted) = 33.3%
s = 3.996 with 106 − 4 = 102 degrees of freedom

Source	Sum of Squares	df	Mean Square	F-ratio
Regression	886.225	3	295	18.5
Residual	1629.090	102	15.9715	

Table 3.7. (Continued)

Variable	Coefficient	s.e. of Coeff	t-ratio
Constant	5.672440	5.6280	1.01
English	0.204717	0.0717	2.86**
High school grad	0.161807	0.0598	2.70**
Born in Vermont	−0.098379	0.0363	−2.71**

Sanders 1988

R^2 = 32.9% R^2 (adjusted) = 30.9%
s = 8.202 with 106 − 4 = 102 degrees of freedom

Source	Sum of Squares	df	Mean Square	F-ratio
Regression	3365.06	3	1122	16.7
Residual	6861.35	102	67.2681	

Variable	Coefficient	s.e. of Coeff	t-ratio
Constant	−1.484820	14.990	−0.099
High school grad	0.566085	0.1202	4.71**
Median age	−0.897451	0.2703	−3.32**
Born in Vermont	0.397343	0.0765	5.20**

SOURCES: See source note for Table 3.2.

NOTE: XXX = perfect correlation.

*Significant at the .05 level.
**Significant at the .01 level.

the 1980s, espoused many traditional socialist programs and policies in his six campaigns for statewide office since 1986, but he also used his independent label and refusal to affiliate with any organized socialist third party as a tool to portray himself as someone who fought for average Vermonters rather than party leaders and their affiliated special interests. While Sanders's appeal to liberals and leftists born out of state, and to voters who were disenchanted with standard party politics, has gained him many supporters and votes, his increasing success in his statewide campaigns in the 1980s and early 1990s also relied heavily on his ability to attract the types of Vermont voters who never belonged to the Republican party and who probably had begun to feel left out of the state Democratic party, which is increasingly controlled by activists born out of state and by the educated and Yankee voters who used to vote Republican.

In 1986, Sanders won 14 percent of the vote for Vermont governor, doing best in areas that had younger voters and more native-born Vermonters. It is possible that some of his popularity among these voters may have derived from some antagonism among younger, native-born Vermonters to the influx of young professionals from other states. Sanders in his 1986 campaign called for controlling the costs of utilities, health care, and housing—costs that have increased greatly with the arrival of young professionals from other states—while the two major party candidates tended to emphasize environmental and budgetary issues.[31]

Sanders surprised many in 1988 when he received 36 percent of the vote in the race for U.S. Representative from Vermont, losing to Republican Peter Smith by only 5 percent. Explanations for that strong 1988 showing included the large amount of out-of-state funding he had and his solid administrative record as mayor of Burlington. Also crucial, however, was the mishap by the Democratic candidate in the race, who blurted out a proposal to end federal dairy subsidies (Vermont is the most rural state in the nation with a relatively large number of dairy farmers) and then awkwardly defended the proposal despite public opposition from farmers.[32] The Democrat, Paul Poirier, would normally have done well in French Canadian areas running against a Yankee Republican (due to Poirier's French name), but he received only 19 percent of the statewide vote and lost many French Canadian voters to Sanders.

Sanders's eventual victory over Smith for the House seat in 1990 again resulted from campaign blunders by his opponents, combined with the increased appeal of the independent socialist among the traditional Vermont Democratic constituency. Democratic candidate Dolores Sandoval, a black University of Vermont professor in a state that is 0.2 percent black, received her party nomination mainly because of the lack of alternatives, despite her finishing last in the four-person primary for the same House seat in 1988. After she called early in the campaign for legalization of drugs and cutting off aid to Israel if they didn't negotiate with the Palestinians, Sandoval was discounted as a serious candidate by her opponents and by the Vermont media.[33] In the month before the election, Republican incumbent Smith got in trouble by quickly endorsing the negotiated budget package that came out of Bush's negotiations with congressional leaders and that called for middle-class tax increases. After the package was defeated, Smith achieved national publicity by vocally

31. Paul Teeter, "Candidates Meet in Mild Debate," *Rutland Daily Herald,* October 2, 1986.

32. "2-Party System Rocked," *Burlington Free Press,* November 9, 1988.

33. Phil Duncan, ed., *Congressional Quarterly's Politics in America 1992* (Washington, D.C.: Congressional Quarterly, 1991), 1513.

disagreeing with several Bush policy stands at a Vermont campaign appearance to which Bush had traveled as a show of support for Smith in his reelection race.[34]

While Smith was apparently embarrassing himself, Sanders gained support by opposing any tax increases for the middle class, issuing his usual call to raise taxes mainly on the wealthy. And while Sanders, surprisingly, was able to take political advantage of conservative attitudes toward higher taxes, even more surprising was his support from the National Rifle Association, which had been angered by Smith's vote for banning semi-automatic weapons.[35] (Sanders voted against the Brady gun control amendment requiring a five-day waiting period for the purchase of handguns his first few years in office.) Sanders won with 56 percent of the vote, compared with 40 percent for incumbent Smith and 3 percent for Democrat Sandoval. In 1990, Sanders maintained the core support he has always had among some of the activists born out of state, but opposition to taxes and gun control tend to be much less popular among these activists than among the traditional conservative Democratic constituency. His victory margin clearly came from the types of voters—Vermont-born, frequently of French ancestry—who had increasingly supported him with each statewide election up to 1990.[36]

And it is this constituency that distinguishes Sanders's success from the Democratic shift in presidential elections and from the John Anderson voters in 1980. While Democratic presidential candidates have been losing votes in their old French Canadian strongholds, but gaining more votes in English Yankee parts of Vermont, Sanders recaptured some of the old New Deal constituency, not just with messages of economic populism but with occasional opposition to the socially liberal policies favored by non-native Vermonters and by the types of voters switching to the Democrats in presidential elections, many of whom supported John Anderson in 1980.

John Anderson received 14.9 percent of Vermont's vote for president in the general election of 1980, his second best total (behind Massachu-

34. Michael Barone and Grant Ujifusa, The Almanac of American Politics 1992 (Washington, D.C.: National Journal, 1991), 1258.

35. Ibid.

36. By 1994, however, Sanders had voted to ban assault weapons and earned the wrath of the National Rifle Association, which campaigned against him that year. Michael Barone and Grant Ujifusa, The Almanac of American Politics 1996 (Washington, D.C.: National Journal, 1995). Sanders has probably lost most of his base among social conservatives since that time and is relying more heavily on modern Vermont Democrats.

setts) among all the states nationwide. Although some dismissed Anderson's support as derived solely from "wine and cheese" liberals,[37] his votes on Election Day clearly came from a more diverse group both in Vermont and nationwide.[38] The strong correlation in Vermont towns between high votes for Anderson and high abandonment rates for Republican presidential candidates is not difficult to explain, given the state's political history and the analysis above of the reasons for the state's Democratic trend.

As stated earlier, it would be difficult to label Vermont's Yankee voters, who opposed Franklin Roosevelt and the New Deal more than almost any other group in the nation, as historically liberal. Yet most of the Republicans that Vermont has elected statewide since the 1930s could also not be classified as conservatives. As Neal Peirce has stated, "Vermont's 'conservative' leaders—those who frequently win office—would be called outrageous spenders and socialist meddlers in a state like next door New Hampshire, or in many states of the South and the Mountain West."[39]

Vermont Republican George Aiken, elected governor in 1936 and U.S. Senator in 1940, vigorously criticized the New Deal during the 1930s, calling it a "tragedy," and "propaganda,"[40] and claimed that the Roosevelt administration's policies were "alien to the free-thinking people of Vermont and of the nation" and an attempt "for more and more control of all of us and our possessions and resources, public and private."[41] To some, his rhetoric might make him seem like a raving reactionary, but his words merely exaggerated a general dislike of the idea of big government. In practice, Aiken supported some New Deal programs, like Social Security and recreation and conservation efforts, and as a U.S. Senator

37. Henry Fairlie dismissed the "new coalition" of John Anderson as consisting merely of the idle rich, the campus activists and idealists "who will be ripping off the system in Washington in 10 years," and the "cause people" interested in issues like abortion, gun control, and energy conservation. *The New Republic*, June 21, 1980, 10–13.

38. Kevin Phillips, *Post-Conservative America*, 230–231, categorized most of Anderson's best counties nationwide as one of seven types: (1) university locations; (2) ski area / arts-crafts orientation; (3) high-tech industry / suburbia; (4) small-town Yankee / summer resort; (5) affluent suburban; (6) rural/urban Scandinavian; and (7) urban/suburban New England.

39. Peirce, *The New England States*, 275.

40. George Aiken, *Speaking from Vermont* (New York: Frederick Stokes, 1938), 196. Cited in William Doyle, *The Vermont Political Tradition and Those Who Helped Make It* (Barre, Vt.: Northlight Studio Press, 1984), 187.

41. H. Nicholas Muller and Samuel B. Hand, *In a State of Nature: Reading in Vermont History* (Montpelier, Vt.: Vermont Historical Society, 1982), 329. Cited in Doyle, *The Vermont Political Tradition*, 188.

he designed the Food Stamp program, which benefits both the poor who need food and farmers who sell food.[42] In his later years in the Senate, Aiken focused on environmental and rural development programs and received publicity for advocating that the United States declare victory in Vietnam and pull out in 1966.[43]

Many of the Republicans who followed Aiken in Vermont politics similarly distinguished themselves as moderate-to-liberal principled politicians. Ralph Flanders, who lost a primary race for the U.S. Senate as the "conservative" alternative to Aiken in 1940, later won the state's other Senate seat and won national fame for introducing the resolution to censure Senator Joseph McCarthy in the 1950s and for advocating universal disarmament.[44] Republican Ernest Gibson, elected Vermont governor in 1946, made the state income tax sharply progressive and proceeded to fund improvements in education, health care, welfare, and criminal rehabilitation.[45]

The state's two most recent Republican U.S. senators have continued their predecessors' traditions. Robert Stafford promoted environmental concerns, even over the objections of the Reagan administration, worked on the federal student loan program that now bears his name, and regularly scored more than 60 out of 100 on the Americans for Democratic Action scale for liberal voting, before retiring in 1988.[46] His replacement, James Jeffords, regularly had one of the most liberal voting records of any Republican U.S. House member, being the only member of his party to vote against the Reagan tax cuts in that chamber, and Jeffords has maintained his liberal image in the Senate, voting to override Bush's veto of the 1990 civil rights bill.[47]

In 1980, John Anderson's presidential candidacy fit well with Vermont's moderate-to-liberal Republican tradition. Anderson first gained widespread national publicity by, surprisingly, almost winning the Massachusetts and Vermont Republican presidential primaries. When he was unable to match this success elsewhere, Anderson declared his independent candidacy for president and through his campaign emphasized his

42. Doyle, The Vermont Political Tradition, 187.
43. Peirce, The New England States, 283.
44. Ibid., 269.
45. Ibid., 270.
46. Alan Ehrenhalt, ed., Politics in America (Washington, D.C.: Congressional Quarterly, 1983), 1543–1544.
47. Barone and Ujifusa, 1992 Almanac, 1257.

conservative positions on fiscal and budgetary matters, his liberal views favoring personal privacy on abortion and religion, and his opposition to hawkish defense and military views of the world. Anderson's call for discipline, responsibility, and avoidance of simple solutions for complex problems,[48] combined with his ideological views, gained him much support among Yankee and well-educated voters in Vermont, who for years had been voting for like-minded Republican candidates. As national Republican presidential candidates drifted away from such views, these voters increasingly switched to the Democrats, especially when alternatives like Anderson were not available.

In state elections, Republicans who have continued the state party's moderate and liberal traditions have remained very successful, while the occasional state Republican candidates who make the apparent mistake of campaigning on their national party's platform have not. Republican Peter Smith, during his successful candidacy for U.S. Representative in 1988, asserted: "I'm a Vermont Republican. I don't get up in the morning and read what George Bush or Dan Quayle said in order to get my marching orders."[49] And evidence from races for governor and senator in the last twenty years indicates that Vermont Republicans usually win races when adhering to the state party's historical image and lose races when instead they emphasize the national party's recent image.

Richard Snelling, Vermont's only Republican governor in the last twenty years, was first elected in 1976, a year when Democrat Stella Hackel, a relative conservative, won her party primary and vowed to veto any tax increase and to crack down on welfare fraud. Snelling, on the other hand, described himself as a liberal on some social issues and sought support from environmentalists. Despite predictions of a close election, Snelling won easily.[50]

An even better demonstration of Vermont's persistent high support for moderate and liberal Republicans, and dislike of national-style conservative Republicans, is provided by the state's last two elections during the 1980s for the U.S. Senate. In 1986, former popular governor Snelling was the Republican candidate for the Senate, and he lost by 63–35 percent

48. Frank Smallwood, *The Other Candidates* (Hanover, N.H.: University Press of New England, 1983), 231–232.

49. John Dillon, "Smith Plays It Safe in Three-Way Race," *Rutland Daily Herald,* October 14, 1988.

50. *Congressional Quarterly Weekly Report,* October 9, 1976, 2861.

to Patrick Leahy. Just two years later, U.S. Representative Jeffords ran as the Republican candidate for Senate and won by 68–30 percent.

The circumstances of the two campaigns were not the same. Snelling ran a negative campaign against a Democratic incumbent in a year in which several Republican incumbents went down to defeat. Jeffords, on the other hand, was considered an early favorite for the open seat in a year in which a Republican won the presidency.

But while national trends and the powers of incumbency likely played an important role in the widely variant results for the two Republican candidates, these factors should also not be overestimated. First, senators in the last twenty years have not been protected by incumbency by anywhere near the same amount as U.S. Representatives, and many of the supposed advantages of incumbents, such as name recognition and fundraising, did not exist in the Snelling-Leahy race. Snelling was as well known as Leahy in Vermont and spent more than $1.5 million on his campaign in this small state, just slightly less than Leahy spent.[51] Second, Leahy had had trouble defeating lesser-known opponents in his two previous Senate races, winning just 50 percent of the vote each time. And third, while Bush had a strong victory nationally in 1988, his coattails did not reach Congress, and he barely won Vermont. Surely there must be other reasons why a well-known Republican like Snelling, popular enough to regain the governor's seat in 1990,[52] did so poorly in 1986 (only three little-known Republican candidates for the Senate did worse in other states that year), while two years later, Republican candidate Jeffords had the highest victory margin for any Republican candidate for Senate that year, higher even than all the incumbents running.

One of those reasons could be the Republican party image each candidate chose to present. Snelling's entry into the race came after a well-publicized effort by Reagan administration officials to recruit him, and Snelling's use in his campaign of the political consultants who helped Jesse Helms get reelected to the Senate from North Carolina in 1984 further identified the former governor with national Republicans.[53] Snelling's views on issues were fairly close to Leahy's, but the former governor decided to take some conservative positions and attack Leahy's stands on

51. Duncan, Congressional Quarterly's Politics in America 1992, 1514.

52. Snelling died in office in 1991 and was replaced by Democratic Lieutenant Governor Howard Dean, who won a full two-year term in 1992.

53. Michael Barone and Grant Ujifusa, The Almanac of American Politics 1988 (Washington, D.C.: National Journal, 1987), 1211.

defense spending.[54] Unfortunately for Snelling, "his efforts to run as a Reaganite rang false; as governor, he had been a sharp critic of Reagan's budget priorities."[55]

Jeffords, on the other hand, had often flaunted his opposition to conservative Republicanism and Reagan programs and stuck to his positions in 1988, much to the dismay of the conservative minority within Vermont's Republican party.[56] Besides opposing the Reagan tax cuts, Jeffords has been a consistent opponent of the conservative Republicans' social agenda and has repeatedly voted against school prayer legislation and for affirmative action and government funding of abortions.[57] However, it must be remembered that Jeffords is a liberal Republican, not a liberal Democrat. He has favored capital punishment in certain types of cases, opposed some gun control measures,[58] and voted for the January 1991 resolution authorizing President Bush to use military force against Iraq in Kuwait. In 1984, the Vermont Rainbow Coalition, part of a national organization set up by Jesse Jackson to assist in his presidential bid that year, criticized Jeffords's votes for certain nuclear weapons projects. "A vote for Jeffords is tantamount to a vote for nuclear war within four years," said one leader of the group.[59]

Such charges may carry weight with some of the liberal or far-left activists born out of state, but they do not seem to have affected the overwhelming support Jeffords got in all of his campaigns for U.S. House and U.S. Senate. Jeffords has been strongly attacked by both the far left and far right activists in the state, yet Vermont voters' historically strong preferences for liberal or moderate Republicans, when available, over either conservatives or Democrats have continued to appear in Jeffords's elections. Snelling, however, lost much of the benefit from these preferences in 1986 by allowing himself to be portrayed as a Reagan Republican.

Vermont voters' penchant for moderate- to liberal-Republicanism is a factor for which typical critical election realignment theory is unable to

54. Deborah Sline, "Snelling, Leahy in First Debate," *Rutland Daily Herald*, October 6, 1986.

55. Duncan, *Congressional Quarterly's Politics in America 1992*, 1514.

56. According to the *Burlington Free Press*, Vermont papers have received "hundreds of scathing letters to the editor from right-wing Republicans convinced Jeffords has more in common with Bolshevik revolutionaries than Vermont Republicans." James E. Bresser, "GOP Candidate Is Sitting Pretty," *Burlington Free Press*, October 16, 1988.

57. Ibid.

58. Ibid.

59. Jack Hoffman, "Rainbow Attacks Jeffords," *Barre Times-Argus*, October 20, 1984.

account in its focus on partisan shifts across all levels of government. While the national Republican party is steering away from policy stands favored in Vermont, thereby causing a shift to the Democrats in presidential elections, many Republican candidates for state office who adhere to the state party's traditionally moderate views remain successful. Recent state realignments like Vermont's might be federalized, divided between national and state office levels, but the persistent change in voting patterns indicates realignment nevertheless.

However, Democrats in Vermont have also made some strong gains in voting for state offices as well, and the state is not the best example of split-level realignments. Chapter 5 will provide a better case study of a state whose voting patterns in elections for president and for state offices moved in completely opposite directions during the 1980s—Rhode Island.

Vermont's voting patterns do, however, strongly demonstrate the need to move beyond the search for critical election periods as indicative of realignments, because data from the state's towns prove such an effort fruitless. Instead, the state's realignment toward the Democrats in presidential elections over the last forty years has been much more gradual, sometimes moving in fits and starts, but generally continuing to move in one direction over the past thirty years.

Table 3.8 provides voting and demographic data for seventeen Vermont towns and cities. Marlboro and Strafford are the two Vermont towns where the shift toward Democrats in presidential elections has been the largest since the 1950s. Marlboro is predominantly a college town in southern Vermont, while Strafford is located in eastern central Vermont near Hanover, New Hampshire, the home of Dartmouth College. A majority of Strafford residents were not born in Vermont.

The next group of five towns are among those with the ten highest Democratic shifts, but these five towns also contain relatively high numbers of residents born in Vermont. While southeastern Vermont contains the counties with the highest Democratic shifts, these five towns are all in the central part of the state, four of them in northern Vermont. The five towns have high ratios of English to French ancestry, relatively high educational levels, populations of at least 60 percent born in state, and widely varying income levels.

The third group of five towns (starting with Canaan) are all located in the Northeast Kingdom, with its unique voting patterns, and are among the eleven towns and cities in all of Vermont that shifted Republican in

Table 3.8. Republican presidential vote in selected Vermont towns and cities, 1952–1988 (percentage of two-party vote)

Town	1952	1956	1960	1964	1968	1972	1976	1980	1984	1988
Marlboro	83	82	72	42	56	38	38	35	31	28
Strafford	84	86	76	35	59	57	49	47	36	35
Calais	89	87	77	34	67	49	49	43	44	41
Greensboro	88	87	76	41	66	58	50	54	51	41
Marshfield	88	90	78	31	68	55	46	41	47	46
Rochester	90	91	83	41	73	65	64	49	53	51
Worcester	91	92	75	38	71	67	56	50	50	46
Canaan	68	67	54	30	53	69	51	64	75	66
Lemington	69	77	56	46	61	78	67	71	81	79
Norton	41	45	29	18	30	39	37	66	65	61
Jay	49	31	40	31	47	55	51	54	71	57
Westfield	58	41	39	28	48	47	52	58	67	54
Barre Town	56	59	46	24	46	62	54	54	62	60
Milton	61	59	49	33	51	70	55	53	67	59
St. Albans Town	54	51	40	24	47	71	53	55	63	52
Swanton	45	46	32	18	37	70	51	51	60	50
Winooski	24	30	13	8	19	45	39	32	48	41

	Demographic Characteristics of the Towns					
Town	Population*	% English*	% French*	% Born in Vermont*	% High School Grad*	Per Capita Income*
Marlboro	695	16	2	25	83	5,600
Strafford	731	20	5	41	74	6,600
Calais	1,207	21	5	60	80	6,300
Greensboro	677	28	10	65	71	5,000
Marshfield	1,267	15	5	60	73	4,700
Rochester	1,054	18	3	60	75	6,000
Worcester	727	27	5	62	72	5,300
Canaan	1,196	22	29	28	51	5,000
Lemington	108	26	18	22	73	4,800
Norton	184	10	32	29	40	5,900
Jay	302	21	12	63	68	5,500
Westfield	418	12	23	78	64	5,800
Barre Town	7,090	12	15	79	72	6,500
Milton	6,829	10	21	77	69	5,700
St. Albans Town	3,555	13	29	76	58	6,300
Swanton	5,141	17	27	77	55	5,700
Winooski	6,318	5	34	73	56	5,800

SOURCES: See source note for Table 3.2.

*All data come from the 1980 U.S. Census. All percentages are rounded off to the nearest whole number. Income is rounded off to the nearest hundred dollar. Ancestries include only those claiming a single ancestry in either category.

Table 3.9. Republican presidential vote in five Vermont English-ancestry towns (Greensboro, Calais, Marshfield, Worcester, Rochester) and five French-ancestry towns (Milton, Winooski, St. Albans Town, Swanton, Barre Town), 1952–1988 (average percentage Republican)

	1952	1956	1960	1964	1968	1972	1976	1980	1984	1988
Five English towns	89	89	78	37	69	59	53	47	49	45
Five French towns	46	49	36	21	40	64	50	49	60	52

SOURCES: See source note for Table 3.5.

presidential elections between the 1950s and the 1980s. As the demographic figures show, three of these towns—Canaan, Lemington, and Norton—are populated mostly by residents born outside Vermont, many of them probably from New Hampshire and Quebec, on which these towns border. The town of Jay also borders on Quebec, while Westfield borders on Jay. While the latter two towns are populated mostly by native-born Vermonters, their lifestyles, and possibly their politics, have been greatly affected by the presence of the ski resort of Jay Peak. Because of its proximity to Quebec, Jay Peak is the only one of Vermont's major ski resorts that caters more to Quebecois than to New Englanders and New Yorkers.[60] If Massachusettsians and New Yorkers have had some influence on the politics of the rest of Vermont, then it is likely that Quebecois have had a very different type of influence on Jay and Westfield.

The final group of five towns have had the largest Republican trends of the six remaining towns with partisan shifts in this direction outside the Northeast Kingdom. All five towns and cities are large by Vermont standards, all five have high ratios of French Canadian to English ancestry, and four of the towns are located in northwestern Vermont between Burlington and the Quebec border. The towns on average have lower educational levels, but higher incomes, than the five English towns shifting toward the Democrats listed in Table 3.8.

Table 3.9 compares the partisan voting trends of the five English towns with Democratic shifts (Greensboro, Calais, Marshfield, Worcester, and Rochester) with the five French towns with Republican shifts (Milton, Winooski, St. Albans Town, Swanton, and Barre Town). The chart presents the average Republican share of the two-party vote for president from each group of five for presidential elections from 1952 to 1988. As Table 3.9 shows, the patterns for the five English towns is strikingly similar to

60. Taken from a Vermont Vacation-Home Inventory cited in Harold A. Meeks, *Time and Change in Vermont: A Human Geography* (Chester, Conn.: Globe Pequot Press, 1986), 238.

that of Ashfield, Massachusetts (see Table 1.1). The clear trend between 1956 and 1988 is for the Republican share of the presidential vote to decrease in every election, except for the temporary overwhelming Democratic shift in 1964 and the slight Republican upsurge in 1984, which may be due more to John Anderson's effect on the two major party's votes in 1980 than to any increase in Reagan's popularity in these towns. No one election in the data stands out as signifying a critical realignment. The Democrats gained 11 percent more of the vote between 1956 and 1960, 9 percent more between 1960 and 1968, 10 percent more between 1968 and 1972, and 6 percent more between 1972 and 1976 and 1976 and 1980, and in 1988 continued to gain over previous years.

Even comparing the five English towns with the five French towns in the manner of Key's "Theory of Critical Elections," to determine the emergence of divergent voting patterns, provides no clear evidence of a single critical election. The year 1972 was the first in which the Republicans gained votes in the French towns and lost votes in the English towns. But 1980 was the first year in which French town support for the Republicans permanently surpassed English town support, and 1984 was the first year in which it became clear that Republican presidential candidates were much more popular in Vermont's French towns than in Vermont's English towns.

What Table 3.9 and the accompanying data demonstrate is that the process of realignment in Vermont over the last forty years has been gradual, but very large and very clear. To deny that there has been electoral realignment in the state merely because no one- or two-election period where massive voter shifts occurred can be found is absurd. The consistent partisan trend in one direction—toward the Democrats—in Vermont's English towns indicates the continued importance of party cues in presidential voting, despite claims that such cues have been overwhelmed by candidate personalities and transient issues. And as stated earlier, although Vermont has become more Democratic across all office levels, the remaining Republican strength in the state has much more to do with the state party's differences with the national party than with voters ignoring the party affiliations of candidates.

Who are Vermont's new Democrats? Some of them are newcomers to the state from other parts of the Northeast, where they were raised in Democratic families. But a larger number of Vermont's new Democrats were born or raised in Vermont, where the traditional Republican preferences among the state's better-educated and Yankee English voters have

faded in presidential elections in reaction to the Republican party's growing conservative national image. Voters of French Canadian ancestry
seem unenthusiastic about the increased cultural liberalism of their traditional Democratic party, and in some areas have become more Republican. Meanwhile, the state's third-largest ethnic group, the Irish, have
become somewhat more assimilated into Yankee culture than the French
Canadians, and have shown much less tendency to change their partisan
voting habits than the two larger groups.

The Vermont pattern of growing Democratic support among well-educated and English Yankee voters is found in many parts of the Northern
United States. That pattern, however, is not dominant everywhere in the
North, or even in all of New England. Just as national public opinion
surveys might label voters in Vermont who consistently vote Democratic
for president and Republican for Congress as dealigned with no partisan
attachments, these surveys also necessarily mix together the opinions of
voters from all over the nation and at best detect differences only among
large regions, in which realignments may not always be apparent. The
next chapter presents evidence for how a clear realigning trend in one
state can be canceled out statistically by an opposite clear trend in a
neighboring state when data from both are mixed together. Chapter 4
will also attempt to solve an odd puzzle: Why has Vermont become more
Democratic, while neighboring New Hampshire, a seemingly similar
state, became more Republican in the 1970s and 1980s?

Chapter Four

— · ※ · —

As Vermont Goes,
So Goes Maine,
But Not New Hampshire

Over the years, many observers of national or regional politics seem to have tossed New Hampshire and Vermont together as twin states when describing their political environments, often grouping them with Maine as bastions of old Northern New England Yankee culture. In *The Emerging Republican Majority* (1969), Kevin Phillips dismissed all three states, along with the rest of New England, New York, and Michigan, as lost causes for the Republicans in future presidential elections.[1] Ralph Nading Hill wrote a comprehensive history of the two states called *Yankee Kingdom*, which he dedicated in part to "the legendary New Hampshire and Vermont Yankee."[2] At one point in his book, Hill did note that "while Vermont and New Hampshire have aptly been called twin states, they are not identical. Their differences, however, are not as easily counted as their similarities."[3] Even the poet Robert Frost, who lived much of his life in the two states, considered Vermont and New Hampshire "yoke fellows."[4] However, once each state is examined closely and separately, it

---

1. See Phillips's map in *Emerging Republican Majority*, 472. Since that book was published, all three Northern New England states voted for the Republican candidate in every presidential election between 1972 and 1988, including Gerald Ford's losing candidacy in 1976. However, Vermont was clearly trending toward the Democrats during the period, while New Hampshire became even more solidly Republican. Maine remained fairly stable in its partisan preferences relative to the nation in presidential elections between 1968 and 1988. Not until 1992 and 1996 did all three states vote Democratic for president for the first time since 1964—New Hampshire by a significantly smaller margin than the other two.

2. Hill, *Yankee Kingdom*, 6.

3. Ibid., 279.

4. Morrissey, *Vermont*, 50.

becomes obvious that while Maine, New Hampshire, and Vermont have many similar characteristics, grouping the three states together as one political phenomenon is a major error.

Table 4.1 summarizes by decade the results for three types of statewide elections in the three Northern New England states between the 1920s and 1980s, and the data reveal several similarities in the voting patterns of the three states, but also some differences, many of them likely surprising to those who have not closely studied the politics of the three states. Between the 1920s and 1950s, all three states were clearly more Republican than the national average in presidential elections, although New Hampshire was significantly more supportive of Democratic candidates than the other two states. By the 1960s, the three states began to move closer to the national average, largely because of their strong aversion to Barry Goldwater's Republican candidacy. Maine even voted more Democratic than the national average in 1968 because of the presence of Maine Senator Ed Muskie on that year's Democratic ticket as the vice presidential candidate.

Between 1968 and 1988, Maine's presidential voting remained close to the national average, while the other two states not only began moving in opposite directions from each other, but reversed their positions in partisan strength from earlier in the twentieth century. By the 1970s, New Hampshire, the most Democratic of the three states for most of the century, broke off from Maine's and Vermont's pattern and began becoming by far the most Republican of the three in presidential elections. Meanwhile, Vermont continued a trend toward the Democrats and was the only one of the three less supportive of Republican presidential candidates than the rest of the nation during the 1980s.

Gubernatorial and senatorial elections show similar patterns for each state, with occasional differences in the timing. Although Republicans were clearly the majority party in elections for both offices in all three states between the 1920s and 1940s, Democratic candidates for governor and U.S. Senator have greatly improved their performances in Maine and Vermont elections since then. In Vermont, Democrats gained large jumps in support in the 1950s and 1960s in gubernatorial elections, and in the 1970s and 1980s in senatorial elections, while in Maine the Democrats made large gains in voting for both offices during the 1950s and 1970s. Democrats were actually much stronger than Republicans in gubernatorial and senatorial elections in Maine during the 1970s and 1980s.[5]

___

5. It is interesting that Democratic gubernatorial and senatorial candidates did better in

Comparing New Hampshire with the other two states in gubernatorial and senatorial elections reveals a pattern similar to that found in comparing the three states' presidential voting before the 1980s. Between the 1920s and the 1940s, New Hampshire was majority Republican, but it was generally the weakest Republican state of the three. From the 1950s to the 1970s, Democrats grew stronger in elections for governor and senator in New Hampshire, as they did in Maine and Vermont. But in the 1980s, New Hampshire began to diverge sharply from the other two states in elections for these two offices, just as it did in presidential elections, and New Hampshire became the most Republican state in Northern New England in elections for all three offices discussed—the opposite of its position earlier in the century.

In the 1990s, New Hampshire began to join the rest of New England in Democratic preferences, at least in presidential elections. In 1992, the state went for Clinton by a 1 percent margin, his smallest in the Northeast, where he won every state. Clinton's victory in New Hampshire, however, could have been considered a fluke, due to Perot's 23 percent of the vote in the state. But by 1996, Clinton won New Hampshire by a healthy 10 percent margin and did about as well there as he did nationally. New Hampshire also elected a Democratic governor in 1996 for the first time since 1980.[6] (See Table 4.2.)

This could indicate the beginning of a process where New Hampshire fits in more closely with the rest of New England, as Kevin Phillips predicted in 1979. Yet New Hampshire still shows marked differences from the political preferences of its two Northern New England neighbors. In 1996, New Hampshire was still the least Democratic state and the most Republican state by far out of all of New England in the presidential election. And following the 1996 congressional elections, New England's delegation to the U.S. House of Representatives consisted of eighteen Democrats and only four Republicans (plus an independent, Bernie Sanders of Vermont). Of those four Republicans, two came from New Hampshire, which elects only two members to the House.[7] New Hamp-

---

Maine than Democratic presidential candidate Franklin Roosevelt during the 1930s. In 1932, Maine elected Democratic Governor Louis Brann at the same time that it was rejecting Roosevelt and voting Republican for president. Brann won reelection in 1934 and gained 49 percent of the vote in a U.S. Senate election in 1936, the year that Maine became one of only two states to reject Roosevelt a second time. Other Democratic candidates in Maine also did better in the 1930s than in the decade before or afterward.

6. New Hampshire and Vermont remain the only two of the fifty states where governors serve two-year terms.

7. The other two were from western Connecticut.

Table 4.1. Votes for president, governor, and U.S. senator in Vermont, New Hampshire, and Maine since 1920, by party (percentage of vote)

Decade	President				Governor			U.S. Senator		
	National	Vt.	N.H.	Me.	Vt.	N.H.	Me.	Vt.	N.H.	Me.
1920s	57-35	74-24	60-38	69-29	73-26	56-44	61-39	71-29	60-40	63-35
1930s	38-59	57-42	49-49	56-42	64-36	55-44	52-48	59-41	53-47	54-46
1940s	45-53	58-42	49-51	53-46	72-28	54-46	66-34	67-33	55-45	65-35
1950s	56-43	72-28	64-36	68-31	57-41	56-44	50-48	67-33	60-38	52-47
1960s	44-51	49-50	47-52	44-56	48-52	46-54	50-50	73-27	55-45	51-49
1970s	54-44	59-40	59-39	55-43	51-44	48-45	36-45	55-42	48-50	45-52
1980s	54-42	51-42	63-32	54-42	49-47	55-45	39-46	51-48	58-40	44-56

SOURCES: 1920s–1940s from *Congressional Quarterly's Guide to U.S. Elections*; 1950s–1970s from *America Votes*; 1980s from *The Almanac of American Politics*.

NOTES: Percentage of vote is expressed as % of the Republican vote, then a hyphen, then % of the Democratic vote. The percentages are decade averages rounded. "National" stands for national vote in presidential elections.

Table 4.2. Presidential election results in the New England states, 1992 and 1996 (percentage)

State	1992			1996		
	Clinton	Bush	Perot	Clinton	Dole	Perot
Maine	39	30	30	52	31	14
New Hampshire	39	38	23	49	39	10
Vermont	46	30	23	53	31	12
Massachusetts	48	29	23	62	28	9
Rhode Island	47	29	23	60	27	11
Connecticut	42	36	22	53	35	10

SOURCES: 1992 results from *America Votes 20*; 1996 results from *Congressional Quarterly Weekly Reports*, January 18, 1997, 188.

NOTE: Figures are rounded to the nearest whole number.

shire's two U.S. senators are also Republican at this writing, making it the only entirely Republican state delegation in Congress east of the Mississippi River. In addition, all the other congressional Republicans in New England are considered moderates at the national level, while New Hampshire's congressional Republicans are significantly more conservative than those elsewhere in New England.

Despite some recent trends, then, New Hampshire remains distinctly more Republican and conservative than its New England neighbors. In close presidential elections in the near future, New Hampshire is still likely to split with the other New England states, especially its "twin" state of Vermont—a circumstance that is unusual but not unknown in the two states' electoral histories. Between 1948 and 1988, Vermont and New Hampshire were two of just seven states to vote for the Republican presidential candidate ten out of eleven times.[8] And between 1856 and 1932, both states voted Republican in every presidential election except 1912 and 1916, when New Hampshire narrowly chose Democrat Woodrow Wilson for president. (Wilson gained less than a majority of the vote in New Hampshire in each election and beat Republican candidate Charles Evans Hughes in the state by only 56 votes in 1916.) Even when the state split from Maine and Vermont by voting for Roosevelt in 1936,

8. The one exception was 1964. The other five states are Indiana, North Dakota, South Dakota, Nebraska, and Kansas. No state voted Republican in all these elections. Maine voted Democratic twice in the period—in 1964 and in 1968, when Muskie was the Democratic candidate for vice president. Oregon would have been an eighth state, voting for the Republican candidate in nine out of ten presidential elections between 1948 and 1984, but Oregon supported Dukakis in 1988.

New Hampshire still gave the Democrat less than a majority of its vote and was Roosevelt's third worse state, after Maine and Vermont.

Between 1856 and 1988, the overwhelming devotion of New Hampshire and Vermont to the Republican party may have made them seem politically like twin states. To find an electoral split between the states as large as the one that has appeared in recent elections, it is necessary to go back in history all the way to the 1836–1852 period, when the Democrats and the Whigs were the two dominant parties.

New Hampshire voted for the Democratic candidate in all five presidential elections of the period, while Vermont supported the Whig candidate in each of the elections—including 1852, when Franklin Pierce of New Hampshire was the Democratic candidate. (At that time, the Maine vote was more similar to that of New Hampshire than of Vermont, supporting the Democratic candidate in four of the five elections.) James Sundquist notes that this seemed odd for New Hampshire and Vermont, "which were settled by people of the same stock, were comparable in economic structure, and shared a common intellectual and religious tradition. Yet through some accident of development, New Hampshire became a Democratic state and Vermont a Whig state, not by narrow margins but by overwhelming ones."[9] Richard McCormick makes similar observations:

> One of the most intriguing problems that strikes the student of New England politics in the Jackson era is the extraordinary contrast between the strength of the Jacksonians in New Hampshire and their weakness in Vermont. Why should these neighboring states have diverged so widely in their political allegiance? New Hampshire in 1836 was the most heavily Democratic state in the nation; Vermont produced the most lopsided Whig majority. The problem is all the more perplexing because before 1824 and after 1856 the two states exhibited similar political tendencies. We do not have adequate studies of either of these states for the period on which we might base explanations of their contrasting behavior. I should suggest, however, that in addition to any explanations in terms of social, economic, or cultural differences, due weight should be accorded to the factor of political leadership.[10]

9. Sundquist, Dynamics of the Party System, 54.
10. Richard P. McCormick, The Second American Party System (Chapel Hill: University of North Carolina Press, 1966), 96–97.

Table 4.3. Statistical comparison of the three Northern New England states

Variable	Vermont	New Hampshire	Maine	United States
% Claiming pure English ancestry	15.4	14.5	23.0	10.5
% Claiming pure French ancestry	11.1	12.2	13.1	1.5
% Claiming pure Irish ancestry	4.4	5.7	5.0	4.6
% Claiming some English ancestry	34.8	33.1	40.4	21.9
% Claiming some French ancestry	28.3	25.8	23.7	6.0
% Claiming some Irish ancestry	19.5	20.9	17.9	17.7
% Born in state	64.2	51.6	75.7	n.a.
% High school grad	71.0	72.3	68.7	68.6
% College grad	19.0	18.2	14.4	17.0
% White (non-minority)	98.6	98.0	98.4	80.3
Population density per sq. mile	58.5	118.6	34.7	65.7
Per capita income (1989)	$16,371	$20,267	$16,248	$17,596
1990 Unemployment rate (%)	5.0	5.6	5.1	5.5
% Total state income (1989) from:				
Construction	9.5	9.6	8.8	6.2
Manufacturing	22.3	24.2	21.4	19.7
Transportation/communication	5.2	4.3	5.1	6.6
Wholesale/retail trade	16.5	18.0	17.1	16.0
Finance/real estate/insurance	4.9	6.1	4.9	7.0
Services	24.8	25.4	23.1	25.5
Government	11.4	16.9	12.4	15.6
Agriculture	1.7	0.3	0.9	1.6

SOURCES: First nine variables (pure English ancestry through college graduates) from *1980 Census of Population: General Social and Economic Characteristics* (Washington, D.C.: U.S. Department of Commerce, Bureau of the Census 1983); next four variables (% white through unemployment rate), *Almanac of the Fifty States* (Palo Alto, Calif.: Information Publications, 1992); Final group of variables (percentage of state income per industry), *State + Metropolitan Area Date Book 1991* (Washington, D.C.: U.S. Department of Commerce, Bureau of the Census, 1991).

n.a. = not applicable.

In the current era, Vermont and New Hampshire have begun diverging electorally to an extent not seen since 1852, with Maine following closer to Vermont's pattern. While this chapter will not attempt to explain why Vermont and New Hampshire differed so greatly in the 1836–1852 period, it does offer an analysis of the modern divergent electoral trends. Besides emphasizing the role of social, economic, and cultural factors in the recent electoral trends, the analysis will also give due weight to the factor of political leadership, in keeping with McCormick's suggestion.

Table 4.3 provides statistics for a social, economic, and cultural comparison of Vermont, New Hampshire, Maine, and the United States as a whole. Ethnically and racially, the three states are nearly identical, with only Maine standing out as somewhat more English than the others. In average educational levels achieved, residents of Vermont and New Hampshire are about the same, while Maine's residents lag behind. But on two social statistics and one economic statistic, New Hampshire differs sharply from Maine and Vermont. First, New Hampshire's population contains a significantly smaller proportion of residents born within the state (barely 50 percent in 1980) than Vermont's or Maine's; second, New Hampshire's population is significantly more urban; and third, New Hampshire residents have significantly higher incomes.[11]

Based only on Table 4.3, one might conclude that New Hampshire's recent voting patterns have differed from those of Maine and Vermont because New Hampshire is wealthier and more urban and has been influenced by Republican-leaning voters moving there from other states. However, such a simple conclusion would be in error.

One way to dispute the effects by themselves of income and population density on New Hampshire's voting patterns is to compare the state with other wealthier and more urban states in the Northeast. Of nine states in New England and the northern Mid-Atlantic region (New York, New Jersey, and Pennsylvania), all but Vermont and Maine are more urban and more densely populated than New Hampshire, and four (Massachusetts, Connecticut, New York, and New Jersey) had higher per capita incomes than New Hampshire in 1989.[12] Yet none of these more urban and higher income states has been trending Republican in presidential elections in the last forty years as New Hampshire has. Three of the nine Northeastern states supported Dukakis in 1988, and only New Jersey and Maine joined New Hampshire in voting for Bush at a higher rate than the national average that year, although at nowhere near the margin of victory in New Hampshire. Wealthy Connecticut and New Jersey voted for Clinton by significantly higher margins than New Hampshire in 1996.

However, just a look at where the Republican trend is occurring in New Hampshire, at both the county and at the township level, provides

11. New Hampshire also has the reputation among some of being significantly more industrial than Vermont, but statistically, New Hampshire's manufacturing base is only slightly larger than Vermont's. The impression may arise from the concentration of industry in densely populated portions of southern New Hampshire, while Vermont has many small manufacturing cities spread throughout the state and has a significantly higher proportion of population living in rural areas.

12. U.S. Bureau of the Census, *Statistical Abstract of the United States 1991* (Washington, D.C.: U.S. Department of Commerce, 1991).

even stronger evidence that the few social and economic differences between New Hampshire and Vermont do not provide an adequate explanation of their political differences. Although the state as a whole has trended Republican, only two of New Hampshire's ten counties actually showed Republican gains in presidential elections between the 1950s and the 1980s; most of the others showed Democratic gains during that period. One of the counties with Republican gains, Hillsborough, on the state's southern border with Massachusetts, contains the cities of Manchester and Nashua and more than a quarter of the state's population. Besides having far more people than any other county, Hillsborough County also has had by far the highest partisan shift in presidential elections of any county in New Hampshire since the 1950s, pushing the statewide vote totals in a Republican direction.

Hillsborough County, with its urban population and the second highest per capita income of any county in the state, may seem to confirm some of the assumptions that could be made about New Hampshire's and Vermont's divergent voting trends from the data in Table 4.3 (although the percentage of the county's residents born in New Hampshire is above the state average), but the second New Hampshire county that has shown strong Republican gains again casts doubt on a method that relies solely on social and economic characteristics to explain differing state voting patterns in Northern New England.

This second county, Coos, covers the northernmost portion of New Hampshire, up to the Canadian border. Coos County has the lowest average income and average educational level in the state, as well as the highest percentage of residents born in state. The county contains only one small city, Berlin, is otherwise completely rural, and is probably best known politically as the location of Dixville Notch, where the town's small number of residents gather at midnight every election day to cast the first votes in the state and the nation. Coos County's rural nature, low incomes, high numbers of residents born in state, and strong Republican trends make New Hampshire's Republican trend as a state seem further unlikely to be a result only of high population density, high incomes, and influence from residents born elsewhere.

The only characteristic under study that Coos and Hillsborough counties do have in common is ethnic ancestry. These two counties are the only ones in the state where residents of French ancestry outnumber those of English ancestry. Yet New Hampshire and Vermont have similar French ancestry percentages (see Table 4.3), so ethnic ancestry does not provide a clear explanation for political differences between the states as a whole.

The relationship of ethnicity and other variables to partisan voting in the two states is shown in Table 4.4. The types of towns most likely to be shifting toward the Democrats in New Hampshire are basically the same as in Vermont. Towns that have a higher educational level, a higher level of English ancestry, and higher numbers of non-natives to the state are more likely to be shifting Democratic in both states, while towns with lower educational levels, higher French ancestry, and high numbers of native-born residents are more likely to be shifting Republican. Most remarkable is that the correlations between the three ancestry variables and the partisan shifts in presidential elections are almost exactly equal for the two states, as are the correlations between the native-born variable and the partisan shift. By itself, Table 4.4 makes the voting patterns in the states appear to be identical, which of course is not at all true.

If Vermont had more people among the groups trending Democratic, and New Hampshire among the groups trending Republican, the paradox of their political differences could be solved. But Vermont and New Hampshire have similar percentages of English, trending Democratic, and French, trending Republican, and nearly equal educational levels. New Hampshire has a much smaller proportion of residents born in state (native-born) than Vermont does, but in both states, towns with relatively few native-born are trending Democratic, and New Hampshire as a whole is not. Vermont's per capita income is lower than New Hampshire's, and lower-income towns seem to be trending Democratic in both states, but only when other factors are taken into account. By itself, income level in a town has no significant relationship to a partisan trend in either state.

Table 4.5 provides an interesting supplement to Table 4.4. While the partisan *direction* of each demographic group in Table 4.4 appears similar for the two states, Table 4.5 shows that the *magnitude* of the partisan gains among the groups differs greatly by state. Table 4.5 demonstrates that while the five New Hampshire towns with the highest percentage of English ancestry residents and the highest percentage of non-natives have become more Democratic in presidential voting, these towns have not shifted at anywhere near the same magnitude as the five corresponding Vermont towns. For instance, New Hampshire's five towns with the highest percentages of residents born out of state contain very few people born in New Hampshire, while Vermont's most non-native towns are more evenly split between residents born in state and people born out of

Table 4.4. Relationship of eight variables to Democratic gains in Vermont and New Hampshire presidential elections in towns and cities of more than 2,500 people, 1952–1956 and 1984–1988

	Correlation coefficient	
Variable	Vermont	New Hampshire
% English ancestry	.45**	.49**
% French ancestry	−.77**	−.73**
% Irish ancestry	.17	.18
Town population	−.07	−.29**
% High school grad	.32*	.60**
% College grad	.31*	.59**
Per capita income	−.01	.21
% Born in state	−.48**	−.54**

Multiple regression of eight variables on the Democratic shift in presidential elections for towns and cities of more than 2,500 people. Only variables that contribute to the overall model are listed.

Vermont

$R^2 = 71.7\%$ R^2 (adjusted) $= 69.3\%$
$s = 5.887$ with $52 - 5 = 47$ degrees of freedom

Source	Sum of Squares	df	Mean Square	F-ratio
Regression	4124.74	4	1031	29.8
Residual	1628.96	47	34.6588	

Variable	Coefficient	s.e. of Coeff	t-ratio
Constant	29.17810	6.1680	4.73
College grad	0.354376	0.1442	2.46*
English	0.781450	0.1992	3.92**
French	−1.012310	0.1464	−6.91**
Income	−0.003289	0.0010	−3.19**

New Hampshire

$R^2 = 64.8\%$ R^2 (adjusted) $= 63.0\%$
$s = 7.483$ with $83 - 5 = 78$ degrees of freedom

Source	Sum of Squares	df	Mean Square	F-ratio
Regression	8032.41	4	2008	35.9
Residual	4367.09	78	55.9883	

Table 4.4. (Continued)

Variable	Coefficient	s.e. of Coeff	t-ratio
Constant	12.63910	7.4670	1.69
College grad	0.448098	0.1044	4.29**
Born in N.H.	− 0.341715	0.0588	− 5.81**
Income	− 0.002417	0.0009	− 2.78**
English	1.056400	0.1683	6.28**

SOURCES: Demographic data for both states from *1980 Census of Population: General Social and Economic Characteristics*; Vermont electoral data from *Primary and General Elections: Vermont, 1974–1988*, and *Vermont Legislative Directory and State Manual*, 1950–1972; New Hampshire electoral data from *New Hampshire Manual for the General Court*.

NOTE: N = 52 for Vermont; N = 83 for New Hampshire.

 *Significant at the .05 level.
**Significant at the .01 level.

Table 4.5. Comparison of partisan gains for several variables in Vermont and New Hampshire towns and cities of more than 2,500 people, 1952–1956 and 1984–1988

Average shift toward Democrats in presidential elections in five most English towns:
   Vermont = 24.6% shift   (average 22.6% pure English ancestry)
   New Hampshire = 11.6% shift   (average 26.8% pure English ancestry)
Average shift toward Republicans in presidential elections in five most French towns:
   Vermont = 6.2% shift   (average 26.3% pure French ancestry)
   New Hampshire = 18.5% shift   (average 28.1% pure French ancestry)
Average shift toward Democrats in presidential elections in five towns with highest percentages born out of state:
   Vermont = 26.4% shift   (average 57.6% born out of state)
   New Hampshire = 12.8% shift   (average 83.8% born out of state)
Average shift toward Republicans in presidential elections in five towns with highest percentages born in state:
   Vermont = 0.0% shift   (average 77.7% born in state)
   New Hampshire = 5.5% shift   (average 76.2% born in state)

SOURCES: See source note for Table 4.4.

NOTE: N = 52 for Vermont; N = 83 for New Hampshire.

state. Yet Vermont's more balanced towns have shifted Democratic much more heavily than the almost completely non-native New Hampshire towns. The same types of patterns exist for towns with high levels of French ancestry and high numbers of native-born shifting Republican in both states. The most French towns and most native-born towns have trended Republican much more in New Hampshire than they have in Vermont.

While demographic groups in each state are trending in the same direction, the groups are shifting at greatly contrasting magnitudes, Republican gainers overtaking Democratic gainers in New Hampshire, and vice versa in Vermont. Clearly another variable, another explanation, remains to be found. This variable must have affected all demographic groups, causing French, native-born, and less-educated voters to trend Republican at a higher rate in New Hampshire than in Vermont, and English, non-native, and well-educated voters to trend Democratic at a lower rate in New Hampshire than in Vermont.

As shown earlier, the reasons for these diverging trends lie not in the differing demographic characteristics of the two states. Differing levels of income, percentages of native-born, and population density may have helped create variant political settings in New Hampshire and Vermont, but by themselves these social and economic differences cannot explain the clearly opposite political trends in the two states. Instead, another variable, one that may depend partly on the few differing demographic characteristics of the two states, is necessary for a full understanding of the politics of New Hampshire and Vermont. This variable is the combination of political environment and political leadership in the two states—the arena in which politics and voting take place, and the types of people who have most influenced that arena. Just as Richard McCormick assumed earlier that political leadership must have affected the unexpected wide political contrasts in New Hampshire and Vermont in the 1824–1856 period, the same assumption can be not only made but also substantiated for the 1970–1990 period, when the partisan patterns of the two states diverged rapidly.

Any casual observer of New Hampshire's first-in-the-nation presidential primary every four years should be familiar with the state's famous "no tax" pledge. The pledge, made by candidates for political office, promoted by the *Manchester Union Leader*, the state's largest newspaper, and apparently supported by many or most of the state's voters, began in the 1962 gubernatorial election, when both major party candidates, at the urging of *Union Leader* editorials, took a pledge to veto any proposed sales or income tax for the state.[13] New Hampshire is currently one of only two states (the other is Alaska) without either broad-based tax; it depends instead on state taxes on horse racing, alcohol, cigarettes, hotels, restaurants, and business profits, a state lottery, and local property taxes for revenue. Vermont has had a state income tax since 1931.

13. Eric P. Veblen, *The Manchester Union Leader in New Hampshire Elections* (Hanover, N.H.: University Press of New England, 1975), 63.

New Hampshire's "no tax" pledge is not simply a statement of opposition to taxes, but an actual pledge to veto any broad sales or income tax. Otherwise, the *Union Leader* goes on the attack against candidates unwilling to take the pledge. Since the pledge began, taxes have "been the dominant issue in New Hampshire gubernatorial elections."[14] Much evidence from political campaigns and the activities of longtime *Union Leader* publisher William Loeb illustrate the importance of the no-tax pledge in New Hampshire elections.

William Loeb first came to national prominence through his strident editorials and seemingly slanted news coverage during campaigns for the New Hampshire presidential primary, but his history as owner of the *Union Leader* began with his purchase of the paper in 1946. Loeb claimed to have penetrated the American Communist party in the 1930s, thereby gaining a strong understanding of the party's secretive strategies. Over the years, Loeb's stands on communism led him to support U.S. Senator Joseph McCarthy's hearings on communist infiltration of the federal government in the 1950s and to call the senator and presidential candidate George McGovern a tool of the communist conspiracy in 1972.[15]

Although Loeb claimed to be a populist conservative, supporting unions, profit-sharing with employees, and engaging in "pro-working-class, anti-upper class rhetoric,"[16] the newspaper publisher consistently supported politicians like U.S. Senator Styles Bridges of New Hampshire. Bridges, the most conservative New England senator during his tenure in Congress, used his office to help many special business interests and accumulated a great deal of personal wealth during his congressional career before his death in 1961.[17]

Perhaps the best known or most notorious of New Hampshire politicians strongly supported by Loeb was Republican Meldrim Thomson, elected governor on his third try in 1972. During Thomson's first month in office, he sent an administrative assistant to search through business tax returns of political enemies, and Thomson himself went to a Massachusetts organized crime records center seeking to inspect files of political

14. Ibid., 98.
15. Ibid., 2–3.
16. Ibid., 5–6. Note that Loeb's professed style of populist conservatism is of the same sort that Kevin Phillips predicted would create the emerging Republican majority in 1969, and the same sort that Pat Buchanan used in 1992 to make the state's Republican primary his most successful performance anywhere in the nation. Buchanan won the New Hampshire Republican presidential primary in 1996.
17. Peirce, *The New England States*, 296–297, 307.

enemies like Democratic U.S. Senator from New Hampshire Thomas McIntyre. The state supreme court ruled that the business tax searches were illegal, but Thomson said he was entitled to interpret the state constitution himself, and "not as it is understood by others."[18] McIntyre testified before the New Hampshire state legislature that Thomson's actions represented "misuse of official authority for either vengeful politics or, to put it gently, bizarre and inexplicable purposes. . . . Good lord, enough's enough. This is America. . . . This is New England!"[19]

During the remainder of his first year in office, Thomson attacked the liberal views of environmentalists and college campuses, canceled a border agreement with Maine with no prior warning (leading to the arrest of a Maine lobsterman in disputed waters), began a crusade to locate an oil refinery in New Hampshire, and sent letters to U.S. Senators Sam Ervin and Lowell Weicker, accusing Watergate investigators of "Gestapo tactics." Weicker returned the letter with a note: "Some nut is using your letterhead and signing your name to it."[20] Thomson's close ties to Loeb were confirmed by a *Concord Monitor* reporter who wrote that at least 138 calls had been made between Thomson's office and Loeb's home during the governor's first one and a half years in office.[21] Thomson was raised in Georgia, suggesting that New Hampshire voters may be more tolerant of Southern-style conservatism than Vermont voters appear to be.

While Loeb had occasional success promoting and electing candidates like Thomson, the publisher's overall biggest influence on New Hampshire politics came through his paper's persistent insistence that candidates take the no-tax pledge, which has affected not only Republican candidates, but Democrats in New Hampshire as well. In 1962, the Republicans divided in a bitter party split that led the incumbent Republican governor, who had lost the primary for renomination, to endorse the Democratic gubernatorial candidate. Democrat John King won the governor's office that fall after taking the no-tax pledge and advocating a legal ban on communist speakers at state colleges.[22] King won reelection in 1964 and 1966 and continued to support policies "so conservative that the Republicans, at least on a programmatic basis, had little reason to

18. Ibid., 334.
19. Ibid., 335.
20. Ibid., 335–336.
21. Ibid., 336.
22. Veblen, *The Manchester Union Leader in New Hampshire Elections*, 60.

quarrel with him."[23] Although the *Union Leader* never endorsed King in his races for governor, fearful of detracting from other Republicans on the ballot, the paper was never antagonistic toward King during campaigns until he ran for the U.S. Senate in 1968 against incumbent Republican Norris Cotton, a longtime favorite of Loeb. King knew the *Union Leader* would oppose him in this campaign, so he went out on a limb by supporting gun control and expressing reservations about the Vietnam War. A *Union Leader* editorial called King a "turncoat," and Cotton won reelection.[24]

Democratic candidates for governor who followed King continued to take the no-tax pledge and advocate conservative policies until 1982. After opposition to Thomson grew after he allowed the company building the Seabrook nuclear power plant to bill customers for the cost of construction, the Democrats regained the governor's office, electing Hugh Gallen in 1978. In 1981, the National Guard had to be called out in New Hampshire to provide basic state services when public employees stayed home in a protest over tiny wage increases. The state's bond rating was also downgraded twice in nine months the following year. So in 1982, Gallen, a popular governor before then, refused to take the no-tax pledge. He lost reelection to Republican John Sununu, who did take the pledge.[25] In his concession speech on election night, Gallen blamed his loss on "that stupid pledge."[26]

The pledge invaded the Republican presidential primary in 1988 when George Bush took the pledge while opponent Bob Dole refused. "Bob Dole had the Iowa momentum [from winning that state's presidential caucuses], but while he talked ominously of the need for painful solutions, George Bush was traveling from truck stop to Catholic college with three-term governor Sununu, an enthusiastic pledge-taker, promising that he would back 'no new taxes' and challenging Dole to do the same."[27] Bush's victory in the New Hampshire primary was widely attributed to the tax issue.

National political observers have berated the effect that the no-tax

---

23. Peirce, *The New England States*, 308.

24. Veblen, *The Manchester Union Leader in New Hampshire Elections*, 60–61.

25. Peirce and Hagstrom, *Book of America*, 204.

26. Richard F. Winters, "New Hampshire," in Alan Rosenthal and Maureen Moakley, eds., *The Political Life of the American States* (New York: Praeger, 1984), 287.

27. Barone and Ujifusa, *Almanac of American Politics 1992*, 760. In 1996, Dole, not wishing to repeat his New Hampshire primary mistake of 1988, signed the no-tax pledge long before the primary. He lost the primary anyway to fellow pledge-taker Pat Buchanan.

pledge has had on New Hampshire. Neal Peirce wrote: "When one looks at New Hampshire public life over most of the years since World War II, one finds an appallingly smug and uncreative atmosphere, and in many policies the prototype among the fifty states of the unresponsive and irresponsible society."[28] Yet New Hampshire's conservative fiscal policy preceded the pledge. "The powers-that-be in New Hampshire tend to convert *all* policy to questions of economy-in-government for the obvious purpose of keeping taxes down and keeping a tight check-rein on the service and regulatory functions of government," wrote Duane Lockard in the 1950s.[29]

By the 1940s and 1950s, New Hampshire was already electing leaders who were generally more conservative than those elected in Vermont or even in Maine. While Vermont's U.S. Senator Ralph Flanders and Maine's U.S. Senator Margaret Chase Smith were denouncing McCarthy and his tactics, New Hampshire's Senator Styles Bridges demanded to know the name of "the master spy, the servant of Russia who moves the puppets . . . using them and using our State Department at will."[30] Lockard noted in the 1950s that New Hampshire Republicans were split between the "less-conservative" and the "more conservative,"[31] unlike the moderate and liberal Republicans usually elected in Vermont. Therefore, the *Union Leader*'s promotion of the no-tax pledge by the 1960s reached an audience in New Hampshire already used to electing conservative politicians and politicians already willing to take strong conservative stands to get elected, a very different situation from that in Vermont.

Once the pledge took hold, New Hampshire revenue sources were already much smaller than in Vermont, which had created a state income tax in 1931, and government services in the former state were kept at a minimal level.[32] As mentioned in Chapter 3, Vermont Governor Ernest Gibson made the state income tax more progressive in 1940s and funded improvements in education, health care, and welfare, helping to begin a tradition of strong government services in the state. Dartmouth College

28. Peirce, *The New England States*, 286.
29. Lockard, *New England State Politics*, 47.
30. Peirce, *The New England States*, 297.
31. Lockard, *New England State Politics*, 50.
32. In 1991, New Hampshire state taxes per capita were $565, the lowest in the nation by far (the next three lowest were South Dakota at $796, Tennessee at $870, and Texas at $923). Vermont state taxes per capita at $1,207 were close to the national average of $1,235. See *The World Almanac and Book of Facts 1993*, 137. New Hampshire does have some high local property taxes, but these revenues are unavailable for any statewide services.

political scientist Richard Winters has written that the difference in revenue sources between the two states has been the key to the vastly differing spending policies of the states. In Vermont, a strong source of revenue has caused politicians to campaign in support of favored spending programs, which in turn creates interest groups seeking to maintain or increase the funding.[33]

Republicans in Vermont who have tried to borrow from the politics of New Hampshire have not been successful. In a very close race to replace Richard Snelling as governor in 1984, Democrat Madeline Kunin campaigned on job creation, environmental issues, and new state programs. She called for a state mini-Superfund that would charge a fee to companies dealing with hazardous wastes. The revenue would be used to begin identifying toxic waste sites until the federal government began providing enough money. She also promoted high technology industries that she believed created jobs without hurting the environment.[34] When her Republican opponent challenged Kunin during a debate to take a pledge not to raise taxes, she said she was opposed to raising taxes, but asked that the debate move away from pledges she labeled as campaign rhetoric.[35] Kunin won in November.

While the *Manchester Union Leader* has not elected every candidate it has supported in New Hampshire, its emphasis on the no-tax pledge—taken by dozens of the state's political leaders, who get elected to office by voters who have historically given majorities to many very conservative politicians—has found a welcome political environment, which has allowed the paper's views not only to influence but often to dominate the state's politics.[36]

And the influence of the *Union Leader* and its no-tax pledge provide a key difference between the politics of New Hampshire and Vermont. In Vermont, no newspaper has taken or likely could take the position of extreme journalistic political influence on state politics found in New Hampshire. For instance, no Vermont newspaper, including Vermont's largest daily, the *Burlington Free Press*, takes the strident editorial and

33. Richard Winters, "Political Choice and Expenditure Change in New Hampshire and Vermont," *Polity* 12 (1980), 598–621.

34. Elizabeth Slater, "Kunin Stumps Vermont as Nation Watches," *Barre Times-Argus*, October 29, 1984.

35. Bob Sherman and Jack Hoffman, "Kunin, Easton Debate: Issues Are a Casualty," *Barre Times-Argus*, September 13, 1984.

36. William Loeb died in 1981, but his wife Nackey has largely continued the *Union Leader*'s editorial and political traditions.

overtly political tone found in the *Union Leader*. Eric Veblen has written: "The *Free Press* is far less vigorous in its political advocacy than the *Union Leader*," adding that many Vermont politicians disputed the value of *Free Press* editorial support, "but not a single New Hampshire political figure [interviewed] called the *Union Leader* unimportant in influencing voters."[37]

However, even if the *Free Press*, which has had a somewhat conservative reputation in the past, or any other Vermont paper wanted to dominate the state's politics, media competition and circulation patterns make that unlikely.[38] The *Union Leader* has more than twice the weekday circulation, and three times the Sunday circulation, of its closest New Hampshire competitor, an advantage not held nearly as strongly by the *Free Press* in Vermont.[39] In addition, the *Union Leader* is the only New Hampshire daily paper distributed statewide, while the *Free Press* is sold only in northern Vermont.[40]

The *Free Press* has not only greater newspaper competition but also greater television competition in its efforts to be a source of news for Vermonters. The Burlington area airwaves carry stations for all the major networks, while New Hampshire has only one commercial television station (in Manchester), which competes with Boston stations for viewers, with the Boston stations carrying relatively little New Hampshire political news.[41] And if the *Union Leader*'s circulation advantages and relative lack of television competition have not been enough by themselves to allow the newspaper to dominate state political coverage, the practice, at least in the past, among many of the state's smaller newspapers of relying on wire service stories for local coverage has provided further distribution of *Union Leader* political viewpoints, as the wire services use the Manchester paper heavily as a source of local news.[42]

Voters in New Hampshire who read the *Union Leader* do not agree mindlessly with every editorial stand it takes, but the newspaper most definitely influences politicians and the issues they emphasize in campaigns, with the no-tax pledge becoming a permanent feature of guberna-

37. Veblen, *The Manchester Union Leader in New Hampshire Elections*, 81.
38. Loeb even owned a small Vermont daily, the *St. Albans Messenger*, whose limited circulation allowed nowhere near the same political impact as the *Union Leader*.
39. *Editor and Publisher International Year Book 1991*.
40. Veblen, *The Manchester Union Leader in New Hampshire Elections*, 83–84.
41. Ibid., 10–11.
42. Peirce, *The New England States*, 305–306.

torial campaigns. Many voters, including Republicans, have actually been inclined to oppose any candidate favored by the newspaper. One moderate Republican in 1966 began his U.S. Senate primary campaign by taking public stands purposely to attract attacks from the *Union Leader* and thereby arouse public attention and support from those who disliked Loeb.[43] "Whatever specific influence the *Union Leader* may have on candidates' issue positions, . . . interviews strongly suggest that politicians always take the newspaper into account when formulating their campaign strategies," wrote Eric Veblen.[44] And whether voters have agreed or disagreed with the editorial positions and political tone taken by the newspaper, enough have relied on it as a source of news to allow the no-tax pledge to influence elections greatly.

The few demographic characteristics that differentiate Vermont and New Hampshire may have accentuated the extent of their political divergence. New Hampshire's overall higher income levels may have made its voters more disposed toward supporting the no-tax pledge, and the state's population density and more urban nature may have allowed more influence for the largest city's (Manchester's) newspaper. New Hampshire's larger percentage of residents born out of state may include many who moved to New Hampshire specifically to avoid taxes, although, as noted earlier, towns with low percentages of residents born in the state are just as likely in New Hampshire as in Vermont to be increasing in Democratic support.[45]

But based on Tables 4.4 and 4.5, the no-tax pledge seems to have cut across all demographic groups, depressing the numbers of voters inclined to switch to the Democrats, and increasing the number inclined to switch to the Republicans. New Hampshire joined Vermont and Maine in becoming increasingly Democratic across all office levels in the 1960s and early 1970s (Table 4.1), but by the late 1970s New Hampshire reversed direction, dramatically split with its two neighbors, and has become in the 1990s by far the most Republican state in New England and one of

43. Veblen, *The Manchester Union Leader in New Hampshire Elections*, 25.
44. Ibid., 57.
45. Three authors writing on New Hampshire politics of the 1960s and 1970s correctly disputed the common notion that migrants to New Hampshire were mostly conservatives avoiding taxes, but incorrectly believed, based on the Democratic gains of the 1960s and early 1970s, that the newcomers might continue to push the state further toward the Democrats. See Peirce, *The New England States*, 312–313; and Robert E. Craig and Richard F. Winters, "Party Politics in New Hampshire," in Josephine F. Milburn and William Doyle, eds., *New England Political Parties* (Cambridge, Mass.: Schenkman Publishing Company, 1983), 139–183.

the most Republican states in the nation, the 1996 presidential election being a notable exception. Although national Republicans were campaigning on opposition to Democratic spending programs by the 1960s, other issues, such as the Vietnam War, civil rights in the South, social disorder, and environmental protection, competed with basic economic issues for attention in presidential elections in Northern New England. Racial and civil strife led to strong gains for the Republican party in the South, but in New Hampshire many held more liberal views on noneconomic issues. While New Hampshire voters supported some politicians who were very conservative on all issues, in part due to *Union Leader* influence, public opinion in the state on noneconomic issues was probably closer to that in Vermont and Maine than to that among Southern whites, so New Hampshire joined its neighbors in the 1960s and early 1970s era in becoming more Democratic, albeit at a lesser pace.

Once such issues as Vietnam, Watergate, and racial discrimination in the South faded from political prominence in the late 1970s, economic concerns could take precedence in New Hampshire elections. In the mid-1970s, Republicans in Congress, such as Jack Kemp, began heavily promoting a new and controversial economic theory called supply-side economics, which claimed that cutting taxes would actually increase revenue to the federal government through economic growth. When Ronald Reagan made tax cuts and supply-side economics a centerpiece of his 1980s presidential campaign, he tapped into a theme that was very familiar and strongly supported by New Hampshire voters.

As the national Republican party increasingly became identified as the party of low taxes, with the Democrats identified as the opposite, and as the tax issue increasingly became a central theme of congressional and presidential campaigns (Democratic presidential candidate Walter Mondale actually vowed to raise taxes in 1984), New Hampshire voters increasingly shifted toward the Republican party. At the same time, in Vermont, the low-tax theme did not dominate state politics and had much less impact on state voters.

The 1988 *Almanac of American Politics* said low taxes in New Hampshire were "part of the state's local, not presidential, politics."[46] But by 1980 an issue that had started in local politics became firmly a part of Republican presidential politics, and a new national party image increased support for Republicans at all levels in New Hampshire.

---

46. Barone and Ujifusa, *Almanac of American Politics 1988*, 721.

Because of New Hampshire voters' overwhelming concern with taxes, any appeal the national Democratic party may have had to the state's potential liberalism on social or environmental issues was submerged by the party's perceived willingness to raise taxes. Meanwhile, national Republicans in the 1980s campaigned for tax cuts or asked Americans to read lips saying no new taxes. But Vermont politicians of recent years have not had such an obsession with taxes. Instead, both Republicans and Democrats in Vermont campaign on issues like who can best protect the environment and how best to administer state services.

Maine, without the *Union Leader*, without a traditional no-tax pledge, and with a recent tradition of moderate Republicanism (Senator Margaret Chase Smith denounced McCarthyism in 1950, and Senator William Cohen voted to impeach President Nixon as a member of the House Judiciary Committee in 1974), has had voting patterns that were much more similar to Vermont than to New Hampshire in the last forty years. As in Vermont, the first Democratic breakthrough in Maine came after Republicans bitterly divided during a gubernatorial race in the early 1950s, leading to the election of Democrat Edmund Muskie as governor in 1954.[47] And although Democratic Governor Kenneth Curtis had made a no-new-taxes pledge in his 1966 campaign, he proposed a new income tax for Maine in 1969 in order to add to revenue from the state sales tax enacted in 1951. The Republican leader of the State House of Representatives supported the proposal, which narrowly passed both houses of the legislature. Curtis gained reelection in 1970, and a 1971 ballot referendum to repeal the income tax failed.[48] So while Maine and Vermont currently have both general sales and income taxes, New Hampshire stands out as having neither.

Yet even in New Hampshire a moderate-to-liberal Republican element has existed, even if it has not dominated the party to the same extent as in Maine and Vermont. In Chapter 3, the discussion of Vermont politics demonstrated the longtime popularity of moderate and liberal Republicans in state elections, which also seemed to appear in support for the 1980 independent presidential candidacy of John Anderson. Within towns in Vermont, there was a high correlation between support for Anderson and a Democratic trend in presidential elections overall between 1952 and 1988, indicating that some of the Democratic gains in the state

47. Kenneth P. Hayes, "Maine Political Parties," in *New England Political Parties*, 187.
48. Peirce, *The New England States*, 390.

have come from areas with disaffected Republicans. As stated before, most parts of New Hampshire have also shown Democratic gains in presidential elections, despite being overwhelmed by a few large population centers with huge Republican gains. An analysis of voting patterns in towns in New Hampshire that have in the past favored moderate or liberal Republicans over conservatives provides additional evidence of the effect of recent national Republican party strategies on its traditional bases in Northern New England.

New Hampshire's historical presidential primary provides excellent data with which to measure support for moderate and liberal Republicans in the state's towns. New Hampshire's primary, as the first in the nation, includes the names of all party candidates on its ballot, frequently providing choices of widely varying ideologies, before any begin to drop out. In 1964 and in 1980, New Hampshire Republicans were presented a broad spectrum of candidates, including liberals, moderates, and conservatives, in the presidential primaries. New England Republicans in early 1964 had not yet been affected by any of the changes that would occur later in national party strategies, so that year's primary election provides some evidence of what type of Republican ideology New Hampshire party members supported at the time. And although Republican John Anderson appealed to some liberals in both parties in the primary elections of 1980, most voters who leaned toward the Democrats probably voted in the close Democratic primary between President Jimmy Carter, Ted Kennedy, and Jerry Brown, rather than switch to a Republican registration to vote for Anderson. Therefore, the 1980 primary also provides strong evidence of the ideologies of those who considered themselves Republican at that time in New Hampshire.

In early 1963, New York Governor Nelson Rockefeller, a liberal Republican, was considered the front-runner for his party's nomination in 1964, despite his divorce in 1961.[49] But in May 1963, Rockefeller married Margaretta "Happy" Murphy, a woman eighteen years younger and a mother of four, whose children were in the custody of their father.[50] Rockefeller's standing in the polls fell immediately.[51] The *Union Leader*'s attacks on

49. John H. Kessel, *The Goldwater Coalition* (Indianapolis: Bobbs-Merrill Company, 1968), 44.

50. See Theodore H. White, *The Making of the President 1964* (New York: Atheneum Publishers, 1965), 79; and Harold Faber, ed., *The Road to the White House* (New York: New York Times, 1965), 22.

51. Kessel, *Goldwater Coalition*, 45.

Rockefeller, which included calling him a "wife-swapper," did not help his campaign for the New Hampshire primary either.[52]

The immediate beneficiary of Rockefeller's problems in 1963 was Senator Barry Goldwater of Arizona, by far the most conservative entrant in the Republican primaries. Goldwater gained the support of the *Union Leader* and took the lead in New Hampshire polls. But in early 1964, Goldwater made a number of controversial statements (for instance, calling for Social Security to be made voluntary, and indicating a willingness to withdraw from the United Nations), presented fairly hawkish attitudes toward national security, ran what observers claimed to be a poor campaign effort, and succeeded in frightening or antagonizing many New Hampshire voters.[53]

Two write-in efforts led by volunteer organizations also began in New Hampshire for former Vice President and former Republican presidential candidate Richard Nixon, a centrist within the party at that time, and for former Massachusetts Senator and current Ambassador to South Vietnam Henry Cabot Lodge, a relative liberal. The media seemed to assume that the write-in efforts would not have any success, and generally ignored them until a few weeks before the primary, when polls showed Lodge might get a significant share of the vote.[54] Lodge ended up winning a surprise victory in the Republican primary, with 35.5 percent of the vote, compared with 23.2 percent for Goldwater, 21.0 percent for Rockefeller, and 16.8 percent for Nixon.[55]

Lodge, a longtime supporter of social welfare programs, civil rights measures, and foreign aid,[56] had expressed disinterest in the nomination, but his protests were not taken seriously.[57] After his victory in New Hampshire, Lodge thanked voters for their support but added, "I do not plan to go to the United States. I do not plan to leave Saigon. I do not intend to resign [the ambassadorship]."[58]

Lodge's victory in New Hampshire, combined with Rockefeller's showing and Goldwater's poor performance, indicated that New Hampshire

---

52. Faber, *Road to the White House*, 22.
53. Goldwater's performance leading up to the 1964 New Hampshire primary is chronicled in Kessel, *Goldwater Coalition*, 60–62; White, *Making of the President 1964*, 103–105; and Faber, *Road to the White House*, 23–24.
54. Kessel, *Goldwater Coalition*, 63.
55. Ibid.
56. Ibid., 51.
57. Faber, *Road to the White House*, 17.
58. Ibid., 29.

Republicans still tended to favor liberal and moderate members of their party over strong conservatives in 1964. Lodge's victory over Rockefeller probably indicated a preference for a native New Englander from neighboring Massachusetts who "represented the New England patrician tradition of public service which still lingered within the GOP" in 1964, over a New Yorker who "evoked images of excessive wealth and Eastern establishment power."[59]

The 1980 Republican primary presented a similar range of choices, but with a very different outcome. Former Governor Ronald Reagan of California, an ardent conservative who had almost won the party's presidential nomination in 1976, was considered the front-runner. Former Texas Governor John Connally and Illinois Representative Phil Crane were also positioned on the most conservative end of the political spectrum. Kansas Senator Bob Dole, the party's vice presidential nominee in 1976, represented a more traditional Midwestern variant of conservatism.

The moderate-to-liberal wing of the party was represented by Tennessee Senator Howard Baker, former Texas Representative, Director of the CIA, and Ambassador to China George Bush, and Illinois Representative John Anderson. Baker had achieved fame as Senior Republican on the Senate Watergate Committee and was considered a moderate conservative. Bush, who had been born and raised in New England before moving to Texas, was generally conservative on economic and defense issues, but far more liberal than most of his opponents on social issues in 1980—favoring the Equal Rights Amendment and abortion rights, for example. (Not until Reagan chose Bush as his vice presidential nominee was Bush reborn as a social conservative.) John Anderson, however, positioned himself to the left of all his primary opponents, announcing his support for gun control at a local meeting of conservative gun owners and calling for a fifty-cent federal tax on gasoline to promote energy conservation. Reagan won the New Hampshire primary with 50 percent of the vote. The three moderates and liberals were next, with Bush at 23 percent, Baker at 13 percent, and Anderson at 10 percent. Reagan apparently captured virtually all of the conservative vote, leaving his three most ideologically similar competitors with 3 percent of the vote between them.

In 1964, a majority of New Hampshire Republicans voted for liberal

---

59. Nicol C. Rae, *The Decline and Fall of the Liberal Republicans from 1952 to the Present* (New York: Oxford University Press, 1989), 30, 62.

candidates from their party in the presidential primary, while less than 25 percent supported the representative of the party's most conservative wing. By 1980, however, a majority of New Hampshire Republicans were willing to support their party's most conservative candidates. Many factors other than ideology played a role in both years' primaries, and the increase in conservative support over the period does not necessarily indicate an increase in the conservatism of New Hampshire's Republican voters, although *Union Leader* political coverage and the willingness of local politicians to take no-tax pledges had probably moved public opinion in a conservative direction by 1980. But an analysis of town voting patterns, and of support for various primary candidates, does present solid evidence that areas that had traditionally supported moderate and liberal Republicans have strongly increased in support for Democrats in presidential general elections.

Bush and Anderson did well in 1980 in the same towns in which Lodge did well in 1964, while Reagan's best performances in 1980 followed the Goldwater pattern in 1964 (see Table 4.6). Rockefeller in 1964 and Baker in 1980 also performed better in the moderate-to-liberal-leaning towns, and Nixon did better in 1964 in the more conservative towns, although their correlations are not quite as strong as the other five candidates.

The most important finding, however, is that in towns where Goldwater and Reagan did best in 1964 and 1980, the residents are voting Republican more and more in the November general election, while in towns where Lodge, Bush, and Anderson performed well in 1964 and 1980, the Democrats have made big gains in fall presidential elections (Table 4.6). As the national Republican party has become increasingly dominated by Goldwater and Reagan-style conservatives, members of the party's traditional moderate and liberal wings in Northern New England and many other Northern areas (as later chapters will show) have abandoned the party in the November presidential elections. These voters may remain registered as Republicans—clearly many still were in 1980 when they voted for Bush or Anderson in the primaries—but have become disenchanted with the candidates nominated by their national party.

The electoral realignment of Vermont toward the Democrats in the last forty years occurred on a gradual but continuous basis (see Chapter 3) and is therefore not obvious to those who are searching only for the quick critical realignments that have dominated discussions in the political science literature. The present chapter has demonstrated some of the problems of relying on national survey data to detect realignments among

Table 4.6. Correlations of Republican primary votes and Democratic gains in New Hampshire presidential elections, for the 229 towns and cities where more than 50 people voted in the 1964 and 1980 Republican presidential primaries

1964 Candidate	Correlation Coefficient for Democratic Gain in Presidential Elections 1952–1956 to 1984–1988	1980 Candidate	Correlation Coefficient for Democratic Gain in Presidential Elections 1952–1956 to 1984–1988
Goldwater	−.34**	Reagan	−.52**
Lodge	.28**	Bush	.42**
Rockefeller	.10	Anderson	.53**
Nixon	−.11	Baker	.12

Correlation Between New Hampshire Towns' Votes for an Individual Candidate in 1964 and an Individual Candidate in 1980

1980 candidate	1964 candidate			
	Goldwater	Lodge	Rockefeller	Nixon
Reagan	.46**	−.46**	−.18**	.30**
Bush	−.41**	.38**	.12	−.19**
Anderson	−.34**	.39**	.20**	−.37**
Baker	−.18**	16*	.06	−.09

SOURCE: *New Hampshire Manual for the General Court.*

*Significant at the .05 level.
**Significant at the .01 level.

the population. A national survey cannot differentiate voting patterns among the states and within the states and is unable to capture the sharp divergence of political behavior of neighboring states, such as New Hampshire and Vermont.

The case studies of New Hampshire and Vermont have shown the important role of decisions by political leaders and others involved in politics in shaping the political environment of a state. In New Hampshire, the presence of the *Union Leader* and its dominance of the state's political coverage, and the willingness of political leaders to take the paper's no-tax pledge, have expanded support for conservatism in the state and tilted political dialogue rightward, leading to increased support for the national Republican party. In Vermont, political leaders have pushed through state income and sales taxes, and attempts to focus on a no-tax pledge have been resisted by many political leaders and unenforced by the Vermont media, so that when the national Republican party turned increasingly conservative, the state's traditionally moderate-to-liberal Republican voters began switching to the Democrats.

Chapter 5 proceeds to another problem with the standard study of voter realignments in American political science: the assumption that an increase in split-ticket voting and a decline in party identification in surveys indicate a strong decrease in the importance of party symbols and ideology when voting. An analysis of recent politics in Rhode Island proves that such an assumption is inaccurate.

Chapter Five

⟶⊷⊶⊷⟵

Rhode Island and Federalized Realignment

In 1980, Vincent "Buddy" Cianci, the Republican candidate for governor in Rhode Island, remarked: "Running in Rhode Island as a Republican is like being the Ayatollah Khomeini at the American Legion convention."[1] Before the 1980s, national studies of state party politics clearly

---

1. "In Rhode Island It's Volatile Republican Against Low-Key Democrat," *Boston Globe*, October 16, 1980, 34, cited in John Kenneth White, *The Fractured Electorate: Political Parties and Social Change in Southern New England* (Hanover, N.H.: University Press of New England, 1983), 72. Rhode Island has a recent history of electing odd, or colorful, politicians, of which Cianci, the mayor of Providence, is among the most prominent. Cianci first won his office in 1974, having run as the "anti-corruption candidate." While in office, a magazine accused Cianci of having committed rape while a college student in Wisconsin—a charge that Cianci denied. In 1982, Cianci decided to bolt the Republican party and won reelection for mayor as an independent in a close three-way race. In 1984, he pleaded no contest to a charge of assault against a man who Cianci claimed was having an affair with his estranged wife. Cianci had hit the man several times, burned him with a cigarette, and threatened to hit him with an ashtray and a log while Cianci's police chauffeur and others watched. The court gave Cianci a five-year suspended sentence and put him on probation. Although he was not charged in a city corruption scandal that was uncovered at the same time and that led to thirty indictments and sixteen prison sentences for city officials and workers, Cianci resigned his office after the assault conviction. After working as a popular radio talk-show host for several years, Cianci ran again as an independent for the Providence city mayor's office in 1990, again winning a close three-way race. Opponents went to court to block him from regaining the mayor's position, using a 1986 amendment to the state constitution that prohibited convicted felons from holding political office in the state until three years after their sentence and probation had been served—a condition Cianci would not meet until 1992. The Rhode Island Supreme Court ruled in December 1990 that the amendment did not apply to Cianci, who was convicted before the amendment took effect, and Cianci took office as mayor as scheduled. For some of the details of Cianci's career, see " 'Buddy' Bids for Redemption," *Newsweek*, August 13, 1990, 39; Lawrence Ingrassia, "Amazing Comeback: Buddy Cianci Is Toast of Providence," *Wall Street Journal*,

placed Rhode Island as one of the most Democratic states, or even as a one-party Democratic state. Yet between the Civil War and the 1920s, Rhode Island politics were dominated by Republicans as strongly as in Vermont.

It took the 1928 Democratic presidential candidacy of Catholic Al Smith and the 1930s New Deal policies of President Roosevelt—so popular with the Catholic working-class voters who dominated Rhode Island, and so unpopular with the Protestant Yankee voters who dominated Vermont—to tear the politics of the two states in separate directions, at least for the next twenty to thirty years. Rhode Island—by far the most Catholic state in the nation,[2] and one of the most working-class and industrial in the 1930s as well—gradually increased its support for Roosevelt New Deal policies and the Democratic party through the 1930s, 1940s, and 1950s. While in the 1920s and 1930s the state gave a larger share of its vote to the Republican presidential candidate than to the nation as a whole, by the 1960s it gave Republican presidential candidates more than 10 percent less than their national share of the vote in all three elections of the decade. Support for the Democrats was also overwhelming in other statewide voting. The entire congressional delegation remained in Democratic hands from 1941 until 1977, and Republicans won only five of twenty-six gubernatorial elections between 1932 and 1982.

Yet, like Vermont politics, Rhode Island politics had clearly changed again by the 1980s. In 1976, the state elected its first Republican U.S. senator since 1930, in 1980 it chose its first Republican U.S. Representative since 1938, and in 1982 it elected its first Republican secretary of state since the 1930s. Republican strength in state elections reached its peak in 1988, when Rhode Island reelected a Republican U.S. Senator, reelected a Republican governor, and elected two Republicans to fill both its seats in the U.S. House of Representatives, voting out one of only two Democratic incumbents to lose reelection to the House that year. In 1989, Rhode Island's congressional delegation was the second most Republican (75 percent) of any state east of the Mississippi River, behind only New Hampshire's entirely Republican delegation.

June 21, 1990, A1; "Court Says Felony No Bar to Seating of Mayor," *New York Times*, December 21, 1990, A22.

2. In 1975, Rhode Island was more than 64 percent Catholic; in no other state were Catholics the majority. Marion I. Wright and Robert J. Sullivan, *The Rhode Island Atlas* (Providence: Rhode Island Publications Society, 1982), 125.

Such a result might lead to the conclusion that Rhode Island had been joining with New Hampshire by moving in the opposite partisan direction from Vermont in the 1975–1990 period. Yet such an assertion would overall be a great misinterpretation of Rhode Island's recent voting patterns, for while the state showed great support in 1988 for the Republican party in the offices listed above, in that same year Rhode Island gave 56 percent of its vote to Democratic presidential candidate Michael Dukakis, his highest share of any state in the nation. (His home state, Massachusetts gave Dukakis 54 percent.)

Rhode Island, one of the most Democratic states in the nation since the 1930s, remains so at the presidential level, but not at the congressional or gubernatorial level. The state may actually have developed a politics almost opposite to that in many Southern states; in Rhode Island, Democrats continued to dominate at the presidential level, while Republicans won many of the other high-profile statewide elections in the 1980s.

Before 1988, Rhode Island was the Democrats' best state in all three presidential elections of the 1960s (1960, 1964, and 1968); it was Ronald Reagan's worse state by far in 1980, giving him 37 percent of the vote (his second worse state gave him 41 percent); and in 1988, Dukakis did better in Rhode Island than Franklin Roosevelt did in winning the state twice in the 1930s. (The state's realignment actually began in 1928, and presidential voting stayed close to the national average as late as 1956, when Eisenhower received a higher percentage of the vote in Rhode Island than he did nationally. This provides some more evidence that the realignment process is often much more gradual and punctuated than critical reelection theorists seem to imply.)

In Vermont, realignment toward the Democrats has occurred at all office levels, and in New Hampshire, support for the Republicans has grown at all levels. But Rhode Island presents a completely different electoral pattern, in which one party dominated at the presidential level (and in the state legislature as well), while another party over a fifteen-year period greatly increased its support in voting for statewide offices (or semi-statewide, in the case of congressional districts). National observers might perceive such split-ticket voting as evidence of dealignment and a decline in the importance of party cues. Even New England political scientists in the late 1970s and early 1980s believed that the increased use of media advertising by Republicans, which often did not include the candidates' party designations, indicated that Republican victories were due to personal popularity of the candidates and not their party labels.[3]

Yet, characterizing the increase in split-ticket voting in Rhode Island as a result of a decrease in the importance of party cues does not present the most accurate picture of the causes of the state's recent voting patterns. Many of the successful Republican candidates were quite obscure before their election campaigns, casting doubt on the personal popularity theory, and even if they did not identify themselves as Republicans in advertising, they all emphasized one theme—a theme that was probably a main reason for their victories, and a theme that the state electorate increasingly identified with Republicans in state elections.

After dozens of years of corrupt Republican leadership of the state following the Civil War, the Democrats took over the state almost totally in 1935, under circumstances that could reasonably be considered a coup d'état.[4] The Democratic party, dominated by Irish Catholics but generally supported by other ethnic Catholic groups in the state as well, tended

3. Victor Profughi, "Rhode Island: The Party Is Sick, but It Isn't Dead—Yet," in *New England Political Parties*, 92–93; White, *The Fractured Electorate*, 110.

4. In 1935, newly elected Democratic Governor Theodore Francis Green, a millionaire lawyer of Yankee ancestry, joined with other Democratic leaders to contest the elections of two Republican state senators who the Democrats claimed were elected fraudulently. On January 1, 1935, with the new senate assembled, Democratic Lieutenant Governor Robert Quinn refused to swear in the two contested Republicans until ballots were recounted in their towns. Without these two Republicans, the state senate was divided between twenty Democrats and twenty Republicans, with Quinn as the tie-breaker. The senate created a Democratic-dominated committee, which determined that Democrats had won the contested elections. Green and the legislature then fired all five Republican judges on the five-member State Supreme Court, an action permitted by the state constitution. Green and the Democrats also eliminated many state boards and commissions controlled by Republicans, and they reorganized the state government with stronger gubernatorial power. Soon after the "coup," Green made a radio address in which he defended his actions by comparing them with the democratic ideals of colonial founder Roger Williams. For details of these events, see Lockard, *New England State Politics*, 191–192, and William G. McLoughlin, *Rhode Island: A History* (New York: W. W. Norton & Company, 1986), 201–203. The Republicans would have been hypocritical to claim victimization from these actions, for they had corruptly held on to the state government for years through grossly malapportioned legislative districts, restriction of voting rights for foreign-born citizens, and vote-buying and bribery financed by wealthy supporters. The *New York Times* therefore praised Green's overthrow of the old corrupt Republican leadership, but the editor of the *Chicago Tribune* declared Green's actions unconstitutional and ordered one star cut out of the flag that flew over the newspaper's building—which was replaced after the editor learned that flag desecration was illegal. McLoughlin, *Rhode Island: A History*, 203. Green was elected to the U.S. Senate in 1936, where he served until 1961, retiring at the age of ninety-three— the record for oldest member of the Senate until Strom Thurmond of South Carolina broke it in 1996.

to continue the state's history of dominance by machine politics, albeit by a different party and by different ethnic and socioeconomic groups. As long as most Rhode Islanders lived in urban areas and remained relatively poor and uneducated, the Democratic machine, through political favors and neighborhood friendships, could easily elect almost all its favored candidates to office. In addition, memories of the old Republican machine, which often favored wealthy business interests, remained strong. Rhode Island College professor Victor Profughi noted in the 1970s that his students, mostly Catholic, still saw the mill owners and the Providence elite as the enemy. "They may have no clear image of the Democrats," he commented, "but they certainly do of the Republicans."[5]

As the children of urban Catholics got better educations and moved out to the suburbs, however, their ties to the political machines were cut. The rampant corruption of the state's dominant party and the frequent incompetence of its leaders, publicized constantly by the state's leading newspaper, reminded suburban, educated voters of the decaying cities they had left behind and the school-taught distaste for machine politics, and these voters increasingly listened to the messages put out by Republican candidates. These messages were able to change the images of both major parties in the state—the Republicans for the better and the Democrats for the worse.

The Republican party, almost immediately after losing its corrupt hold on the state's politics in the 1930s, turned around and began to attack the Democratic party for corruption. The Republicans usually only gained the attention of their traditional Yankee supporters, except when blatant examples of corruption, incompetence, or election-stealing led to occasional defeats of Democratic gubernatorial candidates.[6]

But by the late 1970s, the Republican party had the right combination of resources to gain a larger and more lasting foothold among the elector-

5. Peirce, *The New England States*, 149.
6. In 1956, Democratic governor Dennis Roberts held a slim election-night lead over Republican Christopher Del Sesto, a former Democrat who was popular among the state's Italian voters. But after absentee ballots were counted, Del Sesto took the lead. Roberts took the election to court, claiming that the absentee-ballot law he had signed, permitting such ballots to be cast before election day, violated the state constitution, which stated that absentee ballots must be cast on the day of the election. On Inauguration Day of 1957, the State Supreme Court ruled 3–1 (the majority including two Democrats and one Republican appointed by Roberts the year before) that absentee ballots cast before Election Day were invalid, which made Roberts the winner. Lockard, *New England State Politics*, 194–195. Del Sesto came back to beat Roberts in 1958 but was unable to gain reelection after that.

ate: a medium for repeating its anti-corruption and anti-incompetence messages—television advertising—and a better-educated population that was not connected with the urban Democratic political machines. This better-educated population was more receptive to the message that not only appeared in advertising but also was subtly reinforced by the *Providence Journal-Bulletin*, Rhode Island's only statewide daily newspaper, which has overwhelming circulation advantages over its small, more local competitors. The state Republican committee has not always coordinated a party-wide effort to focus on opposition to corruption and incompetence as a dominant campaign theme in every election, but so many individual Republican candidates have successfully adapted the theme that the electorate increasingly began to identify many Democrats as old-fashioned, incompetent, party-machine political hacks.

Rhode Island's Democratic machine, based in the industrial cities of Providence, Pawtucket, Woonsocket, and Central Falls, has long relied on the traditional tools of strong urban political organizations—government jobs, padded payrolls, personal favors, and friendship.[7] At a time when old-style political machines have become an anachronism in most of the nation, the continuing strength of Rhode Island's Democratic organization may be surprising. Dr. Richard Gabriel commented in 1970:

> What is most striking about politics in Rhode Island is that in an age in which presumably most people have come to expect efficiency and integrity of their governments, where suburban growth has reduced the population, both relative and absolute, of the urban center, and where civil service regulations have become the bulwark against patronage, machine or "old style" politics still exists to extent that it does in the state.[8]

The tension between the supporters and politicians of the old urban political machines, which are still usually able to dominate the Rhode Island Democratic party, although with diminishing strength, and suburban, better-educated voters was used by the Republicans in the 1980s to gain an advantage in state elections. But the state Republican theme has not translated to the presidential level, where old-style machine influence in the national Democratic party ended by the early 1970s, and

7. Richard A. Gabriel, *The Political Machine in Rhode Island* (Kingston, R.I.: Bureau of Government Research, University of Rhode Island, 1970), 14.
8. Ibid., 3.

where Republican administrations have sometimes had more difficulty with accusations of corruption than Democratic administrations have had in recent years. Nor have the Republican messages resonated on any permanent basis in state legislative elections, where neighborhood ties can play a strong role anywhere in the state, and where urban machine politicians are perceived as having little influence on the choice of candidates in suburban and rural areas.

Therefore, the combined impact of a general preference for the liberal policies of national Democrats, and the reaction against the types of Democrats who have often dominated the state's politics, led to an electoral pattern in Rhode Island that can best be categorized as federalized realignment. The term "federalized realignment" means that partisan realignment has occurred differently in nationwide elections than in statewide elections, not because of dealigning forces like transient candidate popularity and absence of party cues in voting, but because of a consistent pattern of viewing the national parties and the state parties in different contexts, and a consistent pattern of split-ticket voting for rational reasons based on the long-term party images, which differ between the state level and the national level.

Rhode Island is probably best known during its first two hundred years of history for two events: its founding by Roger Williams, who left the Puritan colony of Massachusetts Bay to establish a new colony with religious freedom; and the state's refusal to attend the constitutional convention of 1787 and to ratify the U.S. Constitution until 1790 (the last of the thirteen colonies), when the first president and Congress had already been in office for more than a year. Rhode Island objected to the Constitution at first because it lacked a Bill of Rights and because it would prevent the state from continuing its popular practice of printing enough paper money to allow farmers to pay their debts.

Once agreeing to statehood, Rhode Island became dominated by business-led machine politicians (Republicans after the Civil War) who restricted suffrage until the 1920s. The Democratic party machine took over in the 1930s, thanks to an upsurge in voting by the new Catholic arrivals to the state, and while less stifling than the Republican machine of earlier years, the Democrats continued fraudulent practices in order to win elections. Duane Lockard commented in 1959: "Rhode Island cannot match the flamboyant and flagrant corruption that has flourished in Louisiana, but it does offer a formidable challenge."[9]

9. Lockard, *New England State Politics*, 209.

Yet, as Neal Peirce notes, "despite an oppressive political order, the independent tradition [of Rhode Island, as symbolized by Roger Williams's founding and the temporary opposition to the U.S. Constitution] survived into the nineteenth and twentieth centuries."[10] Even though its demographics and recent political history were vastly different from those of Maine, New Hampshire, and Vermont, Rhode Island actually maintained into the 1980s some of the ornery independent political practices popular in Northern New England. By 1990, Rhode Island, Vermont, and New Hampshire were the only states in the nation that elected governors and other statewide officials to two-year terms, and several attempts to lengthen terms to four years had been turned down by Rhode Island voters.[11] Most Rhode Island communities also still depend on town meetings to decide local financial matters. Despite often dismal attendance, attempts to eliminate town meetings have been voted down in most towns. Before 1992, Rhode Island's state legislators, who meet as a whole only briefly each year and can commute easily from home, received the second lowest salaries in the nation (only New Hampshire's were lower), and the necessary constitutional amendment to raise their salaries had been rejected by voters at least eight times since World War II.[12]

Rhode Island's differences from its Southern New England neighbors, and its similarities to New Hampshire and sometimes Vermont, were also demonstrated during the 1980s through the Rhode Island government's continued refusal to require auto insurance for drivers and mandatory seat-belt use in cars.[13] In 1985, despite the testimony in favor of seat-belt legislation by public safety "experts," the auto industry, most leading politicians, the state police, and a group of witnesses whose relatives would be leading normal lives if they had only worn seat belts, the State House of Representatives rejected a mandatory seat-belt use measure by a 58–32 vote. The leading legislative opponent of the measure called it "a frightening erosion of individual freedom."[14]

10. Peirce, *The New England States*, 142.
11. In 1992, Rhode Island voters finally approved a state constitutional amendment to lengthen gubernatorial terms to four years. The amendment was approved this time because a two-term limit for governors was included.
12. Katherine Gregg, "R.I. Suit Would Outlaw Pensions for Assembly," *Providence Journal*, November 14, 1987.
13. Rhode Island did finally pass mandatory seat belt use and mandatory auto liability insurance legislation by the 1990s.
14. Doug Cumming, "The Low-Cost Insurance of Wearing a Seat Belt Remains Tough to Sell," *Providence Journal*, July 28, 1985. The New York State commissioner of motor vehicles

Rhode Island's distrust of government leaders, as demonstrated by voters' continued support for town meetings and for low salaries for state legislators, and periodic dislike of government meddling, such as requiring seat-belt use or auto insurance, often causes the state to surprise national observers, who might assume that its support for social welfare programs signifies support for big government.[15] That was the case in late 1983 and early 1984, when a proposed "Greenhouse Compact" for Rhode Island was getting national media attention. The compact was touted by economists and the media as an exciting innovation in industrial policy. The plan, designed in large part by business consultant Ira Magaziner and supported by most of the state's political leaders, involved "a comprehensive strategy for encouraging new industries to grow [hence the name 'greenhouse'] and bolstering older industries through direct government action" directed by an appointed state commission.[16]

At a time when the concept of industrial policy was gaining a large following among some academic and political leaders across the nation, "the Greenhouse Compact was generally regarded by those in the field as the most comprehensive and ambitious state economic development program ever put together."[17] The *New York Times* reported that Magaziner had been asked to speak at a National Governors Association summer conference and that compact supporters "have to an extraordinary degree, taken their message directly to the voters trying to inform them about the Rhode Island economy, and to educate them about what it will take to insure the state's industrial future."[18]

But while the national media, most state politicians, and some economists and local financial leaders showed much excitement in the plan, Rhode Island voters had decidedly less enthusiasm. In a special election to set up and fund the compact, 80 percent of them rejected the plan. In no town or city did the compact receive more than 31 percent of the vote. Supporters of the plan believed they had put together a winning

---

even visited Rhode Island to urge passage of the bill. John Kiffney, "N.Y. Official Urges R.I. to Insist upon Laws for Seat Belts," *Providence Journal*, February 14, 1985.

15. Rhode Island for a long time provided unemployment benefits for striking workers from an insurance fund paid for by employers. After much controversy, this benefit was ended in the 1980s.

16. Dan Stets, "Greenhouse Vote Provides Lesson for Industrial Plans Across U.S.," *Providence Journal*, June 17, 1984.

17. Ibid.

18. Tamar Lewin, "Putting Industrial Policy to a Vote," *New York Times*, June 10, 1984, sec. 3, 4.

coalition of labor, education, government, and business leaders. But as Brown University economics professor Allan Feldman noted, "the average Rhode Island voter looked at this extremely complicated plan and really didn't understand it, but understood it to the extent that it was going to funnel $250 million in public money through the hands of a small group of people, including bankers and state government people and politicians and union presidents, and the average voter was repulsed by that idea."[19]

Rhode Islanders, in general, frequently do not trust politicians, do not trust the government, and sometimes do not trust politicians in government to tell state citizens how to vote or take care of themselves. In years past, the state's residents would not let government leaders mandate forms of religious worship, and refused for as long as possible to submit to a national government authority. And in the 1980s, state voters did not want to be told to wear seat belts or buy auto insurance, and voters ignored politicians' views on town meetings and economic development. Although voters in other states also often oppose the wishes of political leaders, Rhode Island's periodic resistance to government authority seems to have been part of popular political culture both in the 1780s and in the 1980s.

And what issues did Republicans stress when they won their first Senate seat since the 1930s in 1976, the state's two House seats in the 1980s after forty years of complete Democratic dominance, and the governor's office in 1984 for the first time since the 1960s? First, they stressed independence: independence from party bosses, independence from political machines, and independence from the party of most people's parents. Second, they stressed a refreshing change: change from a history of corruption, and change from a history of incompetent leaders who embarrassed the state. Rhode Island Republicans began to win elections based on voter distrust of and distaste for the longtime ruling Democrats in the state.

Martin Shefter has chronicled how reform movements in New York City, made up of various groups of professionals, have used charges of

---

19. Brian C. Jones, "Greenhouse Defeated in All 29 Communities," *Providence Journal*, June 13, 1984. Ira Magaziner, the architect of the Greenhouse Compact, made news in 1993 as the director of President Clinton's Health Care Task Force, serving under Hillary Rodham Clinton. His poor track record of selling economic development programs in New England did not appear to have been held against him by his longtime friend, Bill Clinton. The complicated policy recommendations of the task force went nowhere in Congress.

corruption throughout the twentieth century to attack the city's Democratic machine.[20] Such a line of attack has also been used by Republicans in Rhode Island ever since the Democrats consolidated control of all major political offices in the state. In a poll on the 1976 gubernatorial campaign, two of the three issues voters most remembered being discussed by the candidates were machine politics and corruption in government, both issues that had been emphasized by the Republican candidate. Yet when asked the basis for their voting decision, jobs, the second most memorable issue, clearly ranked first.[21] The issue of machine politics was still not influencing enough voter decisions, as Democrats remained dominant in the state through the 1970s. John Kenneth White, writing in the early 1980s, still called Rhode Island a clear one-party Democratic state, similar in nature to Key's descriptions of party politics in the 1950s South.[22]

But by 1989, with Republicans controlling four of the five most visible statewide or semi-statewide offices, the fortunes of the "half-party," as White labeled the Republicans,[23] had changed. Republicans were also elected during the 1980s to the usually less visible offices of secretary of state (for the first time since 1938) and attorney general, the latter office occupied for two years by Sister Arlene Violet of the Sisters of Mercy. Violet, a lawyer sometimes nicknamed "Attila the Nun" for her aggressive style, was forced to resign from her order by the Bishop of Providence for disobeying the Pope's edict against clerics (including nuns) running for political office.[24]

In a discussion of the rise of the Republicans, two factors important to the state's politics must be kept in mind. First, Republicans elected to state offices in Rhode Island are not Reaganite conservatives; they are often more liberal than their Democratic opponents. In 1984, the Repub-

20. Martin Shefter, *Political Crisis / Fiscal Crisis* (New York: Basic Books, 1987).
21. Profughi, "Rhode Island: The Party Is Sick . . . ," 85.
22. John K. White, "One-Partyism in Rhode Island," in *New England Political Parties*, 261.
23. Ibid., 264.
24. David R. Carlin Jr., "Facing the Canons," *Commonweal*, January 27, 1984, 38. Violet wasn't the first Republican Catholic clergyman or nun to run statewide for office in Rhode Island. In 1970, the Reverend John McLaughlin, wearing priestly garb through the campaign, unsuccessfully challenged Democratic Senator John Pastore in his reelection bid. McLaughlin was a Jesuit priest who had been raised by Democratic parents but who had become a Republican. After losing, McLaughlin worked as a speechwriter for the Nixon White House and defended the president's activities during the Watergate scandal. Peirce, *The New England States*, 160. Today, McLaughlin is best known as the host of the weekly political talk show "The McLaughlin Group."

lican candidate for governor called for more spending on welfare and social programs, while his Democratic opponent said the state could not afford such increases.[25] Republican U.S. Representative Claudine Schneider, who in 1986 won the highest percentage for a Republican candidate for her office in Rhode Island since 1878, opposed President Reagan's position on two-thirds of major roll-call votes in 1986, more often than all but one other House Republican.[26] None of the recent successful Republican candidates for statewide office could be considered a conservative, a characteristic Rhode Island has more in common with Vermont than with New Hampshire.[27]

A second factor that is key to understanding recent Republican successes in Rhode Island is the role of the state's longtime leading newspaper, the *Providence Journal*, which has Republican ownership and has never been uneager to bring attention to any perceived misdeeds and embarrassments of the Democratic party machine and Democratic elected officials. Despite the paper's Republican ownership, many of its reporters would consider themselves liberals and Democrats, and the paper has always tried in recent years to provide balanced political coverage.[28] But corruption and incompetence are issues on which conservative or moderate Republican publishers and well-educated liberal reporters are generally in agreement, and the temptation to devote large amounts of coverage to the political screwups of old-style Democrats is too difficult for the paper to resist. A brief history of the state's major election campaigns between 1976 and 1988 provides ample evidence of how Republican candidates used the theme of machine politics and Democratic

25. Bruce DeSilva, "GOP on Upswing in Rhode Island," *Hartford Courant*, October 31, 1984.

26. Alan Ehrenhalt, ed., *Politics in America 1988* (Washington, D.C.: Congressional Quarterly Press, 1987), 1541.

27. A 1992 *Congressional Quarterly Weekly Report* provided the results of ABC News exit polls from 1988's "Super Tuesday" multistate presidential primaries for ten of the states that again participated in 1992's Super Tuesday (Rhode Island, Massachusetts, Maryland, Georgia, Florida, Tennessee, Mississippi, Louisiana, Oklahoma, and Texas). 1988 primary voters from both parties were asked to identify their own ideological preferences. Less than half (48 percent) of Rhode Island Republicans identified themselves as conservative, the only one of the ten states where this occurred (54 percent conservative in Maryland, 55 percent conservative in Massachusetts, between 59 percent and 70 percent in the seven Southern states among Republicans). Rhode Island also tied for the fewest conservative Democrats, with only 18 percent of Democratic primary voters identifying themselves that way. (Maryland also had 18 percent, Massachusetts had 20 percent, and the Southern states had between 27 percent and 35 percent.) *Congressional Quarterly Weekly Report*, March 7, 1992, 561.

28. Peirce, *The New England States*, 145–146.

bumbling to appeal to voters' distrust and frequent antagonistic feelings toward government leaders.

Sometimes the Republicans allowed the issue to be raised by Democrats and then have took advantage of the ensuing battles among their opponents. In 1976, Cadillac dealer Richard Lorber spent half a million dollars, most of it his own, in a Democratic primary against Governor Philip Noel to replace a retiring U.S. senator. Lorber, previously a political unknown in the state, won a slim victory by running a campaign with a strong antigovernment theme and charging Noel with being a political hack with a record of scandal.[29] Democratic leaders in the state were shocked by the primary results, and Noel refused to endorse Lorber. In November, Republican John Chafee coasted to victory with 58 percent of the vote as the first Republican in Congress from Rhode Island since 1941. Chafee's victory is sometimes attributed to his personal popularity (he had been elected governor three times in the 1960s before losing reelection in 1968), but he had also lost a race for the Senate four years earlier, when he had been heavily favored over a Democratic incumbent who was untainted by scandal, Claiborne Pell, who retired from the Senate in 1996.

The 1980 victory of U.S. Representative Claudine Schneider was less connected to the machine politics issue, as incumbent Democrat Ed Beard had run against the machine in a primary to win the seat in 1974.[30] (He did begin receiving party leader endorsements for reelection by 1978, though.) But by 1978, Schneider could attack Beard as an incompetent legislator addicted to foreign junkets.[31] Beard's pet cause in Congress seemed to be the establishment of a federal boxing commission, an idea of limited interest to many Rhode Islanders. Schneider surprised most observers by almost winning in 1978, she did win in 1980, and she received increasingly higher winning percentages in every reelection through 1988 before attempting an unsuccessful run for the Senate in 1990. Schneider was regarded by most political observers as an "independent" or "maverick" Republican in the House, always scoring highly in the Americans for Democratic Action ratings of liberal voting records in Congress.

Schneider's win in 1980 was the first of three successful challenges of

29. *Congressional Quarterly Weekly Report*, September 18, 1976, 2533.
30. Beard's profession was housepainter, which he proudly noted by putting a paintbrush on the front of his congressional office door in Washington.
31. *Congressional Quarterly Weekly Report*, October 11, 1980, 3068.

Rhode Island Republican women against traditional Democratic male officeholders. Susan Farmer, elected secretary of state in 1982, and Sister Arlene Violet, elected attorney general in 1984, each accused the low-profile incumbent Democrats of ineffectiveness. Like Schneider, both the other women had previously been unknown to the state's voters, lost on their first tries, but succeeded on their second.

And Farmer and Violet may also have been helped by a historical reapportionment mess in the state in 1982. In April 1982, the State Senate, run by the Democrats and Majority Leader Rocco Quattrocchi, passed a reapportionment plan based on 1980 census figures. The plan put a reformist State Senate Democrat in the same Providence district as the Republican Senate minority leader. The two redistricted senators and the state Republican party filed suit, claiming illegal gerrymandering, and a Rhode Island court found the plan unconstitutional. The legislature then passed another senate reapportionment plan, which the Republicans threatened to challenge in court. While awaiting legal action, the legislature, the governor, and the attorney general (all Democratic-controlled offices) decided to use the 1974 district lines for the 1982 election. The Republican party again filed suit, and in August a federal judicial panel called use of the 1974 lines in 1982 unconstitutional and ordered the State Senate elections postponed until "a constitutionally permissible apportionment plan is devised."[32]

In 1983, federal judges adopted their own redistricting plan, based partly on the legislature's second plan and partly on Republican recommendations, and scheduled State Senate elections in June. In the election, Republicans gained fourteen senate seats, to increase their numbers from seven to twenty-one in the fifty-member body, their highest representation since 1964. Outside of Providence, the state's largest city, Republican candidates as a whole won more votes than Democrats.[33] Quattrocchi subsequently lost his leadership positions in the Senate and in the state Democratic party.

By 1984, state voters had overwhelmingly rejected the Greenhouse Compact, which was supported by most politicians, and an out-of-state paper was commenting:

32. Karen Ellsworth, "GOP Bid to Halt Election Denied," *Providence Journal*, July 31, 1982; Karen Ellsworth and Thomas E. Walsh, "Court Blocks Using 1974 Lines in Election, Special Vote Now Likely," *Providence Journal*, August 12, 1982.
33. M. Charles Bakst, "GOP Wins 21 Seats in Senate Elections, Tops Expectations," *Providence Journal*, June 22, 1983.

For the first time in memory, being a Republican does not seem to be a liability in a Rhode Island general election, and the party is making a serious bid for a share of the power. . . . Events of the past three years have tainted the longtime image of the Rhode Island Democratic party as the party of the ordinary person. Increasingly, it has been seen as the party of patronage, privilege, corruption, and machine politics. . . . In the past three years, the Rhode Island news media have been filled with reports of wrongdoing by Democratic officeholders and appointees. Reports on bribery, kickbacks, perjury, theft, and conflict of interest touched so many agencies and officials that the *Providence Journal* ran box scores to help readers keep track. For many Rhode Island voters, the last straw seemed to be the 1982–1983 gerrymandering scandal that lasted for nearly a year.[34]

In 1984, the Republicans dropped back down to eleven seats in the Senate, indicating less a resurgence of Democratic support than a lack of strong interest in the institution among most Rhode Island voters. Besides the small salary, the state legislature serves just two months a year, and in a state with one senator per 19,000 residents, most candidates are well known personally among voters. This provides an advantage to the Democrats, who, as the longtime dominant party, attract the most politically ambitious individuals. In addition, much of the voting for state legislatures, as in the South, is habitually Democratic, and voters often know little about legislative candidates outside of personal contact.

In the much more visible governor's race of 1984, however, memories of recent Democratic party activities played a larger role in voter decisions. The Democratic primary pitted Warwick's Mayor James Walsh against State Treasurer Anthony Solomon. Walsh, a creature of party bosses, according to Solomon, attacked Solomon for accepting an endorsement from Quattrocchi.[35] Solomon, despite the support from Quattrocchi, labeled himself "the independent Democrat" and won the primary. But in the general election, Republican candidate Edward DiPrete relied on a "toss the bums out" mood and campaigned on the slogan "The change we need."[36] The *Providence Journal* called "independence

---

34. Bruce DeSilva, "GOP on Upswing in Rhode Island," *Hartford Courant*, October 31, 1984.
35. *Congressional Quarterly Weekly Report*, August 18, 1984, 2035.
36. *Congressional Quarterly Weekly Report*, October 13, 1984, 2588.

from Rhode Island's old political order, a hunger for change," the year's key issue.[37] DiPrete won with 60 percent of the vote.

In 1986, Democratic U.S. Representative Fernand St. Germain's Republican opponent called St. Germain scandal-ridden and a liar, accusing him in a televised debate of accepting bribes and keeping his tax returns secret. St. Germain denied all accusations and denied that he was being investigated by the House Ethics Committee (even though the committee was investigating him, as St. Germain admitted after the debate).[38] That November, St. Germain won 58 percent of the vote, his lowest percentage since 1966.

Because St. Germain represented the Rhode Island district that contained most of the state's French-Canadian and Portuguese populations, which generally remain the poorest and least educated among the state's ethnic groups, his district's voters may have taken a little longer to join the rest of the state's anticorruption mood. In September 1988, a *Congressional Quarterly Weekly Report* stated: "St. Germain will appear on no one's list of vulnerable incumbents this year"[39] despite continued investigations and revelations about his private finances. And after St. Germain's 55–45 percent September primary victory over a virtually unknown opponent, a later *Weekly Report* still said that Republican opponent Ronald Machtley was not regarded as likely to improve on the Republican performance in the district in 1986.[40]

Machtley, another political unknown, became the Republican candidate only when the state party favorite, who had lost to St. Germain in 1986, failed to file his candidacy papers in time because of a campaign mishap. In November, Machtley won "the House race upset of the year," according to one *Weekly Report*, with 56 percent of the vote.[41] Again, national news sources were surprised that the state's voters reacted so strongly against its political leaders.

In 1988, Republicans Schneider, Chafee, and DiPrete were also all reelected, indicating the continued strength of the Republican party. Yet the DiPrete race also indicated the continuing importance of corruption

37. M. Charles Bakst and Thomas E. Walsh, "DiPrete, GOP Set to Celebrate," *Providence Journal*, November 4, 1984.
38. M. Charles Bakst and Katherine Gregg, "St. Germain, Holmes Clash in Acrimonious TV Debate," *Providence Journal*, October 18, 1986.
39. Ronald D. Elving, "St. Germain Expected to Clear Another Hurdle," *Congressional Quarterly Weekly Report*, September 3, 1988, 2481.
40. *Congressional Quarterly Weekly Report*, September 17, 1988, 2600.
41. *Congressional Quarterly Weekly Report*, December 31, 1988, 3618.

as a political issue, this time with a Republican under attack. Before the election, DiPrete was accused of profiting from a government land sale that netted his family company $2 million in one day, and of showing favoritism on one government contract—the latter a minor charge by Rhode Island standards. In the last debate, two days before the election, each gubernatorial candidate asked questions of his opponent. All the Democrat Bruce Sundlun's questions dealt with ethics and charges of corruption.[42] DiPrete won the election with only 51 percent of the vote.

Despite DiPrete's performance in 1988, the elections between 1976 and 1988 make it clear that the issues of machine politics, corruption, and incompetence have been winning several elections for the Republicans. Stressing the theme of antagonism toward established party leaders, so prominent in the state's recent and colonial political history, Republican party candidates have changed the longtime habits of the state's citizens when voting for the most visible political offices below the presidency.

While the Republican campaign issues have tended to influence all voter groups in the state, the issues have had more appeal to the groups that are most receptive to such messages and least tied to Democratic machine politics. Voting data for Rhode Island towns and cities can identify the effects of the recent Republican strategies in competitive elections, and can also show that some of the same areas that have swung to the Republicans in state elections have been trending toward the Democrats in presidential elections.

In the tables and text below, several demographic, economic, and educational variables will be used to compare town voting trends in a similar manner to that used in the earlier chapters, on Vermont and New Hampshire. However, Rhode Island's ethnic composition is much more heterogeneous than that in Northern New England, making simple correlations less accurate than multiple regressions, which account for all variables when analyzing the factors behind political trends.

Rhode Island as a whole is largely made up of five separate ethnic groups of European origin. Rounding off to the nearest whole number, the 1980 U.S. Census found 13 percent of Rhode Islanders claiming pure Italian ancestry, while pure English, French, and Irish ancestry were claimed by 8 percent each, and Portuguese by 7 percent. No other pure

---

42. Russell Garland, "Ethics, Past Policies Dominate Final Debate," *Providence Journal*, November 7, 1988.

ethnic ancestry was claimed by more than 2 percent of the state population. The ethnic distribution divides up even more closely when partial
ancestry is considered. About 22 percent claim some Irish background,
21 percent claim English, 20 percent Italian, and 19 percent French
(mostly French Canadian, as in Northern New England).[43] The census
did not publish figures for partial Portuguese ancestry in 1980.

Such a close ratio between the four largest ethnic groups in the state
caused the Democratic party, during its years of almost complete control
of the state's politics, to balance the four-member congressional delegation with one from each ethnic background.[44] Portuguese voters, left out
of this balance, continue to have little representation from their ancestry
among the state's leading politicians, although they are the state ethnic
group with the largest number of recent immigrants (many from the
Azores) and were probably the fastest growing in the 1980s. African
Americans are relatively insignificant in the state as a voting group, making up 3 percent of Rhode Island's population in 1980, less than 1 percent
in thirty-one of the state's thirty-nine cities and towns, and more than 3
percent only in Providence and Newport (with its strong naval presence).[45]

Four of the large ethnic groups in Rhode Island each tend to dominate
a certain region of the state: the French in the northern mill areas, the
Portuguese in the eastern fishing and shipbuilding areas next to Narra-
gansett Bay, the Italians in Providence and the suburbs that border on it,
and the English in the less densely populated western and southern portions of Rhode Island. The Irish are more spread out in numbers and are
the only group to make up at least 10 percent of the population (in
partial ancestry) in each of the state's cities and towns. The Irish presence is especially strong in towns where the English are the largest group,
the Irish being the second largest group in thirteen of these fifteen towns
and a very close third to the French in the other two. Therefore, in simple
correlations, English and Irish voting patterns would appear similar, although the two groups often vote very differently.

In presidential elections, the voting patterns in Rhode Island's individual towns and cities are similar to those in Vermont and New Hampshire
and the Massachusetts towns included in Table 1.1, although usually to

43. 1980 Census of Population: General Social and Economic Characteristics (Washington,
D.C.: U.S. Department of Commerce, Bureau of the Census, 1983).

44. Peirce, The New England States, 152.

45. Wright and Sullivan, Rhode Island Atlas, 103.

Table 5.1. Rhode Island decade averages in presidential voting, 1920s–1990s

Decade	United States	Rhode Island
1920s	57-34	58-40
1930s	38-59	42-54
1940s	45-52	42-58
1950s	56-43	55-45
1960s	44-51	29-70
1970s	54-44	49-51
1980s	54-42	44-51
1990s	39-46	28-53

NOTE: The first number represents the average Republican percentage of the vote and is separated from the second number, which represents the average Democratic percentage of the vote, by a hyphen.

Average Republican percentage of the vote for two presidential elections (each year's percentage rounded off to nearest whole number before both election years are averaged)

Election Years	United States	Rhode Island
1952 + 1956	56.0	54.5
1960 + 1968	46.5	34.0
1984 + 1988	56.0	48.0

SOURCES: 1920–1992, *Congressional Quarterly's Guide to U.S. Elections*; 1996, *Congressional Quarterly Weekly Report*, 188.

a lesser degree. Many towns of mainly English-Irish ancestry, and towns with higher educational levels, have slowly been increasing their share of the vote for Democrats in presidential elections, while towns mainly containing other Catholic ethnic groups shifted dramatically toward the Democrats in the 1960s and rebounded toward the Republicans ever since, although often still at levels below the Republican support found before the 1960s, a pattern demonstrated by the Catholic Massachusetts towns of Somerville and Quincy in Table 1.1.

Because heavily Catholic Rhode Island contains more population in towns of the latter type, unlike in Vermont, the state as a whole has not continued to turn more Democratic since the 1960s. However, as Table 5.1 shows, Rhode Island did vote slightly less Republican in the 1980s than in the 1970s (thanks in part to John Anderson's 14 percent of the vote in 1980), while the United States as a whole voted slightly less

Democratic, so the state's trend in presidential voting continues to be strongly tilted toward the Democrats relative to the nation.

A small number of predominantly English-Irish and relatively well-educated Rhode Island towns show the pattern, found in dozens of Vermont towns, of a continuous gradual shift since the 1950s toward the Democrats in presidential elections, but none of the Rhode Island shifts comes close to matching the magnitude of those found in Vermont. The relative heterogeneity of Rhode Island's most English towns means that other ethnic groups usually have a strong influence within each town, and many of these groups, after extreme swings toward the Democrats in the 1960s due in large part to the presidential candidacy of John Kennedy, have returned to a closer partisan balance when voting, although still more Democratic than in the 1950s. Because a comparison of 1950s presidential votes and 1980s presidential votes of the type made in earlier chapters would mix together two very different types of partisan shifts—the great Catholic swing of the 1960s and the more gradual trends among certain other voter groups—this chapter will make a different comparison.

Table 5.1 provides the statewide and nationwide averages for the Republican percentages of the presidential vote in 1960 and 1968. These two years represent the beginning of the gradual trend toward the Democrats found in many Vermont towns. The data for 1964 is excluded here because of the temporary overwhelming swing toward the Democrats of that election year among almost all Northern U.S. voters. As Table 5.1 shows, the United States voted about 10 percent more Republican in the 1984 and 1988 presidential elections than in 1960 and 1968, while Rhode Island voted 14 percent more Republican in the later two elections. Yet thirteen Rhode Island towns, one-third of those in the state, either voted more Democratic in this latter period or voted only slightly more Republican (less than 5 percent), despite the much larger national and state Republican trends.

These towns generally have two characteristics in common. First, twelve of these towns are among the fifteen in the state where English is the most common ancestry named by residents in the U.S. Census.[46] In the thirteenth town, Irish is the most common ancestry, with English

---

46. The town of New Shoreham, better known as Block Island, is excluded from this figure—as it will be from all town data in this chapter—because of its tiny voting population and incomplete published census information.

close behind. A second characteristic held by most of these Democratic-trending towns is above-average educational levels for the state, a trait held by nine of the thirteen towns, with only one of the thirteen at below-average educational levels. Because the trends of these towns toward the Democrats relative to the nation has continued since the 1960s—while many of Rhode Island's most Catholic towns and cities realigned heavily toward the Democrats only in the 1960s—comparing voting trends between the 1960s and 1980s allows for a better comparison of Rhode Island's voting trends with those of Northern New England.

The data in Table 5.2 strongly indicates that Democratic trends and Republican trends in presidential elections for Rhode Island since the 1960s closely match the patterns found in Vermont and New Hampshire during the same period, 1950–1980. As in Northern New England, English and well-educated areas of Rhode Island are trending Democratic, while French and less-educated areas are most likely to be trending Republican. Irish areas in all the states so far examined seem not to be part of any partisan trends. In addition, the Democratic shift in Rhode Island highly correlates positively to a strong vote for John Anderson in the fall 1980 election, again hinting at the presence of disenchanted liberal Republicans in the trend toward the Democrats.

Two other variables also play interesting roles in Rhode Island's recent politics. Population growth between 1970 and 1980 is included here to test for any influence on political trends of the naval pullout from Rhode Island facilities in the mid-1970s. The Navy shut down many of its operations in the state in this period, and several towns where naval personnel lived lost population during the decade.[47] While some of Rhode Island's larger cities also lost population during the decade, the population-density variable in a multiple regression should account for the different influences on population loss. Once all factors are considered, population losses in the 1970s seem not to be a significant factor in presidential voting trends in the state.

However, population density itself does seem to play a role. When examined alone in a correlation, big cities seem to be trending Republican, and small towns Democratic. However, once ancestral variables are

47. The U.S. Department of Defense announced additional shutdowns of Rhode Island military facilities in 1992, which included some of the few operations left from the 1970s and a few added since then.

Table 5.2. Relationship of many variables to a shift away from Republicans in Rhode Island presidential elections for 38 of 39 towns and cities, 1960–1968 and 1984–1988

Variable	Correlation Coefficients	
	Democratic Shift	Nov. 1980 Anderson Vote
% English ancestry	.79**	.58**
% French ancestry	−.58**	−.51**
% Irish ancestry	.29	.58**
% Italian ancestry	−.21	−.22
% Portuguese ancestry	−.25	−.31
% High school grad	.65**	.85**
% College grad	.53**	.80**
Per capita income	.30	.48**
% Owner-occupied housing	.43**	.35*
% Born in Rhode Island	−.34*	−.38*
Median age	−.26	−.34*
% Population growth 1970–80	.37*	.65**
Population density	−.34*	−.43*
% Anderson vote Nov. 1980	.65**	XXX

Multiple Regressions (insignificant factors excluded)

1960s–1980s Democratic Shift

Variable	t-statistic
% English	7.12**
% French	−3.75**
Density	2.06*
R^2 (adjusted) = 72.0%	

Nov. 1980 Anderson Vote

Variable	t-statistic
% High school grad	4.11**
% College grad	2.44*
Per capita income	−2.12*
R^2 (adjusted) = 75.0%	

SOURCES: Ancestry, education, income, and born in Rhode Island variables from 1980 *Census of Population: General Social and Economic Characteristics* (U.S. Department of Commerce, Bureau of the Census); housing and age variables from 1980 *Census of Population and Housing; Summary Characteristics for Governmental Units and Standard Metropolitan Statistical Areas;* population growth and density variables from Marion I. Wright and Robert J. Sullivan, *The Rhode Island Atlas* (Providence: Rhode Island Publications Society, 1982), based on information gathered in the 1980 U.S. Census; 1960s voting data from *The Rhode Island Manual* (Providence: Office of the Secretary of State of Rhode Island); 1980s voting data from *America Votes.*

NOTES: Ancestry variables are for those claiming pure ancestries. Data for the town of New Shoreham is excluded. XXX = perfect correlation.

*Significant at the .05 level.
**Significant at the .01 level.

considered, it seems to be mainly the French cities that are trending most Republican, and medium-size English towns that are trending most Democratic; high population density becomes positively related to a Democratic trend. Heavily Italian Providence, for instance, was Rhode Island's fourth most Democratic city in the 1960 presidential election, behind two mainly French cities and one mainly Portuguese city, but in 1988, Providence gave Dukakis his largest victory in the state.

While Rhode Island's most English and best-educated towns are likely to be trending Democratic in presidential elections, these same towns seem to be the most supportive of the anti-corruption, anti-incompetence campaign themes of state Republicans and frequently become the most likely to turn against Democrats in state elections when such accusations are made. And in these campaigns, the English and well-educated towns are not joined in their political trends by some of Rhode Island's larger non-French cities, as in presidential elections, because the Republican state gains in the well-educated and English areas occur precisely because of an aversion to the Democratic politics practiced locally·in the larger cities.

In Vermont, as noted in the discussion of Bernard Sanders's statewide campaigns, analysis of town voting for state offices can be tricky because of the friends-and-neighbors syndrome, where a candidate does especially well in the portion of the state where he or she lives, or, as is often the case in Rhode Island and many other states, a candidate does especially well among members of his or her own ethnic group, who like the surname they see on the ballot.[48] The friends-and-neighbors syndrome was strongly demonstrated in the 1990 U.S. Senate election results for Republican Claudine Schneider against incumbent Democrat Claiborne Pell.[49] Pell's 1984 Republican opponent was a little-known token candi-

---

48. For example, William Marutani, a Philadelphian who ran often in the 1980s for elected judicial offices in Pennsylvania, was very successful in getting votes from heavily Italian sections of Philadelphia. Marutani's name and ancestry are Japanese.

49. Pell was best known during his Senate service as the senior Democrat on the Foreign Relations Committee and as the sponsor of the college aid federal grant program that currently bears his name. But the highlight of the 1990 campaign probably came from Pell's interest in parapsychology. During the Iraq-Kuwait crisis, a Pell staff member, whose duties included research on paranormal phenomena, discovered that when he played speeches backward made by Bush administration officials about the Persian Gulf, he could detect the codeword "Simone." The aide alerted the Defense Department to this possible breach of national security. Pell admonished the aide, but found the discovery interesting. Schneider could not really take advantage of Pell's eccentricity because she was at the time appearing in late-night half-hour "infomercials" for Anthony Robbins "Personal Power" cassettes. Schneider claimed that the

date, and Schneider did about 11 percent better in 1990. (Pell was one of the few statewide Democratic candidates who consistently escaped being tainted by the state party's machine politics image, because of his patrician image and status as one of the richest members of the Senate from mainly inherited wealth.) But a vastly disproportionate amount of Schneider's improved Republican vote came from the towns and cities she represented in the U.S. House. Of the twenty towns that were entirely within Schneider's congressional district, she improved the 1984 Republican vote for senator by more than 11 percent in seventeen of these towns, but of the eighteen towns entirely not in her district, she improved the Republican vote by more than 11 percent in only two. One city, Providence, is divided between the state's congressional districts and is not included in this analysis.

Despite the analytical problem of friends-and-neighbors voting, there are some consistent findings for the state for several elections where Republicans, many previously obscure to the public, used the issue of corrupt, incompetent machine politics to defeat Democratic candidates. Table 5.3 provides evidence from the Republican gains made in the 1984 governor's race in which Republican Edward DiPrete defeated Democrat Anthony Solomon by 60 percent to 40 percent after the Republican candidate in 1982 lost by an overwhelming 73 percent to 24 percent margin. As mentioned earlier in the chapter, DiPrete's campaign focused on a "toss the bums out" message following the state's legislative reapportionment debacle.

The Rhode Island towns that are trending toward the Democrats in presidential elections in the last thirty years are basically the same towns that have been the main impetus behind the increased success of Republicans in statewide elections of the last fifteen years (see Table 5.3). Both party's gains have come from the more-English, better-educated towns in the state, with English ancestry perhaps playing a stronger role in the Democratic presidential gains, and high educational levels playing a main role in the Republican state gains. The low Republican increase in Italian areas for the 1984 gubernatorial candidate is probably related to the Italian ancestry and name of the 1982 Republican gubernatorial candidate. (DiPrete, the 1984 candidate, is also of Italian ancestry.)

The largest difference in the Democratic presidential gains and the

---

Robbins program, which basically promotes assertiveness, self-confidence, and positive thinking, had helped her battle Hodgkin's disease in the 1970s.

Table 5.3. Comparison of Democratic gains in Rhode Island presidential elections, 1960s and 1980s, and Republican gains in gubernatorial elections, 1982 and 1984, for 38 of 39 towns and cities

Variable	Correlation Coefficients	
	Democratic Gains, 1960s–1980s Presidential Elections	Republican Gains, 1982 and 1984 Gubernatorial Elections
% English ancestry	.79**	.52**
% French ancestry	−.58**	−.38**
% Irish ancestry	.29	.48**
% Italian ancestry	−.21	−.33*
% Portuguese ancestry	−.25	−.17
% High school grad	.65**	.73**
% College grad	.53**	.71**
Per capita income	.30	.49**
% Owner-occupied housing	.43**	.42**
% Born in Rhode Island	−.34*	−.40**
Median age	−.26	−.21
% Population growth 1970–80	.37*	.12
Population density	−.34*	−.51**
1982–84 Repub. gov. vote gain	.50**	XXX

Multiple Regressions (insignificant factors excluded)

1960s–1980s Democratic Presidential Shift

Variable	t-statistic
% English	7.12**
% French	−3.75**
Density	2.06*
R^2 (adjusted) = 72.0%	

1982–1984 Republican gubernatorial shift

Variable	t-statistic
% College grads	5.26**
Density	−2.51*
Italian	−2.46*
R^2 (adjusted) = 61.0%	

SOURCES: See source note for Table 5.2.

NOTE: Presidential figures are repeated here from Table 5.2. XXX = perfect correlation.

*Significant at the .05 level.
**Significant at the .01 level.

Republican state gains occurs with the population density variable. Once other factors are taken into account, high population density is positively related to the Democratic shift and negatively related to the Republican shift. In other words, Rhode Island's non-French cities remain strongly Democratic in presidential elections and in state elections, but many of the suburban and rural parts of the state have been frequently voting more Republican in state elections, while at the same time voting increasingly Democratic in presidential elections.

It is precisely these suburban and rural voters, well educated and not connected to the urban political machines, who have been most receptive to the state Republican campaign themes of opposition to corruption and incompetence. In 1940, Rhode Island's three largest cities—Providence, Pawtucket, and Woonsocket—contained 52.6 percent of the state's population. These three cities, the main centers of state industrialization in the nineteenth century, probably to this day contain the most numbers of voters supportive of traditional machine politics, in which friendship, loyalty, and government jobs and favors often play a stronger role than merit and competence. (Buddy Cianci was reelected mayor of Providence in 1990 and in 1994 and is no longer a member of a party machine, but his old-fashioned style of politics and his personal behavior would gain him few votes for any office in many towns of the state.) By 1980, these three cities contained only 28.9 percent of Rhode Island's population.[50]

Many whose ancestors arrived in one of these cities as new immigrants have moved to the suburbs and will not tolerate the type of politics and behavior among elected officials that may have been supported or allowed by their parents or grandparents. As the population proportion of the cities supportive of traditional Democratic state politicians has continued to shrink, Republicans have gained an opening among the growing proportion not tied to the state's old style of political leadership. Yet the issues that have often dominated state politics in recent years have had little effect on the choices of Rhode Island voters in presidential elections, and therefore divergent electoral trends have occurred at different office levels in the state.

Congressional election results show the Rhode Island towns that became more Democratic in presidential elections between the 1960s and the 1980s also became more Republican in congressional elections between 1978 and 1988. There is a strong positive correlation between

50. Wright and Sullivan, *Rhode Island Atlas*, 72–73.

Table 5.4. Correlations of Democratic gains in Rhode Island presidential elections, 1960s and 1980s, with Republican gains in congressional elections, 1976–1988

Republican Share of the Vote for U.S. Representative	
Second Congressional District	First Congressional District
1976, Ianitti, 23%	1984, Rego, 31%
1978, Schneider, 47%	1986, Holmes, 42%
1980, Schneider, 55%	1988, Machtley, 56%

1976–1978 Republican Second Congressional District gain correlation to 1960s–1980s Democratic presidential gains for 20 Rhode Island towns and cities = .30.*

1984–1988 Republican First Congressional District gain correlation to 1960s–1980s Democratic presidential gains for 18 Rhode Island towns and cities = .62.*

SOURCES: 1960s presidential elections from *Rhode Island Manual*; 1980s presidential elections from *America Votes*; 1976, 1988 congressional elections from *The Journal-Bulletin Rhode Island Almanac* (Providence: Providence Journal-Bulletin); 1978, 1980, 1984, 1986 congressional elections from *Official Court of the Ballots Cast* (Providence: Rhode Island Board of Elections).

*Data for Providence are excluded from both districts; the city of Providence is divided between the two districts.

towns trending Democratic in presidential elections over twenty years, and towns trending Republican between 1984 and 1988 in House elections for the First Congressional District, the district which fourteen-term incumbent Fernand St. Germain lost to Republican Ronald Machtley over the issue of corruption in 1988 (see Table 5.4). There is also a positive correlation between the Democratic presidential trend and Republican gains between 1976 and 1978 in House elections for the Second Congressional District. By the time of Republican Claudine Schneider's victory over Democratic incumbent Ed Beard in the Second District in 1980 using the issues of incompetence and ineffectiveness, Schneider had increased her support in all towns of her district.

Recent electoral patterns in Rhode Island show elements of voting behavior usually associated with dealignment, such as split-ticket voting and a tendency to reelect incumbents of both parties who are not tainted with accusations of corruption or incompetence. However, these voting behaviors have existed at times earlier in the state's history and were common by the 1950s and 1960s, when Republican gubernatorial candidates often did much better than presidential candidates or other state-wide candidates before the advent of mass media advertising in state races. In 1964, Republican Barry Goldwater received 19 percent of Rhode Island's vote in the presidential election, while Republican Governor John Chafee was reelected with 61 percent of the vote. (Unlike congressional elections, Republicans did have some success in gubernatorial elections before the mid-1970s, often by stressing the same types of issues that were later used successfully by Republican candidates in all statewide and congressional elections.)

But one aspect of voting behavior usually associated with dealignment—a decreased significance of party cues and messages when voting—would make labeling recent Rhode Island electoral behavior as mere dealignment inaccurate. Democratic strength at the presidential level remains high precisely as a result of the images the states' voters have of both major national parties. And the gains made by Republicans at the state level are also due precisely to each party's image within the state. The key distinction in the divergent voting patterns is not the dominance of candidate personalities over party messages; instead, Rhode Island voters have different images of the Democratic party at the national level and at the state level, and of the Republican party at each level. A preference of one party at the presidential level and another at the state level results not from an absence of any party attachments, but from consistent party attachments that differ by office level, creating a federalized form of realignment.

It might be too early to label the Republican state gains of the mid-1970s to late 1980s as a long-term realignment, although the length of the period over which the gains occurred makes it impossible to label them as temporary "deviating" elections as well. In 1990, lingering memories of his 1988 scandal, along with Rhode Island's faltering economy and budget problems, led to a huge defeat for Republican Governor DiPrete, who lost 74 percent to 26 percent on Election Day, a dismal performance for an incumbent. In addition, a Democrat running against a Republican with ties to DiPrete replaced Schneider in the House seat she left to run for the Senate, returning the congressional delegation to an even split between the parties. The news was not all bad for Republicans, however. Congressman Machtley surprised some by winning reelection at about the same margin at which he had beaten St. Germain two years earlier.

And tales of corruption, scandal, and incompetence, most of which involved Democratic politicians, were rampant again in the state during 1991 and 1992. On January 1, 1991, Rhode Island's brand-new governor, Bruce Sundlun, started his term by closing down forty-five state-chartered banks and credit unions insured by a private state fund. Some 300,000 of Rhode Island's million residents had deposits in the affected institutions. The crisis began when Joseph Mollicone, the vice chairman of the insurance fund and the head of one credit union reputedly associated with organized crime, allegedly embezzled $13 million and disappeared in November 1990. (Mollicone turned himself in to the authorities in 1992.) The state insurance fund used up its reserves to cover the embezzlement, leaving it nearly broke. Most of the affected institutions were able to get federally insured, but several remained closed as depositors waited for their money. Sundlun pledged to pay back everyone who lost money up to $100,00 in a time of severe state budget cutbacks, but many impatient depositors organized numerous angry demonstrations, demanding more immediate payment.[51]

After the banking crisis began, it was revealed that Republican Attorney General Violet had issued a report to the Democratic-dominated legislature in 1985 warning that the insurance agency was severely underfunded, but legislators with ties to the industry had blocked any reforms. It was also revealed that one Democratic urban state legislator who was vice president of an affected credit union had actually withdrawn $200,000 of his money three days before Sundlun shut it down. The legislator claimed he had had no inside information at public hearings in July 1991.[52]

Also during 1991, a former Democratic mayor of Pawtucket was convicted of extortion, a judge pleaded guilty to fraud, another judge was indicted for bribery, and state pension records revealed that checks were being mailed to dead people and that more than two hundred friends and relatives of legislators were receiving specially approved pensions for part-time state jobs. Governor Sundlun declared that 1991 was the year in which "the dishonesty, greed and corruption that rotted our system was exposed for all to see."[53]

51. Barone and Ujifusa, *Almanac of American Politics 1992*, 1101; Elizabeth Kolbert, "Long Hot Summer of Political Sleaze Leaves Rhode Islanders Boiling Mad," *New York Times*, August 27, 1991, A16.
52. Kolbert, "Long Hot Summer," A16.
53. "Rhode Island Scandals Ignite Revolt by Voters," *New York Times*, February 23, 1992, 26.

The exposure continued in July 1992, when a suburban reform-minded Democratic state legislator filed a police complaint stating that a State Senate bill had been stolen from the clerk's desk in the senate chambers. The bill, which would have limited the borrowing authority of the Rhode Island Convention Center Authority, had been passed by the state House of Representatives but could not be voted on by the senate during the legislature's short session because it had disappeared. The clerk who discovered the bill was missing claimed that it must have been stolen during the only few minutes in which he left his desk during an eight-hour time period. He said angrily that he had heard such episodes in the past referred to as "pocket vetoes."[54]

While Sundlun and articles in the New York Times portrayed reactions to the scandals of the early 1990s as stronger than any in the past, these episodes actually seemed to be a continuation, although possibly at an increased rate, of those of the past, with the banking crisis perhaps having greater effect because of its personal impact. In the last twenty years, allegations of corruption and incompetence in state government have benefited the Republican party in Rhode Island, and 1992 was no exception. Sundlun, a millionaire businessman before entering office, remained untainted by charges of political corruption or incompetence when he won reelection easily in 1992, despite or perhaps because of his actions in the credit union scandal the year before. By 1993, though, Sundlun's popularity dropped after his previously unacknowledged seventeen-year-old daughter filed a paternity suit.[55] In 1994, he lost the Democratic party primary for reelection and was replaced as governor in 1995 by Republican Lincoln Almond, a former U.S. Attorney for Rhode Island best known for prosecuting two allegedly corrupt Democratic mayors in the state.

But even by 1992, Republicans were able to shake the temporary legacy of scandals and a poor economy under DiPrete's final years as governor, and Republican candidates swept elections for the lower statewide offices of secretary of state, attorney general, and general treasurer. Republican Representative Machtley was also reelected with 70 percent of the vote, retaining his party's hold on half the state's congressional delegation. However, while the Republicans had another banner year in 1992 in

---

54. Michael Pare, "'Pocket Veto' Defeats Proposal in State Senate," East Greenwich Pendulum, July 22, 1992, 1.
55. Congressional Quarterly Weekly Reports, February 19, 1994, 409.

elections for Rhode Island state offices, the party's presidential candidate, George Bush, received just 29 percent of the vote in the state, which tied for his worst performance nationwide. By mid-1997, while Democrats again controlled three of the four members of the state's congressional delegation, Republicans held four of the five offices elected statewide in Rhode Island government.

The next chapter contains evidence from what may be an even stronger example of federalized realignment: Upstate New York. Bordering on Vermont, this region in presidential elections follows closely the Vermont pattern in trending toward the Democrats in presidential elections. At the same time, however, most Upstate New York counties remain overwhelmingly Republican in state legislative races because of issues that dominate state politics. Chapter 6 also provides additional case studies from the Upper Midwest and the Pacific Northwest that will strengthen the arguments from preceding chapters by analyzing the Democratic shifts that are similar to the Vermont pattern in other states. As in Vermont, those shifts have generally been gradual and, as with Vermont and New Hampshire, have been shaped by the unique political environments of each state.

Whatever happens in Rhode Island in the near future, the state's Democratic party retains a strong and sometimes dominant city machine faction that in the foreseeable future can offer plenty of candidates that can be easily attacked by Republicans as being corrupt or incompetent. In 1980, Buddy Cianci thought that running in Rhode Island as a Republican was like speaking as the Ayatollah Khomeini before a veterans' group. But by the mid-1980s, running as a Republican in Rhode Island symbolized opposition to and rejection of the corrupt and incompetent one-party leadership of the past. Maybe that's why Buddy Cianci does not run as a Republican anymore.

Chapter Six

———⸺◆⸺———

Northern Realignment
West of New England

If Vermont stood out as the only one of the fifty states to see major gains for the Democrats since the 1950s, and Rhode Island stood out as the only state to see a federalized form of realignment in the 1970s and 1980s, then this book would be of specific interest mostly to followers of New England politics. Yet the trends demonstrated in Vermont and Rhode Island, as well as the countertrend seen in New Hampshire, exist not only in New England but also throughout much of the rest of the nation.

The one New England state not discussed in any depth so far—Connecticut—has generally followed the trend toward the Democrats found in most of New England, though not always to as large an extent. Between the 1950s and 1980s, Connecticut showed small gains for Democratic candidates in presidential elections, and by the 1990s went strongly for Clinton twice. But Connecticut remains the second most Republican state in New England, after New Hampshire, and in mid-1997 had the only two Republican U.S. House members in the region outside New Hampshire.

Part of the reason that Connecticut's partisan trends have not been as strong as much of New England is that the southwestern part of the state has become an extended suburban part of the New York City area and is influenced much more by New York media and popular culture than the media and culture of New England. Yet the New York City suburbs are not extremely conservative themselves, and the New England brand of politics remains strong in Connecticut, as elsewhere in the region. Connecticut's two Republican members of Congress are both considered moderates in the national party, and in the 1990s the traditional brand of New England independent liberal Republicanism reasserted itself in Connecticut.

In 1990, former Republican U.S. Senator Lowell Weicker was elected governor on the ticket of "A Connecticut Party"—an independent vehicle for expressing his distaste for traditional Democratic and Republican politics in the state. As governor, Weicker pushed through the legislature the state's first income tax and lowered the more regressive state sales tax. Weicker chose not to run for reelection in 1994, and the independent party he created may lose its significance without his public leadership, but in 1994 its candidate for governor did receive 19 percent of the vote, and a candidate for the U.S. House in eastern Connecticut won 15 percent. That House candidate, David Bingham, had supported John Anderson for president in 1980, Weicker for governor in 1990, and Perot for president in 1992, and was endorsed by the New London daily newspaper,[1] symbolizing the type of New England voter and attitudes that since the 1960s have been most likely to become disenchanted with the new national Republican party.

In 1996, Connecticut's only conservative Republican member of the U.S. House lost reelection. Meanwhile, moderate Republican Nancy Johnson barely won reelection in a surprise near-upset in which her Democratic opponent nicknamed her "Stonewall Johnson" amid accusations that she was stalling in her investigation of ethical lapses by Republican Speaker of the House Newt Gingrich.

Connecticut, like most of New England, has trended Democratic in recent presidential elections, and its voters have shown a distaste for national conservative Republican politics. This clear gradual trend toward the Democrats in presidential voting between 1952 and 1988 has occurred throughout much of the northern tier of the United States, an area that follows a pattern similar to the westward migration of New England Yankees in the nineteenth century. Certain pockets in this area, however, like New Hampshire, have increased their support for Republicans despite the Democratic gains in surrounding counties. And Rhode Island is not the only Northern state to have opposite partisan realignments at differing levels of government in the last twenty years. The counties of Upstate New York perhaps demonstrate even better than Rhode Island how voters, when deciding among candidates, can focus on

---

1. Barone and Ujifusa, *The Almanac of American Politics 1996*, 263.

different priorities for different levels of office within a federal system, leading to a federalized realignment.

"Upstate New York" is the term commonly used to label the counties of New York State north of New York City that contain almost all the state's geographical area but a minority of its population.[2] For one hundred years following the Civil War, Upstate New York, like Vermont, remained solidly Republican. By the late 1800s, "the upstate-downstate rivalry became the predominant political fissure in the state, with the Democrats the protectors of New York City and the Republicans in control of upstate."[3] In 1956, when the nation gave Republican President Eisenhower 57 percent of their votes to 43 percent for Democrat Stevenson, New York City supported Stevenson 51–49 percent, while the rest of the state went overwhelmingly for Eisenhower, 71–29 percent. Seven counties in Upstate New York gave more than 80 percent of their votes to Eisenhower. The solid support for Republicans in the part of the state north of New York City was comparable to that of Vermont, Eisenhower's best state in 1956, on which Upstate New York borders.

Like Vermont, though, Upstate New York has grown increasingly Democratic in its presidential voting preferences in the last forty years. All of New York State's sixty-two counties actually voted more Democratic in the 1984–1988 presidential elections than they did in the 1952–1956 period.[4] But as in Rhode Island, many of these areas had a quick, or perhaps "critical," realignment toward the Democrats in 1960 due to the popularity of candidate John Kennedy in Catholic areas. These areas voted much more heavily Democratic in presidential elections in the 1960s than in previous decades, but they have since stabilized their partisan support or grown more Republican (although not to 1950s levels). Therefore, as in the last chapter on Rhode Island, the presidential election data that follows compares the 1960 and 1968 elections with the

2. Upstate New York in 1990 still contained less than half the state's population, with a majority living in New York City or Long Island.

3. Peter W. Colby and John K. White, "The Politics of New York State Today," in Peter W. Colby and John K. White, eds., New York State Today (Albany: State University of New York Press, 1989), 9.

4. The average increase in Democratic support between the two presidential election periods was at least 8 percent in all but six of the state's counties. The exceptions were Kings County (Brooklyn, 7 percent), two counties in the outer orbit of the New York City area—Putnam (1.5 percent) and Sullivan (the Catskill Mountains, 3.5 percent)—and three counties in the southern part of western New York: Steuben (Corning, 6.5 percent), Cattaraugus (5.5 percent), and Chautauqua (Jamestown, 7.5 percent).

1984 and 1988 elections in order to distinguish the gradual trends toward the Democrats found in most New York counties from the Catholic realignment of the 1960s.

The tables that follow present data for fifty of New York's sixty-two counties to represent Upstate New York.[5] Of the twelve excluded counties, five are in New York City and two consist mainly of Long Island suburbs. The four suburban counties immediately north of New York City are also excluded. Finally, one upstate county—Tompkins—is excluded because of its status as a large outlier in the data. While almost all of Upstate New York's counties had an average shift in presidential voting between the 1950s and the 1980s toward the Democrats of 8 to 19 percent, Tompkins, with a shift of 32 percent, was the only one that had a shift of greater than 20 percent.[6] Tompkins County, in which the city of Ithaca is located, as well as Ithaca College and Cornell University, actually had the fourth highest such Democratic gains of any county in the nation during the period covered.[7] While some of Tompkins County's increased support for the Democrats undoubtedly results from the same factors as in neighboring counties, large numbers of faculty and alumni and others attracted to the two large higher-education institutions in Ithaca have settled permanently in the otherwise rural county, causing greater population growth than in neighboring counties, and causing extreme political changes that obfuscate any trends among the locally born population. No such conditions occur to anywhere near the same extent in the remaining fifty counties of Upstate New York.

In 1960, John Kennedy received 53 percent of New York State's support, compared with 52 percent for Dukakis in 1988. If no realignment had occurred in the intervening years, support for each Democratic candidate in each county should have been at similar levels. Yet the pattern of support changed dramatically in twenty years. Dukakis did slightly

5. The twelve excluded counties include Bronx, New York, Richmond, Queens, and Kings in New York City; Nassau and Suffolk on Long Island; Orange, Putnam, Rockland, and Westchester north of New York City; and Tompkins in the upstate Finger Lakes region.

6. Tompkins County has also shifted toward the Democrats by more than twice as much as any other county in the state, since the 1960 and 1968 elections. The Democratic percentage of the major party (Democrats, Republicans) vote for president since 1956 in Tompkins County follows: 1956—22 percent; 1960—34 percent; 1964—64 percent; 1968—43 percent; 1972—41 percent; 1976—45 percent; 1980—49 percent; 1984—51 percent; 1988—59 percent; 1992—67 percent; 1996—64 percent.

7. Tompkins County followed only Dukes (Martha's Vineyard) and Nantucket counties in Massachusetts and Shannon County, South Dakota (Pine Ridge Indian Reservation, which includes Wounded Knee) in its Democratic gains.

worse than Kennedy in five of the six suburban counties surrounding New York City (Nassau, Suffolk, Putnam, Rockland, and Orange), but better than Kennedy in almost all upstate counties—the main exceptions being a few counties on the Canadian border with significant populations of French Canadian ancestry. In sixteen counties, the Republican percentage of the vote declined by at least 7 percent between 1960 and 1988, fourteen of these in central New York areas labeled by the state as the Finger Lakes and Central Leatherstocking regions.

This chapter and the next use counties rather than townships as units of analysis, unlike the more in-depth case studies found in the three previous chapters on New England states. Although township data may be preferable for breaking down populations into smaller and frequently more homogeneous groups, using county data allows certain variables, such as economic conditions and religious affiliation, which are not readily available at the township level, to be introduced. Table 6.1 measures the correlations of several variables against the Democratic shift in presidential voting between the 1960s and the 1980s in Upstate New York.

The data analyzing the components of the Democratic shift in New York's upstate counties provide results similar to those found in Vermont's townships and cities. The upstate counties most likely to be trending Democratic in presidential elections since the 1960s tend to be more English and more Protestant than those trending Republican that tend to be Catholic. It is important to remember, however, that, due to the Kennedy candidacy, the Republican gains in Catholic areas followed a giant swing toward the Democrats in these areas in 1960, which were unlikely to be followed by further increases in support for non-Catholic Democratic candidates. The use of the 1960s data instead of the 1950s data, therefore, helps to identify better the sources of gradual Democratic gains in longtime Republican areas, but it may mislead as to the extent of Republican gains in areas that suddenly shifted heavily Democratic in the 1960s after also being generally Republican in the past. Despite this disclaimer, however, the areas in New York with relatively large French ancestries (mainly near the Canadian border) seem to be among those least likely to be trending Democratic, a result that matches the results for Vermont and New Hampshire.

Once all factors are taken into account, high educational levels, high percentages of English ancestry, and low numbers of Catholics seem to best describe which Upstate New York counties have had the highest

Table 6.1. Relationship of many variables to Republican declines in presidential voting in 50 Upstate New York counties, 1960–1968 and 1984–1988 (for an explanation of each variable, see the table note)

Variable	Democratic Shift	Variable	Democratic Shift
English	.56**	Baptist	.59**
Dutch	.33*	Catholic	− .69**
German	− .06	Church of Christ	.27
Irish	− .14	Episcopal	.55**
French	− .32*	Methodist	.60**
Italian	− .26	Presbyterian	.38**
Polish	− .37**	Anderson in '80	.44**
College grad	.06	Wallace in '68	.03
High school grad	.12	Free Soil	.17
Population	− .24		
Income	− .12		
Poverty	.04		
Unemployment	− .16		

Multiple Regression on 60s and 80s shift away from Republicans

R^2 = 59.6% R^2 (adjusted) = 57.0%

s = 2.388 with 50 − 4 = 46 degrees of freedom

Source	Sum of Squares	df	Mean Square	F-ratio
Regression	387.013	3	129	22.6
Residual	262.407	46	5.70449	

Variable	Coefficient	s.e. of Coeff	t-ratio
Constant	− 2.829010	2.8650	− 0.987
College grad	0.273735	0.1112	2.460*
Catholic	− 0.138484	0.0269	− 5.150**
English	0.363526	0.1146	3.170**

SOURCES: Ancestry, education, population, and economic variables from *1980 Census of Population: General Social and Economic Characteristics;* religious variables from Bernard Quinn et al., *Churches and Church Membership in the United States 1980* (Atlanta, Ga.: Glenmary Research Center, 1982); Anderson vote from *The World Almanac and Book of Facts for 1983* (New York: World Almanac Publications, 1982); Wallace vote and all Republican and Democratic vote percentages from *America Votes.* Free Soil Vote from Walter Dean Burnham, *Presidential Ballots 1836–1892* (Baltimore: Johns Hopkins University Press, 1955).

EXPLANATIONS OF VARIABLES:

  English, Dutch, German, Irish, French, Italian, Polish: % claiming full ancestry in 1980 census.

  College grad, high school grad: % having graduated at each level in 1980 census.

  Population: 1980 county population.

  Income, poverty, unemployment: 1980 census per capita income, poverty levels, and unemployment rates.

Table 6.1. (Continued)

EXPLANATIONS OF VARIABLES: *(continued)*

Baptist, Catholic, Church of Christ, Episcopal, Methodist, Presbyterian: % of county population counted as members in the following church organizations—American Baptist Churches in the U.S.A., Catholic Church, United Church of Christ, Episcopal Church, United Methodist Church, United Presbyterian Church in the U.S.A.

Anderson in '80: % of county vote for independent presidential candidate John Anderson in 1980.

Wallace in '68: % of county vote for independent presidential candidate George Wallace in 1968.

Free Soil: % of county vote for Free Soil party presidential candidate Martin Van Buren in 1848.

*Significant at the .05 level.
**Significant at the .01 level.

Democratic gains in presidential elections, another result that basically matches the results for New England. The use of county data in New York allows religious affiliation to be compared with ancestry, and additional economic variables to be compared with educational levels to see which are the strongest factors in determining Democratic trends. Despite strong positive correlations between most of the large Protestant denominations and Democratic gains, English ancestry seems to remain the stronger explanation of declining Republican support. Catholic religion, however, seem to outweigh the individual Catholic ancestries in explaining Republican gains. High educational levels, meanwhile, continue to be stronger factors than any economic variables in explaining partisan trends.

In Upstate New York, many or most of those claiming English ancestry are descendants of New Englanders who migrated west in especially large numbers after the American Revolution. New Englanders reproduced the political, religious, and educational institutions of their original home towns in their new settlements, and, by 1820, 60 to 75 percent of the entire New York State population was estimated to be of New England Yankee origin.[8]

The Upstate New York data also matches that found in New England in the significant positive correlation found in Democratic gains with relatively high support for John Anderson's presidential candidacy in 1980. As discussed in earlier chapters, Anderson's 1980 third party candidacy, whose significance is now often given little attention by politicians and political scientists, reflected an important reaction among liberal and

8. David Maldwyn Ellis, *New York: State and City* (Ithaca, N.Y.: Cornell University Press, 1979), 31.

moderate Republican voters against the increased conservatism of their party. It is surprising that George Wallace's 1968 third-party vote shows no correlation to any partisan trend in Upstate New York. Wallace received only 5.3 percent of the statewide vote, doing worse in only seven other states, and he was not a significant factor in New York's vote. However, his candidacy did have a strong correlation with partisan trends in much of the rest of the United States.[9]

Finally, an attempt to find a correlation between modern partisan trends and voting behavior in the nineteenth century was not clearly successful. Before the Civil War, several antislavery political parties arose to contest presidential elections and races for other offices. These parties tended to be especially popular in New England Yankee areas that later became core constituencies of the newly formed Republican party. The only presidential election in which one of these parties received a significant share of New York's vote occurred in 1848, when New Yorker and former Democratic President Martin Van Buren ran as the presidential candidate of the Free Soil party, which opposed extending slavery to American territories, and received 27 percent of New York's statewide vote.

The correlation between the Free Soil vote and Democratic gains more than one hundred years later is positive but statistically insignificant. The characteristics of county populations have changed since 1848, making comparisons over such a long period of time difficult. In addition, presidential voting in the pre–Civil War era tended to be influenced more by local politics than is the case now—especially in 1848, when the Free Soil candidate was a former New York Democratic governor. According to James Sundquist, the Free Soil party attracted votes from Democrats allied with Van Buren's "Barnburner" faction of the state Democratic party in New York, some of whom had previously shown no concern with the slavery question, while some antislavery Whigs refused to vote for a former Jacksonian Democrat, preventing the 1848 Free Soil vote from being a totally accurate gauge of antislavery or anti-South attitudes in all New York counties.[10]

Upstate New York has seen a clear, persistent, and gradual trend toward the Democrats in presidential voting since the 1950s and 1960s.

9. The seven states in which Wallace did worse than in New York are Hawaii (1.5 percent), Maine (1.6 percent), Vermont (3.2 percent), Massachusetts (3.7 percent), New Hampshire (3.8 percent), Rhode Island (4.1 percent), and South Dakota (4.8 percent).

10. Sundquist, *Dynamics of the Party System*, 61–65.

Some would refuse to label this trend a realignment unless voters also voted more Democratic for other offices and unless voters identified themselves to pollsters as Democrats. The puzzling emphasis that many political scientists put on answers to polls, rather than on the actual voting behavior that elects candidates to office, is a question of research methodology that has been addressed previously in this book. And the insistence that a "true" realignment must occur in the same partisan direction at all office levels was disputed in the last chapter on Rhode Island, but will be further discussed here.

In Rhode Island, towns with high percentages of English ancestry and well-educated voters have become more Democratic in presidential voting since the 1960s. Yet the same towns turned consistently more Republican in voting for some statewide offices in the 1970s and 1980s. A typical recent analysis of American voting behavior would label such a phenomenon as dealignment, indicating a decline in strong partisan attachments among the electorate and a focus on candidate personalities and transient issues in voting decisions. The discussion in the last chapter proved such an assessment to be an inaccurate description of recent Rhode Island voting behavior. Certain groups of voters in the state became more Democratic in presidential elections and more Republican in voting for state offices, not because of a lack of party identification at any level but because the images each party presented differed greatly between the national level and the state level. The changes in partisan support occurred when voting did not fluctuate wildly from election to election, but persisted in one direction for presidential elections and in another direction in statewide elections.

In Upstate New York, the increases in support for Democratic presidential candidates have not been matched in state legislative elections, where much of the area remains as solidly Republican as ever. While every one of the fifty upstate counties under analysis grew more Democratic in presidential voting between the 1950s and the 1980s, forty of these fifty counties increased their support for Republicans in elections to the New York State Senate in the same period.[11]

There is no statistical correlation between partisan changes in presidential voting and partisan changes in state senate voting for upstate counties between the 1950s and 1980s, and there is a positive but insig-

___

11. The source for New York state legislative election data is the *Manual for the Use of the Legislature of the State of New York* (Albany: New York Department of State, various years).

nificant statistical correlation between increased Democratic support in presidential voting since the 1960s and increased Republican support in state senate voting since the 1950s. But the lack of statistically significant correlations does not eliminate the value of the data in analyzing upstate political trends. The idiosyncrasies of local politics, and the strong advantages of incumbency, do detract from an accurate statistical assessment of state legislative elections on an aggregate basis. Several upstate Republican incumbent state senators ran for reelection unopposed or against only minor party opposition in 1988. But the continued overwhelming support for Republicans in state senate elections, even if any increases in support derive from incumbency, remains a remarkable contrast to the strong increases in support for Democratic presidential candidates in the same region.

And when the only ten upstate counties where the Democrats have gained in state senate elections since the 1950s are identified, the contrast grows even more striking—eight of these counties are located in the metropolitan areas of Buffalo, Rochester, Syracuse, and Binghamton, while the remaining two are in the southwestern corner of the state, the area with the weakest Democratic gains in the upstate region in presidential voting.[12] In a study of New York gubernatorial elections between 1962 and 1982, Martin Shefter noted that although upstate rural areas showed no consistent changes in partisan voting, upstate cities, such as Buffalo, Syracuse, Rochester, Albany, and Binghamton, gave larger and larger margins of victory for Democratic gubernatorial candidates during the period, a pattern that is consistent with the state senate data analyzed above.[13]

While these urban or metropolitan counties have realigned at all levels since the 1950s, forty other upstate counties have all grown increasingly Democratic in presidential voting and increasingly Republican in state senate voting since the 1950s. Again, the question arises as to whether these counties have dealigned and have lacked any consistent voting behavior in the last forty years, therefore leading to divergent partisan trends. Some of these forty counties with large Catholic populations became much more Democratic in the presidential election of 1960 because

12. The ten counties are Albany; Erie (Buffalo); Monroe (Rochester); Genesee (the only county between Erie and Monroe); Onondaga and Madison (Syracuse area); Broome and Tioga (Binghamton area); and Allegany and Cattaraugus (southwestern New York).

13. Martin Shefter, "The Electoral Framework," in Gerald Benjamin and Charles Brecher, eds., *The Two New Yorks* (New York: Russell Sage Foundation, 1988).

of the Kennedy candidacy and have not had divergent partisan trends at different office levels since, but others among these counties have continued to become gradually more Democratic in presidential voting. Almost all these counties also reelected incumbent Republican state senators that were unchallenged by Democrats in 1988.

There are three types of explanations for these divergent partisan trends in many Upstate New York counties. First, the population may be voting entirely inconsistently from election to election at all office levels with no patterns emerging, therefore indicating a complete dealignment. The data suggest otherwise—state senate voting remains solidly Republican, and presidential voting has become increasingly Democratic in every decade. Second, local Democrats may be foolishly passing up opportunities to run in the mistaken belief that they cannot win in these Republican areas, despite presidential voting trends to the contrary. This explanation may have a bit of validity, but it must be noted that even when incumbent Republicans retire and seats open up, new Republicans still usually beat the Democrats. A third type of explanation is that Upstate New York voting behavior may have become federalized, as in Rhode Island.

In Rhode Island, people in highly educated, English ancestry areas have voted more Democratic in presidential elections, partly because of the national Republican party's increased conservatism and emphasis on gaining votes in the South. The same voters became increasingly Republican in many state elections in the 1970s and 1980s, as a reaction to control of the state Democratic party by urban politicians perceived as corrupt or incompetent. The most salient issues for these voters were different at the national level and the state level, and their voting patterns therefore federalized and realigned in two different directions.

The historically strongly Republican population of Upstate New York's mostly English, better-educated areas have also grown increasingly disenchanted with the national Republican party since the 1950s, probably for the same reasons found in most of New England. However, appeals to Southern voters emphasized opposition to civil rights measures, support for conservative moral positions, and the military threat posed by the former Soviet Union, which were not key issues in upstate New York's local elections. State legislative elections have instead been dominated by another key issue for more than one hundred years—the antagonism between Upstate New York and New York City. For years, upstate voters have perceived themselves as paying high taxes to pay for New York City social services that were distributed by corrupt or incompetent city politicians.

In 1984, New York City, with slightly less than 40 percent of the state's population, included two-thirds of state residents on public assistance. City residents also obtained two-thirds of all state spending on public assistance and other social services for that year.[14] This and similar statistics are noticed in Upstate New York, as "politicians from this region regularly can gain publicity in upstate newspapers by portraying themselves as defenders of the state budget against the enormous appetite of New York City."[15]

Not only are public assistance and social services for the poor of New York City unpopular causes in Upstate New York, but Upstaters also feel that much of the state money is filtered through incompetent or corrupt city officials. A 1982 poll found that three out of four Upstate New Yorkers felt there was a "serious conflict" between Upstate and the city and believed that the city was poorly managed and wasteful.[16]

Since the days of Tammany Hall and Boss Tweed, and through recent years of financial troubles, New York City has had a statewide and national reputation for corruption and incompetent administration. (This reputation has begun to change a bit under the administration of liberal Republican Mayor Rudolph Giuliani.) New York City is not unique in this regard. Many other American cities have achieved similar reputations in their states, including the old Democratic machine strongholds of Rhode Island. And as in Rhode Island, the differing salience of issues at the national and state levels has caused a federalized realignment in Upstate New York.

Most Democrats in the New York state legislature represent New York City.[17] The state senate, the only part of New York's government under the control of Republicans for many years, has often been seen as a bul-

---

14. Irene Lurie and Mary Jo Bane, "Social Services," in *The Two New Yorks*, 421.

15. Jeffrey Stonecash, "State-Local Relations: The City and Upstate," in *New York State Today*, 45.

16. Gerald Benjamin, "The Political Relationship," in *The Two New Yorks*, 107.

17. Most of the upstate Democrats represent the cities mentioned earlier as being among the few upstate areas where Democrats have improved their performance in state senate elections since the 1950s. Some of the reasons for Democratic gains in local politics in these areas probably derive from urban problems common to most American cities. Stonecash, "State-Local Relations: The City and Upstate," 47, noted a coalition among legislators from New York City and the upstate cities to seek state funding for urban needs.

wark against complete New York City control of state government, which might have occurred if Democrats became the state senate majority.[18] Most Upstate New Yorkers, therefore, became convinced by local politicians that voting Republican in state senate races was the best way to prevent government by free-spending, corrupt, and incompetent New York City politicians.

In national politics, the Republican party by the 1980s portrayed itself as the savior of conservative social values, the opponent of civil rights measures that went beyond banning simple discrimination, and the best defense against the Soviet military threat. In state legislative races in Upstate New York, local Republicans rarely focused on such issues (there are few racial minorities outside the cities in the area, except for scattered Indian reservations), instead emphasizing their opposition to the spending and programs desired by New York City Democrats.

National Democrats are of course also perceived as being more receptive to urban spending programs than national Republicans, but such issues have either been submerged or just treated as one of many issues in recent presidential campaigns. More important to the realigning voting patterns of New York has been the national Republican party's efforts to capture votes from the traditional political opponents of Northern Yankees in the South and among Catholics. Just as the national Democratic party was unable to maintain a coalition among African Americans and white Southerners, the national Republican party has not had as easy a time joining the interests and values of Southerners to Northern Yankees as it thought it would.

Local Republicans in Upstate New York see no purpose in emphasizing issues that are of interest to Southerners and have continued their traditional political message of opposition to New York City interests, a strategy that has remained successful at winning the votes of most Upstaters outside of larger urban areas. The values and interests of Upstate New Yorkers have not changed dramatically, nor has the political strategy of local Republicans. There have therefore been no great political changes in state senate elections in the area. The political strategy of national Republicans did change after 1960, though, and the voting patterns of Upstaters have therefore changed accordingly. Upstaters remain opposed to the political interests of New York City at the state level and unenthu-

18. This became less of a concern in 1995 after Democratic Governor Mario Cuomo was defeated for reelection by upstate Republican George Pataki.

siastic about the political interests or values of the South at the national level.

To label perfectly consistent political attitudes such as these a "dealignment" would be a distortion, as it was in Rhode Island. Instead, Upstate New York has undergone a federalized realignment—more Democratic at the national level, solidly Republican at the local level.

Similar patterns of realignment emerge west of the Northeast, nowhere more so than in Iowa. For the one hundred years following the Civil War, Iowa's Republican credentials were almost as strong as Vermont's. Between 1856 and 1932, Iowa never gave a majority of its vote to a Democratic presidential candidate (Democrat Wilson won a plurality in 1912), and it elected a Democratic governor just once. The Republican dominance was interrupted temporarily by the Great Depression and New Deal agricultural policy, which led Iowans to vote Democratic for president in 1932, 1936, and 1948.[19]

By 1952, however, the state returned to its historical voting habits, with Eisenhower winning twice easily in 1952 and 1956 and Nixon winning in 1960 with 57 percent of the vote. Iowa was Nixon's seventh best state in 1960, behind only the Great Plains states of South Dakota, Nebraska, Kansas, and Oklahoma and the New England states of Maine and Vermont. The Kennedy appeal was insignificant in Iowa, compared with the Catholic areas of the Northeast. Before the 1960s, Iowa was "by instinct and normal voting pattern Republican, . . . a clear reflection of the Protestant hard-work ethic of its countless county seats and little towns."[20] Early twentieth-century Iowa Republican Senator Jonathan Dolliver even ventured to assert: "When Iowa goes Democratic, Hell will go Methodist."[21]

No direct evidence of Satan's religious conversion yet exists, but by the 1980s there was no doubt about Iowa's political conversion, as the state became one of the most Democratic in the nation in presidential elections. In 1984, Iowa was Mondale's sixth-best state (Mondale did better than Kennedy did in Iowa in 1960), and when Dukakis won Iowa in 1988, it was his second-best state. Dukakis did better than Kennedy had done in ninety-seven of Iowa's ninety-nine counties.

Some might assume that the changes in Iowa's partisan voting habits

19. Roosevelt lost in Iowa in 1940 and 1944, however, when he chose Iowan Henry Wallace and Missourian Harry Truman as vice presidential running mates.
20. Peirce and Hagstrom, *Book of America,* 572.
21. Ibid., 573.

resulted from the state's economic problems in agriculture in the 1980s. No doubt the economic troubles of many farmers helped increase the Democratic share of Iowa's vote, but a closer analysis of the data will show that other factors played at least as large a role as well. In addition, Iowa began increasing its Democratic vote in presidential elections and in state elections by the 1960s, before any farm "crisis"; Iowa is geographically right in the middle of the whole northern tier of states that have trended Democratic since the 1950s, and many of those states have not had similar agricultural economic problems. In Iowa, the economic situation of the 1980s probably only amplified Democratic voting trends that would have existed in any case, just as Vermont's large number of residents that have moved there from other states are not the main source of responsibility for Vermont's Democratic gains but did help amplify them.

Before examining the data to explain Iowa's Democratic trends, it is necessary to discuss whether any Iowa counties should be excluded from the analysis because of glaring inconsistencies with voting patterns in the rest of the state. Reagan and Bush in 1984 and 1988 did worse than Eisenhower in 1952 and 1956 in all ninety-nine of Iowa's counties, and averaged at least 5 percent worse in eighty-nine counties. The ten counties where Reagan and Bush came closest to matching Eisenhower's performance are all in two small corners of Iowa: three in the northwest corner of the state and seven in the southwest corner. Statistics can easily explain the maintenance of high Republican support in one of these areas, but not in the other.

The three northwest Iowa counties are notable in two ways: they are three of the four counties with the lowest percentages of high school graduates in the state, and they are ethnically much more Dutch than most of the rest of the state. Both these characteristics fit in with patterns elsewhere in the state; less-educated and Dutch areas have generally maintained higher Republican support than other areas across Iowa. The educational factor in voting patterns also matches perfectly with that found and discussed in New England. However, New England has relatively few residents of Dutch ancestry, and such ancestry did not play a clear role in Upstate New York voting patterns. But Dutch ancestry in the Midwestern United States does seem to be a significant factor in predicting consistently high levels of Republican support, for northwestern Iowa is not the only part of the Midwest where a Dutch area stands out from surrounding counties that have been trending Democratic.

In Michigan—as in New England, New York, and the rest of the Upper

Midwest—almost all counties voted more Democratic in 1984 and 1988 than they did in 1952 and 1956. Other than a few scattered counties, mostly in the state's Upper Peninsula, there are only two areas, or group-ings of counties, in Michigan that maintained or increased their Republi-can support between the 1950s and the 1980s. Most significant to the statewide vote was the declining Democratic vote in Detroit's high popu-lation suburbs in all the counties surrounding the city, a trend that will be discussed further in Chapter 7. Of less significance to the statewide vote, but of importance to understanding Iowa's voting patterns, is the other area of Michigan that has maintained its historical high levels of Republican support: the counties along Lake Michigan with high per-centages of Dutch ancestry, which includes the cities of Holland and Grand Rapids.

Exactly why the Dutch, "probably the single most Republican ethnic group in the country,"[22] have not joined with other Northern Protestant groups in trending Democratic is not easy to determine.[23] The answer likely derives from original and current settlement patterns among Dutch communities. Many of the original Dutch settlers of Michigan and Iowa emigrated to the United States as religious protesters against the growing liberalism of the Netherlands Dutch Reformed Church during the En-lightenment. Known as the Seceders, these Midwestern immigrants gained a reputation for cultural conservatism and clannishness.[24]

In the 1990s, some of these conservative social characteristics remain strong in the American Dutch Reformed community. In Iowa, the Dutch remain strongly concentrated in certain areas. In Sioux County in north-west Iowa, 55 percent of the population claimed full Dutch ancestry in the 1980 census, a stronger concentration of one ethnic group than that found among any other ethnic group in any county in the state. And the Dutch Reformed Church in the United States has sometimes been known nationally in recent years for personalities and institutions some-what similar to those found in large Texas churches. Television evangelist Robert Schuller, with his elaborate Crystal Cathedral, is Dutch Re-formed, for example, and the Amway Corporation, founded by Dutch

---

22. Barone and Ujifusa, *Almanac of American Politics 1992*, 621.

23. Most of the Dutch settling in western Michigan and northwest Iowa were Dutch Re-formed Protestants, not Catholics.

24. Robert P. Swierenga, "Introduction," in Robert P. Swierenga, ed., *The Dutch in America* (New Brunswick, N.J.: Rutgers University Press, 1985), 3–4.

Reformed members in western Michigan, promotes a similar evangelistic and success philosophy in its corporation.[25]

Whatever the proper explanation for Dutch Republicanism, the continued support of Iowa's three northwestern counties for Republicans seems to be consistent statistically with the rest of Iowa, where most less-educated and Dutch counties have been trending less Democratic than the state as a whole. However, the seven counties of southwestern Iowa that have remained strongly Republican provide no such obvious statistical reasons for their voting patterns. The counties do not stand out from the rest of the state on ethnic, religious, economic, educational, or agricultural grounds. Their only distinction is their regional location in one corner of the state.[26]

This regional location, though, provides the key to an explanation of why these counties are different from the rest of the state, for these counties are all within the Omaha, Nebraska, media market. Almost all counties in Iowa are dominated by Iowa-based media, especially from Des Moines, with other exceptions being Dutch northwestern Iowa, near Sioux Falls, South Dakota,[27] and the area around Davenport in eastern Iowa, which is part of a two-state, four-city metropolitan area (the "Quad Cities"). But the area around Sioux Falls in South Dakota and the Illinois counties in the Quad Cities area have all been trending strongly Democratic, like most of Iowa. The Omaha area notably has not.

In Chapter 3, the three counties of northeastern Vermont known as the Northeast Kingdom stood out from the rest of the state in voting habits, and many towns in the counties seemed more similar politically to neighboring New Hampshire than to Vermont. In Chapter 4, the anomaly of New Hampshire's increasing Republicanism, despite being surrounded by increasingly Democratic states, was in part explained by the influence the state's largest newspaper, the *Manchester Union Leader*, had on the political dialogue in the state. In southwestern Iowa, a similar phenomenon seems to have occurred. Seven counties seem not to fit the political patterns of the rest of Iowa, and the media may again have played an influence in this aberration.

25. Elton J. Bruins, "Americanization in Reformed Religious Life," in Swierenga, *The Dutch in America*, 208.

26. The counties all border on one another with no other counties between them.

27. While this area has been much less likely to trend Democratic than the rest of Iowa, Richard Nixon actually did worse in several counties in northwestern Iowa in 1972 than he had done in 1968, probably due to McGovern's longtime exposure in Sioux Falls media seen in this part of Iowa.

Like New Hampshire with the *Union Leader*, Iowa has a single newspaper that tends to dominate the statewide print media.[28] The *Des Moines Register*, available for home or farm delivery in all of Iowa's ninety-nine counties, was delivered to two out of three Iowa households on Sundays in the early 1980s and is "truly a state rather than a city newspaper."[29] Unlike the *Union Leader*, however, the *Des Moines Register* has had a long liberal or progressive political tradition. At the beginning of the twentieth century, the *Register* was purchased and taken over by Progressive Republicans who were allied politically with local opponents of the state's conservative Republican machine. The newspaper proceeded to be influential in electing a Progressive governor and enacting progressive urban political reforms in Des Moines, which were copied by many other cities around the nation.[30]

Both conservative and moderate-to-progressive Republican politicians have been elected to Iowa statewide office since the turn of the century, including Senator Smith Brookhart, who in the 1920s denounced his party leadership, refused to endorse Calvin Coolidge for president in 1924, and supported public ownership of railroads and utilities, and liberal Republican Governor Robert Ray, who served from 1969 to 1983.[31] Although Iowa's current Republican governor is more conservative, many of the state's recent Republican members of the House of Representatives have been prominent moderates, such as Jim Leach, who headed the liberal Republican Ripon Society in the 1980s, and Fred Grandy, best known for his portrayal of "Gopher" on television's "The Love Boat." So while not all of Iowa's Republicans have been as liberal as those elected in Vermont, the state party does have a strong progressive tradition, which has been supported by the *Register*.

But by the 1970s, the *Register*'s progressive and liberal editorial views became out of step with the national Republican party and closer to the Democratic party. By the late 1960s, the paper was repeatedly editorializing against the Vietnam War and has since expressed many views that are close to the positions of many leading liberal Democrats. "Because of the paper's influence throughout the state, it has been in the twentieth century a major factor in explaining the vitality of liberalism within the

28. Joseph Frazier Wall, *Iowa* (New York: W. W. Norton & Company, 1978), 194.
29. Peirce and Hagstrom, *Book of America*, 576.
30. Wall, *Iowa*, 171.
31. Ibid., 175, 182.

state, not only with respect to economic and political issues, but also in the area of civil liberties."[32]

In Vermont, as the national Republican party began to move away from some of its traditionally moderate views favored by Vermont politicians and many Vermont voters, the party's presidential candidates lost large numbers of votes in the state. And in Iowa, as the national Republican party's views grew more distant from those of some of the state's traditionally Republican voters and from those of the state's most important media source, the party's presidential candidates have lost votes there as well. The *Register*'s editorial views are obviously not the only source of declining Republicanism in Iowa—Table 6.2 shows several other factors that seem to be playing a role. And Rhode Island's largest newspaper, the *Providence Journal*, has been comparatively more conservative but has had little influence in making the state more Republican in presidential elections (it has had more success in state elections, as Chapter 5 notes). The *Register*'s liberal attitudes have had some impact, though, on educated opinion and political discussions in the state.

In one part of Iowa, however, the *Register* has much less influence because the area is dominated by other media sources. That area is the southwestern corner of Iowa. "Beyond the range of Des Moines television stations and the liberal *Des Moines Register & Tribune*, [southwest Iowans] are in the Omaha TV market and get the conservative *Omaha World-Herald*."[33] Surrounded on all sides by counties in eastern Nebraska and in most of Iowa, which voted much more Democratic in the 1980s than in the 1950s, the counties of southwestern Iowa became only slightly more Democratic in the period, and the three Nebraska counties included in the U.S. Census' Omaha metropolitan area all became more Republican (including Douglas County, most of whose population lives in the city of Omaha).

Like Vermont's Northeast Kingdom, southwestern Iowa's voting patterns seem to have been more affected by the voting patterns of another state rather than its own state. And while most of Iowa has been influenced by liberal media sources, the southwest has instead seemed to have been influenced by the more conservative media and politics of the Omaha area. For that reason, seven counties in southwestern Iowa were omitted in the second regression displayed in Table 6.2.

32. Ibid., 171, 182.
33. Barone and Ujifusa, *Almanac of American Politics 1992*, 454.

Table 6.2. Relationship of many variables to Republican declines in presidential voting in Iowa's 99 counties, 1952–1956 and 1984–1988 (for an explanation of each variable, see the table note)

Variable	Democratic Shift	Variable	Democratic Shift
Danish	−.13	High school grad	.42**
Dutch	−.36**	College Grad	.23*
English	.06	Income	.16
German	.08	Poverty	−.10
Irish	.03	Unemployment	.09
Norwegian	.10	Govt worker	.23*
Swedish	−.10	Farm area	−.07
Catholic	.13	Big farms	−.02
Church of Christ	.07	Corn	−.05
Disciples of Christ	.07	Hogs	.01
Lutheran	.04	Dairy	−.01
Luth Mo. Synod	−.08	Beef	−.07
Methodist	.16	Poultry	−.01
Presbyterian	−.04	Anderson '80 vote	.48**
Reformed	−.33**	Wallace '68 vote	−.29**
Density	.02	New England	.07
		1970s pop. change	.05

Multiple Regression on 1950s and 1980s Shift Away from Republicans in 99 Iowa Counties

R^2 = 36.0% R^2 (adjusted) = 32.6%
s = 3.849 with 99 − 6 = 93 degrees of freedom

Source	Sum of Squares	df	Mean Square	F-ratio
Regression	775.096	5	155.000	10.5
Residual	1377.450	93	14.8113	

Variable	Coefficient	s.e. of Coeff	t-ratio
Constant	−40.172700	7.3760	−5.45
High school grad	0.544756	0.0870	6.26**
English	0.652201	0.1700	3.84**
German	0.240941	0.0564	4.27**
Norwegian	0.358750	0.1099	3.27**
Unemployment	0.476245	0.2124	2.24*

Multiple Regression on 1950s and 1980s Shift Away from Republicans in 92 Iowa Counties (7 southwest Iowa counties excluded)

R^2 = 57.2% R^2 (adjusted) = 53.7%
s = 2.696 with 92 − 8 = 84 degrees of freedom

Table 6.2. (Continued)

Source	Sum of Squares	df	Mean Square	F-ratio
Regression	817.095	7	117	16.1
Residual	610.457	84	7.26734	

Variable	Coefficient	s.e. of Coeff	t-ratio
Constant	− 39.730600	5.4880	− 7.24
Density	− 0.013073	0.0048	− 2.75**
High school grad	0.561420	0.0729	7.70**
English	0.502666	0.1284	3.92**
German	0.182910	0.0417	4.38**
Norwegian	0.238254	0.0804	2.96**
Unemployment	0.536301	0.1523	3.52**
Govt worker	0.149267	0.0552	2.70**

SOURCES: Ancestry (except Danish), education, and income and poverty variables from *1980 Census of Population: General Social and Economic Characteristics*; Danish from James Paul Allen, *We the People: An Atlas of America's Ethnic Diversity* (New York: Macmillan Company, 1988); religious variables from Quinn et al., *Churches and Church Membership in the United States 1980*; density, unemployment, govt workers, farm area, and big farms from *County and City Data Book 1988* (Washington, D.C.: U.S. Department of Commerce, Bureau of the Census); 1970s pop change, corn, and livestock from *1987 Statistical Profile of Iowa* (Des Moines: Iowa Department of Economic Development); Anderson vote from *The World Almanac and Book of Facts for 1983* (New York: World Almanac Publications, 1982); Wallace vote and all Republican and Democratic vote percentages from *America Votes*; New England from *Census of Iowa for the Year 1885* (Des Moines: Iowa Secretary of State, 1885).

EXPLANATIONS OF VARIABLES:
   Danish, Dutch, English, German, Irish, Norwegian, Swedish: % claiming full ancestry in 1980 census.
   College Grad, High School Grad: % having graduated at each level in 1980 census.
   Income, Poverty: 1980 census per capita income, poverty levels.
   Unemployment: 1986 unemployment rate.
   Catholic, Church of Christ, Disciples Christ, Lutheran, Luth Mo. Synod, Methodist, Presbyterian, Reformed: % of county population counted as members in the following church organizations— Catholic Church, United Church of Christ, Christian Church (Disciples of Christ), Lutheran Church in America, Lutheran Church–Missouri Synod, United Methodist Church, United Presbyterian Church in the U.S.A., Reformed Church in America (mainly Dutch Reformed).
   Density: Population per square mile.
   1970s pop change: % population increase or decline, 1970–1980.
   Govt Workers, Farm Area: % of earnings in county by government employees and from farms in 1984.
   Big Farms: % of farms with earnings of $100,000 or more in 1982.
   Corn, Hogs, Dairy, Beef, Poultry: 1985 bushels of corn produced, hogs marketed, numbers of milk cows, beef cows, and hens.
   Anderson '80 vote: % of county vote for independent presidential candidate John Anderson in 1980.
   Wallace '68 vote: % of county vote for independent presidential candidate George Wallace in 1968.
   New England: % born in six New England states in 1885 Iowa state census.

   *Significant at the .05 level.
   **Significant at the .01 level.

In simple correlations in Table 6.2, few individual variables significantly identify counties that have trended the most Democratic in the last forty years. As in every other state examined so far, high educational levels clearly relate to a decline in Republican support. And as discussed earlier, Iowa's Dutch counties have been among those most likely to maintain higher Republican support. Also in Iowa, counties with relatively high support for Independent John Anderson in 1980, and with low support for independent George Wallace in 1968, are the most likely to be showing Democratic gains overall. As in New England and Upstate New York, support for liberal Republican Anderson seems to have signaled a disenchantment with the increased conservatism of the national Republican party.

Once several factors are taken into account together, other variables, many of them ethnic, also appear to be factors in recent Democratic gains in Iowa. Iowa follows the New England and Upstate New York pattern, in which areas with high numbers of people with English ancestry have decreased their support for Republicans. Relatively few nineteenth-century Iowans moved to the state directly from New England, compared with the large numbers from the Southern border states and from Ohio, Indiana, Illinois, and Europe. Yet some of those from other Midwestern states, or their parents, had previously lived in New England, and New England Yankee culture tended to have a disproportionate effect on early Iowa society. "Iowa lay within this belt [of New Englander settlements] and soon came to include institutions and values that New Englanders believed to be important. Religious and educational institutions developed quickly in Iowa, both strongly influenced by Protestant church groups and their clergy."[34]

In its 1885 state census, Iowa asked residents their state of birth, but comparing 1885 county populations to voting trends one hundred years later is likely to be unfruitful unless New England Yankees were able to plant permanent, unchanging political cultures. However, there is a positive, albeit nonsignificant, relationship between percentages of residents born in New England in a county in 1885 and an increase in votes for Democratic presidential candidates one hundred years later. Whatever the relationship to nineteenth-century populations, counties that currently have high numbers of English-ancestry residents, once other factors are taken into account, have become more Democratic.

34. Dorothy Schwieder, "Iowa: The Middle Land," in James H. Madison, ed., *Heartland* (Bloomington: Indiana University Press, 1988), 282.

German areas in Iowa also appear to have become more Democratic in the last forty years. Midwestern Germans are perhaps best known politically for their opposition to U.S. involvement in World War I and their isolationism leading up to World War II.[35] Perhaps the English Yankee tradition of frugality in government spending combined with German isolationism to enlarge Iowans' opposition to big defense budgets. (The state's lack of significant military bases probably plays a role too.[36])

Before the 1960s, the Republican party contained the most prominent political isolationists. But since then, the Republican party has chosen presidential candidates like Goldwater, Nixon, Reagan, and Bush, who all supported extensive international interventionism when they said it served American interests, and who all supported large increases in the defense budget. Meanwhile, the Democratic party following the Vietnam War began to contain most of the more prominent isolationist or anti-interventionist politicians, who also distinguished themselves from the Republicans by generally favoring less defense spending.[37] As the national Democrats became the party perceived as more likely to oppose international military involvement and less likely to raise defense spending, any Iowans with frugal and isolationist views would have been enticed to switch from Republican to Democratic voting in presidential elections.[38]

A third ethnic group that has joined with the Germans and the English in trending Democratic in Iowa is the Norwegians. Scandinavians in the United States generally have a liberal reputation, but it probably derives more from the welfare states of modern Scandinavia than from the political activities of Scandinavian Americans. However, Michael Paul Rogin, in a study of Midwestern politics, found that Scandinavians, and Norwegians in particular, were among the strongest supporters of populism, progressivism, and the less conservative elements of the Repub-

35. For lengthy discussions of German isolationism in Wisconsin, see Michael Paul Rogin, *The Intellectuals and McCarthy: The Radical Specter* (Cambridge, Mass.: M.I.T. Press, 1967); and Herbert F. Margulies, *The Decline of the Progressive Movement in Wisconsin* (Madison: State Historical Society of Wisconsin, 1968).

36. Barone and Ujifusa, *Almanac of American Politics 1992*, 437.

37. This distinction between parties is disappearing somewhat with the end of the Cold War, as neo-isolationist Republicans like Pat Buchanan speak out, and Democrats fight hard to protect jobs with defense contractors in their districts or to intervene in foreign conflicts, such as the one in Bosnia-Herzegovina.

38. In the U.S. Senate, however, Iowa Senator Charles Grassley was one of only two Republicans to vote against the Persian Gulf War resolution in January 1991 (the other was Oregon Senator Mark Hatfield). Grassley won reelection with 70 percent of the vote in 1992.

lican party between the 1890s and 1950s.[39] Because of their heritage, Norwegians may have been even more likely than Swedes or Danes to oppose political establishment figures in the United States. Norway was under the political control of Denmark and Sweden for several centuries and did not gain independence until 1905. The tendency of Iowan Norwegians to support liberal Republicans probably predisposed them, along with Germans and English Yankees, to be more likely to switch to the Democrats once national Republicans became more conservative.[40]

Although many studies of voting behavior have focused more on religion than on ethnic ancestry in their analyses, in Iowa, as in Upstate New York, ethnicity seems to provide a better explanation than religious denomination in explaining partisan voting trends in recent years. Except for Dutch Reformed adherents, no other prominent religious group in Iowa stands out in its relationship to voting patterns. Counties with relatively large memberships in the United Methodist Church show the strongest positive relationship with Democratic gains and are actually significantly related at a .10 level (a significance that remains after other factors, including ethnicity, are taken into account).

One notable finding in the Iowa data is that high school graduation rates in each county are much more important than college graduation rates in predicting partisan voting trends. In Upstate New York and in Oregon (discussed later in this chapter), college graduation rates are more significant. The reason for this distinction is not easy to determine. Perhaps the answer lies in the differing political traditions of internationalist, industrial New York and isolationist, agricultural Iowa, or in the statewide influence of the *Des Moines Register,* which is possibly as likely to be read by high school graduates as college graduates. Iowa historian Dorothy Schwieder has commented that, despite the strong emphasis on public education in the state and the high scores of Iowa high school students on standardized exams, young Iowans seem reluctant to apply to top national universities or to pursue all opportunities.[41] While in many states the college-educated elite tend to see themselves as a step above mere high school graduates, such distinctions may be of less importance, at least politically, in Iowa.

39. Rogin, *The Intellectuals and McCarthy.*

40. Not all Midwestern Norwegian areas were mostly Republican before 1960. In Minnesota, the support of many Norwegians for the Farmer-Labor party was transferred to the Democratic–Farmer-Labor party when the two parties merged in 1944. See Fenton, *Midwest Politics,* 75–113.

41. Schwieder, "Iowa: The Middle Land," 293.

Michael Paul Rogin noted that in several Midwestern states various political movements have shown greater strength in certain agricultural product areas. For instance, Wisconsin Senator Joseph McCarthy was particularly popular in that state's corn belt.[42] No such agricultural distinctions seem to appear in Iowa, and a county's dependence on agriculture and the percentage of large farms do not relate significantly to changes in county voting patterns. Once ethnic and educational factors are considered, however, a negative relationship between corn production and Democratic gains, and a positive relationship between hog production and Democratic gains, both strengthen to significance at the .10 level.

Among other variables considered, three more appear as significant factors in explaining recent changes in Iowa politics. High unemployment rates in 1986 are positively related to Democratic gains and provide some support for the argument that voters turn to the Democrats in troubled economic times when Republicans are president. And once southwestern Iowa is excluded, the state's Democratic gains also seem higher in rural areas and in counties with high percentages of government workers. It is not surprising that areas with higher dependence on government employment tend to turn more toward a party that favors more social services and increased government spending, and away from a party that advocates cutting government programs and spending.[43] The more significant finding that comes from excluding southwestern Iowa is that the overall regression model analyzing the factors responsible for the Democratic gains strengthens greatly, indicating that these seven Omaha-influenced counties do not fit well with voting patterns in the rest of Iowa.

The Iowa pattern of increased Democratic support follows the pattern in New England and Upstate New York in many ways, but there are also several distinguishing features, which show that realignment patterns vary in different regions. Historically Republican Oregon, in the Pacific Northwest, on the other side of the continent from New England, provides a third realigning pattern, which, while still similar in many ways

42. Rogin, *The Intellectuals and McCarthy*, 97.
43. The only state not in the U.S. northern tier to vote much more Democratic in 1980s presidential elections than in the 1950s was Maryland. Most Maryland counties actually became more Republican in the period, as did almost all counties in the portions of Pennsylvania, Delaware, Virginia, and West Virginia that border on Maryland. But the heavily populated counties between Baltimore and Washington have shifted by large amounts toward the Democrats in the last forty years, and not coincidentally these counties have seen an explosion of federal government employees among their residents during that time.

to the other two discussed in this chapter, again has its own distinct characteristics.

From 1872 to 1984, only two of the nineteen different Democratic presidential candidates during the period won a majority of Oregon's vote. Franklin Roosevelt and Lyndon Johnson were the two exceptions; both won national landslide victories in their elections. National election victors Grover Cleveland, Harry Truman, John Kennedy, and Jimmy Carter never won in Oregon, and Woodrow Wilson won the state in 1912 with only 39 percent of the vote against a divided opposition, and then lost the state in 1916. For this reason, as well as Republican control of most state offices through the first half of the twentieth century, Oregon was often referred to politically as "the Vermont of the west."[44] In 1988, losing presidential candidate Michael Dukakis joined Franklin Roosevelt and Lyndon Johnson as the third Democrat since 1870 to win a majority of Oregon's vote. (Clinton became the fourth in 1992.)

Oregon is similar to the other states discussed so far in its strong Democratic trend in presidential elections in the last forty years. However, Oregon is the first state under study not to have that trend be statewide. With only a few exceptions, all counties in New England, New York, and Iowa voted at least slightly more Democratic in the 1980s than they did in the 1950s.[45] But Oregon's voting trends are strictly divided on a regional basis. Western Oregon, which contains a large majority of the state's population, trended strongly Democratic; lightly populated eastern Oregon trended just as strongly Republican.

Oregon's original settlers were a mix from New England, the Midwest, and Southern border states. The state's reputation as a western outpost of New England Yankee culture is probably due less to numbers of original settlers than to the political, economic, and social dominance of the state's early New Englanders. Portland and Salem, which later became Oregon's largest city and capital, respectively, were both named after New England cities.[46] "Many of Portland's more prosperous families were of New England origin. . . . The economic and social influence of the Portland dynasties significantly outweighed their strength in numbers and

44. Robert E. Burton, *Democrats of Oregon: The Pattern of Minority Politics 1900–1956* (Eugene: University of Oregon Books, 1970), 138.

45. The only major exception here, as noted in Chapter 4, is Hillsborough County, New Hampshire—the state's most populous county—which swung heavily Republican during the period.

46. Peirce and Hagstrom, *Book of America*, 821.

gave the community such tone that it was often described as a New England village transplanted to the West."[47] Salem was perhaps even more New England dominated. In both cities, "the New England influence was probably most noticeable in Oregon's churches and schools."[48] Large-scale migrations later in the nineteenth century by Yankees, Germans, and Scandinavians from the Midwest or from Europe strengthened support for the Republican party which had been favored by New Englanders in Oregon and by ethnically similar Iowa.[49]

At the turn of the twentieth century, Oregon became one of the top states in supporting the Progressive movement within the Republican party. Along with Wisconsin, "the strongly middle-class, Yankee state of Oregon set the pace for all others in pioneering reform," which consisted of measures like popular initiatives and referendums and direct primaries as well as workplace regulations.[50]

Reform or liberal Republicans dominated the state party until a key period following World War II, when the party leadership was captured by conservatives. "This drove the tempestuous, iron-willed maverick [Oregon Republican] Senator Wayne Morse to change parties."[51] Two years after Morse quit the Republican party in 1952, the Democrats won their first U.S. Senate election since 1914, when the Republicans had divided over Progressivism. As in other states with long histories of support for liberal Republicanism, any perceptions of increased conservatism among Republican politicians lost votes for the party. The Oregon Republican party learned quickly from its mistakes, however, and by the 1960s it regained Oregon's two U.S. Senate seats with popular liberal Republicans Mark Hatfield and Bob Packwood, who both remained in the Senate until 1995.[52] During President Nixon's years in office, Hatfield denounced the president's "Southern strategy" of calculated attempts to

---

47. Dorothy O. Johansen, *Empire of the Columbia* (New York: Harper & Row, 1967), 284.

48. Ibid., 286.

49. Burton, *Democrats of Oregon*, 3.

50. Michael P. Malone and Richard W. Etulain, *The American West* (Lincoln: University of Nebraska Press, 1989), 58.

51. Ibid., 281. Morse is best known nationally for casting one of two votes against President Johnson's Gulf of Tonkin resolution in the Senate.

52. By the 1990s, the two senators had helped to tarnish the clean government reputation of liberal Republicans. Hatfield was accused of various ethical violations involving gifts and favors for himself and his family, while Packwood was accused by many women of sexual harassment in the office. Packwood resigned his seat in 1995, while Hatfield decided not to run for reelection in 1996.

gain popularity among Southern voters and charged that the Republicans were practicing "the politics of revulsion."[53]

The national party ignored Hatfield's scorn and became increasingly conservative into the 1980s, setting the stage for Oregon's realignment in presidential elections. Measuring statistically the key factors in Oregon's realignment process is a somewhat more difficult process than in other states, and for that reason, the data on Oregon will include an extra table below.

Although early Oregon contained a strong New England Yankee presence, followed later by mostly Northern European immigrants and their descendants, regional ethnic distinctions within contemporary Oregon remain nowhere near as strong as they do in the towns of New England or the counties of Iowa. The English-ancestry population contains strong infusions of Southerners and a group mostly unique to the West, the Mormons, who alter the relationship between such ancestry and voting trends found in the states of the Midwest and Northeast. And the patterns of modern white ethnic settlement in the state are relatively indistinct for many groups. The same two counties in eastern Oregon contain the largest percentages of people claiming English, German, and Irish ancestry. The same two counties are first and third in the state in Swedish ancestry, and one of the counties is second in Norwegian ancestry. Some ethnic distinctions do remain among counties in the state, though, in that each of the five groups listed above has its smallest populations in five different areas of the state.

Another factor whose role in Oregon's realignment is difficult to measure is the decline in the timber industry. Because the Democratic-trending section of Oregon overlaps heavily with the state's prime forest lands, it might be assumed that economics played a key role in Democratic gains. Measuring such economic effects statistically are difficult, for problems in the timber industry have varied in different counties, and unemployment rates have fluctuated dramatically in recent years in some counties. However, much evidence suggests that economic prosperity or decline has played at most a small role in Oregon's realignment, as in the states previously studied.

For instance, not all counties in Oregon trending Democratic have a large timber industry. Many of the counties that do depend on timber showed a strong permanent realignment toward the Democrats in the

53. Peirce and Hagstrom, *Book of America*, 827.

1930s and 1940s, a period in which economic factors were more likely to play a role in changing votes, and many continued their Democratic trends during the era of timber region prosperity in the twenty-five years following World War II.[54] By 1980, an Oregon county's high unemployment rate was strongly and significantly related to a gain for Reagan's vote percentage over Ford's vote four years earlier. In other words, Republicans were gaining, rather than Democrats, due to any economic troubles at the time, probably because the Democrats were the party in power nationally, casting doubt on any assumption that Democrats are always the party to gain from a bad economy because of their greater support for government social services. Besides all the evidence stated so far to show that the economic fortunes of the lumber industry are not the main cause of Oregon realignment, the tables below show (1) that Democratic gains started long before the 1980s, which is when the timber industry began a serious decline, and (2) that such factors as high educational levels, which would not be associated with employment in timber, are the key sources of Democratic trends.

One other factor that some might consider as contributing to Oregon's Democratic gains is the state's rapid population growth in the 1970s, which included many environmentally conscious migrants from California. Despite early 1970s Governor Tom McCall's welcome of visitors to Oregon with the added plea "But for God's sake, don't move here," the state's population grew by more than 25 percent in the 1970s.[55] However, Oregon's population increased by much smaller margins in the 1960s and 1980s, and Table 6.3, which includes a measure of each county's Oregon-born percentage of residents, indicates that newcomers to the state have actually played a mixed role in state voting trends, because some of these newcomers were conservatives moving to eastern Oregon. Anyhow, few writers on Oregon politics have attributed the state's Democratic gains to Californian newcomers the way many have misperceived Vermont's realignment as resulting mainly from those born in other states.

From the educational, economic, and population variables used above, it appears that the better-educated, economically better off, and more highly populated sections of the state have been the most likely to trend Democratic, while the lightly populated, less-educated, and poorer coun-

---

54. For voting trends from 1920 to 1956, see the map in Burton, *Democrats of Oregon,* 152. For a description of the fortunes of Oregon's timber industry since World War II, see Malone and Etulain, *American West,* 246–248.

55. Peirce and Hagstrom, *Book of America,* 820–821.

Table 6.3. Relationship of many variables to partisan changes in Republican presidential voting in Oregon's 36 counties between 1952 and 1956 and 1984 and 1988 (for an explanation of each variable, see the table note)

Variable	Democratic Shift	Variable	Democratic Shift
English	−.21	High school grad	.49**
German	−.12	College grad	.66**
Irish	−.49**	Per capita income	.50**
Norwegian	.31	1980 Unemployed	−.41**
Swedish	−.11	Born in Oregon	−.18
Catholic	.27	Population Size	.44**
Church of Christ	.14	Wallace in '68	−.43**
Episcopal	.22	Anderson in '80	.78**
Lutheran	.37*	1892 Prohibition	.48**
Mormon	−.54**		
Assemblies of God	−.23		
Southern Baptist	.05		

Multiple regression on 50s–80s Shift Away from Republicans in 36 Oregon Counties

$R^2 = 72.5\%$ R^2 (adjusted) $= 69.0\%$
$s = 3.859$ with $36 − 5 = 31$ degrees of freedom

Source	Sum of Squares	df	Mean Square	F-ratio
Regression	1220.090	4	305	20.5
Residual	461.654	31	14.8921	

Variable	Coefficient	s.e. of Coeff	t-ratio
Constant	0.075476	3.3560	0.022
College grad	0.608394	0.1319	4.610
Norwegian	3.185550	1.3030	2.440
Mormon	−0.413609	0.1144	−3.620
Irish	−1.32669	0.4450	−2.980

SOURCES: Ancestry, education, economic, population, and Oregon-born variables from *1980 Census of Population: General Social and Economic Characteristics;* religious variables from Quinn et al., *Churches and Church Membership in the United States 1980;* Anderson vote from *The World Almanac and Book of Facts for 1983;* Wallace vote and all Republican and Democratic vote percentages from *America Votes;* 1892 Prohibition vote from Burnham, *Presidential Ballots 1836–1892.*

EXPLANATIONS OF VARIABLES:
   English, German, Irish, Norwegian, Swedish: % claiming full ancestry in 1980 census.
   College grad, high school grad: % having graduated at each level in 1980 census.
   Income, Unemployment: 1980 census per capita income and unemployment rates.
   Catholic, Church of Christ, Episcopal, Lutheran, Mormon, Assemblies of God, Southern Baptist: % of county population counted as members in the following church organizations—Catholic Church, United Church of Christ, Episcopal Church, Lutheran Church in America, Church of Jesus Christ of Latter-Day Saints (Mormons), Assemblies of God, Southern Baptist Convention.

Table 6.3. (Continued)

EXPLANATIONS OF VARIABLES: *(continued)*

Population Size, Born in Oregon: 1980 county population and % born in Oregon.

Anderson in '80: % of county vote for independent presidential candidate John Anderson in 1980.

Wallace in '68: % of county vote for independent presidential candidate George Wallace in 1968.

1892 Prohibition: % of county vote for Prohibition party in 1892 presidential election.

*Significant at the .05 level.
**Significant at the .01 level.

ties have trended Republican. When all factors are taken into account, educational levels take precedence as the key among these factors in relating to partisan voting trends, matching the results found in other Northern states. The two counties showing the largest Democratic gains since the 1950s contain the University of Oregon and Oregon State University, but the education-level voting patterns remain even if these two counties are excluded. However, there appears to be no significant relationship between voting trends and a county's percentage of residents born in the state; in fact, the relationship is in the opposite direction from one that would attribute Oregon's Democratic gains to residents born in other states, such as California.

Among ethnocultural variables, areas of high Norwegian ancestry in Oregon, as in Iowa, have showed strong Democratic trends. Areas of English ancestry do not show a significant relationship, for reasons stated earlier, including the strong presence of Mormonism in eastern Oregon.[56] High percentages of Mormon church membership are the strongest predictor of Republican voting trends in a county, due to the strongly conservative influence of that church's leadership and practices.[57] The most unexpected finding in Oregon may be the relationship between high Irish percentages and Republican trends. In the other states studied so far, Irish ancestry stood out mainly as one of the few ethnic groups to show no significant changes in partisan voting relative to other groups. The reasons for the difference in Oregon are clarified by the data in Table 6.4.

For Upstate New York and Iowa, Table 6.4 indicates a positive relation-

56. Methodist and Presbyterian church memberships are insignificantly related to any voting patterns. Methodist counties come out similar to those with high United Church of Christ membership (see Tables 6.3 and 6.5), while Presbyterian counties show no discernible partisan preferences at any point.

57. More about the political influence of Mormonism in the western United States will be discussed in Chapter 7. Eastern Oregon is contiguous with the southern Idaho and Utah region, where the Mormon religion dominates.

Table 6.4. Relationship of Irish ancestry to Scottish ancestry and Catholic religion in Oregon counties

Correlations Between % Irish and % Catholic in a County	
Upstate New York	.25
Iowa	.19
Oregon	− .35
Correlations Between % Irish and % Scottish in a County	
Upstate New York	.08
Iowa	.48
Oregon	.78

Source: See source note for Table 6.3.

ship between a county's Irish population and a county's Catholic population, but in Oregon, Irish populations are lowest in the most Catholic parts of the state (chiefly northwestern Oregon), signifying that many in Oregon claiming Irish ancestry may be Protestants. Irish Protestants, sometimes called Scotch-Irish, are descended from Scottish settlers in Ireland, whose descendants there have been the source of controversy over Northern Ireland. In the United States, Scotch-Irish immigrants dominated the original white populations of much of central and western Pennsylvania and many of the Southern border states. Additional evidence that the Irish in Republican-trending portions of Oregon may be Scotch-Irish Protestants is the strong relationship between Irish ancestry and Scottish ancestry in counties in the state. In Iowa, the relationship is somewhat weaker, and in Upstate New York, out of the path of Scotch-Irish westward migration, the relationship is near zero, indicating that the state's Irish population is predominantly Catholic.

Kevin Phillips has noted that the Scotch-Irish populations of central Pennsylvania have historically had political tendencies very different from those of much of the Yankee Northeast United States: tending to favor the Jacksonian Democrats over the Whigs before the 1850s, registering even stronger opposition than Yankee New England areas to Catholic presidential candidates like Al Smith and John Kennedy, and, along with southern New Jersey, providing Wallace's best vote percentages in the Northeast above the Mason-Dixon line in 1968.[58] Since the 1950s,

58. Phillips, *Emerging Republican Majority*, 126–138.

South Central Pennsylvania has stood out as the only large geographical portion of the Northeast above the Mason-Dixon Line to trend Republican in presidential elections. Apparently, Irish Protestants in Oregon are following this Pennsylvania pattern.

One other finding from the data in Table 6.3 is that in Oregon, as in other Northern states, a high vote for Wallace in 1968 is negatively related, and a high vote for Anderson in 1980 is positively related, to a county's Democratic gains. The relationship to the Anderson vote is exceedingly high and may come as close to a perfect correlation as is possible with county voting habits, probably indicating a strong preference for liberal Republicans among those who have switched to the Democrats. The Wallace vote was higher, on the other hand, in the areas trending Republican.

An additional interesting finding in the Oregon data is the significant positive correlation between the 1892 vote for the Prohibition party, and recent Democratic party gains in a county. In the 1890s, the Prohibition party was considered progressive and advocated such reforms as women's suffrage, popular referendums, progressive income taxes, and railroad reform, which were similar to some of the demands made by the Populist party of the same time period and by the later Progressive party. Although the Prohibition party's key plank of ending the sale of alcohol was supposed to help the disadvantaged of society to better themselves, many of the movement's supporters also seemed antagonistic toward Catholics and other groups perceived as imbibing too frequently.[59] In Oregon, the party's best performance was in 1892, winning just 3 percent of the statewide vote in competition with the Republicans, the Democrats, and the Populists, but it did better in northwestern Oregon, the same area that has had the highest Democratic gains in the last forty years. Not too much weight should be given to this correlation, but it does show some possible continuity to the political culture in Oregon.

Because Oregon since the 1950s is split between two regions moving in opposite partisan directions, it is possible to pinpoint the large changes in each party's modern social base in the state by examining individually each election over the last forty years, as shown in Table 6.5. In addition, such data also provide clues as to which particular elections played the strongest roles in realignment. Three presidential elections in the last

59. Rogin, *The Intellectuals and McCarthy*, 181.

Table 6.5. Correlations of several variables with Republican presidential voting in 36 Oregon counties, 1952–1988

Variable	1952	1956	1960	1964	1968	1972	1976	1980	1984	1988
English	.02	−.21	−.12	.17	.04	.04	.10	.21	.17	.10
German	−.05	−.14	−.01	−.14	−.05	.06	.18	.09	.10	−.01
Irish	−.16	−.27	−.25	−.02	.06	.18	.06	.40	.38	.27
Norwegian	−.35	−.31	−.32	−.62	−.60	−.61	−.39	−.56	−.56	−.61
Swedish	−.32	−.29	−.29	−.26	−.28	−.29	−.06	−.08	−.12	−.14
Catholic	.22	.34	.30	.19	.15	.06	.17	−.14	−.09	.00
Church of Christ	.13	.10	.03	−.14	.00	.12	.16	−.06	−.01	−.10
Episcopal	−.07	−.03	−.10	−.20	−.19	−.36	−.09	−.25	−.27	−.24
Lutheran	−.21	−.16	−.11	−.26	−.38	−.46	−.26	−.56	−.53	−.50
Mormon	−.22	−.21	−.15	.22	.12	.19	.33	.48	.34	.41
Assemblies of God	−.10	−.18	−.06	.04	.08	.02	−.24	.09	.12	.12
Southern Baptist	.22	.12	.09	.06	.09	.16	.00	.05	.14	.04
High school grad	.25	.37	.40	.02	.12	.00	.33	−.32	−.23	−.27
College grad	.39	.52	.52	.14	.20	−.01	.32	−.38	−.31	−.30
Income	−.19	.00	−.02	−.43	−.44	−.52	−.15	−.63	−.59	−.57
Unemployed in '80	−.24	−.36	−.33	.09	−.07	−.06	−.24	.32	.14	.20
Born in Oregon	−.29	−.26	−.17	−.27	−.06	.11	.00	−.07	.01	−.09
Population	−.07	.10	.13	−.04	−.20	−.31	−.08	−.43	−.44	−.42

SOURCES: See source note for Table 6.3.

EXPLANATIONS OF VARIABLES: See explanations for Table 6.3.

NOTE: Positive correlation = more Republican than state; negative correlation = less Republican.

forty years stand out as crucial in Oregon's realignment of each party's social bases.

In the 1950s, Irish, Mormon, and Norwegian areas were more Democratic than the rest of the state, while high educational levels were the best way to predict a high Republican vote in a county.[60] In 1964, when Republicans nominated conservative Barry Goldwater for president, Mormon areas became more Republican than well-educated areas, and Irish areas became less Democratic, while Norwegian areas became even more Democratic. In 1972, when the Democrats chose liberal George McGovern for president, Oregon's better-educated areas for the first time no longer voted more Republican than less-educated areas, while Irish areas became more Republican. And in 1980, when the Republican party chose Reagan for president and liberal Republican John Anderson ran as an independent, Mormon and Irish areas became even more Republican, and better-educated areas shifted strongly against the Republicans and became solidly Democratic by 1984, when the Anderson alternative disappeared.

That Oregon's realignment occurred from changes in the ideologies of the two national parties was made even more clear in the 1976 presidential election. The Democrats chose relative moderate Jimmy Carter of Georgia, while the Republicans chose relative moderate Gerald Ford of Michigan. Carter had beaten more liberal candidates in the primaries, while Ford had defeated conservative Reagan. Both Ford and Carter came from their parties' traditionally strongest regions from the past—the Midwest and the South, respectively—and both had stronger appeal to their parties' traditional constituencies than other recent nominees, such as Goldwater and McGovern.

When the national parties seemed to return to their more historical ideologies and constituencies, many of Oregon's voters abandoned their recent political trends and reverted to previous voting habits. In 1976, better-educated areas temporarily became solidly Republican again, and Norwegian areas were distinctly less Democratic. Irish areas also became temporarily less Republican. Mormon areas did not change their pattern and continued a solid march toward Republicanism, but areas with high Assemblies of God membership (the largest of the evangelical Pentecostal church organizations, whose membership is largest in less-educated

60. The most Norwegian parts of Oregon had already realigned more Democratic previously during the New Deal era.

Table 6.6. Republican presidential vote in two Oregon counties in specified elections, 1952–1996 (percentage of vote)

County	1952	1956	1960	1968	1976	1980	1988	1992	1996
Lane	64	56	53	49	43	44	40	28	35
Multnomah	55	53	51	44	44	39	37	24	26

SOURCES: *America Votes*, various years, 1952–1992; 1996 data from the Office of Oregon Secretary of State.

parts of Oregon), which had also been becoming somewhat more Republican, switched back to supporting Southern Democrat and self-proclaimed Born-Again Christian Carter.

Elections since 1980 have not offered any more vast changes in each party's social bases in the state, but they have included a continuing statewide trend toward the Democrats in presidential elections. As in Vermont, Oregon's realignment toward the Democrats has been a gradual process, rather than a "critical" period of the sort political scientists are often used to looking for. Although a few elections have seemed the most critical to the realigning process, the trend of areas shifting Democratic has continued gradually with every competitive presidential election in the last forty years. This can be seen with the Republican vote in Oregon's two most populous counties since 1952. Multnomah County, which contains the city of Portland, and Lane County, which contains the city of Eugene and the University of Oregon, together include about one-third of the state's population and therefore influence greatly any statewide voting trends. Omitting the three popular vote landslide presidential elections of the last forty years in 1964, 1972, and 1984, which disrupt the gradual Democratic and anti-Republican trends (although not by much in 1972 and 1984), Table 6.6 presents each county's Republican vote from 1952 to 1996.

In both counties, with only a couple of exceptions when the trend stopped temporarily, the Republican percentage of the vote declined in every reasonably close presidential election between 1952 and 1992. Lane County went from overwhelmingly Republican in 1952, with Eisenhower doing much better there than he did nationally, to becoming solidly Democratic by 1988 for losing candidate Dukakis. The trend in Oregon's largest county, Multnomah, has been almost as strong.

In Oregon, Iowa, and Upstate New York, a gradual realignment toward the Democrats in presidential elections has occurred since the 1950s. These Northern states have all followed the pattern in Vermont, where better-educated areas and areas of high English ancestry (except in Oregon) have led the shift toward the Democrats. All these areas have also historically had a preference for Progressive, liberal, or moderate Republicanism.

Iowa and Oregon have added new factors to the pattern, with Norwegians also trending Democratic, and Midwestern Dutch and Western Mormon areas moving against statewide trends by going Republican. In Upstate New York, as in Rhode Island, realignment has been federalized, with Democratic gains at the presidential level not being matched in state elections, for reasons having nothing to do with the usual connotations of "dealignment." And in Iowa, as in New Hampshire, a portion of the state does not match up with statewide (or region-wide, in the case of New Hampshire) voting patterns partly because of the differing influences of statewide newspapers.

In Chapter 7, recent realignment patterns in other states and other regions of the country will be examined, including other Democratic-trending areas not mentioned so far, many of which have nothing to do with any Northern or Vermont pattern. Also analyzed briefly are the two parts of the nation that have shifted heavily Republican since the 1950s: the South and the Mountain West, centered in Mormon Utah. These two regions have usually provided the strongest bases for Republican presidential candidates in the last thirty years, helping them to win all but one presidential election between 1968 and 1988.

Chapter Seven

―――➤●←―――

Realignment Outside
the North

The Northern trend toward the Democrats in presidential elections that has been most extreme in Vermont is also found in Maine, Upstate New York, Iowa, and Oregon, as shown in previous chapters. And, as discussed in Chapter 2, this regional realignment actually includes most of the Northern United States between New England and the Great Plains, as well as the Pacific Northwest.

The area of early Yankee English settlement, including New England, Upstate New York, northeastern Ohio, and much of Michigan falls entirely within the Democratic-trending region. Farther west, Yankee settlers were joined by Germans and Norwegians, and all of Iowa and Wisconsin, northwestern Illinois, most of Minnesota, Kansas, and North Dakota, and neighboring portions of South Dakota, Nebraska, and Missouri, have all shifted heavily Democratic since the 1950s.[1] A similar pattern emerges in the Pacific Northwest, where well-educated areas from the San Francisco Bay region, up the California coast, through western Oregon, and into Washington state have all shown greatly diminished enthusiasm for the Republican party—environmentalism probably playing a strong role in this section's realignment.

As stated in previous chapters, realignment has taken a different form in each state. In Minnesota, for example, better-educated, English, and German areas have all become more Democratic as in Iowa, but many

---

1. While many counties in the Great Plains states are less Republican than they used to be—hence the Democratic shift—most of these counties still remain majority Republican, and became even more so with the candidacy of Kansan Bob Dole in 1996.

Norwegian areas had already become Democratic before the 1950s, when the Farmer-Labor party joined the Democratic party in the state, bringing many former Republicans with them. In Wisconsin, the history of Progressivism within the Republican party was temporarily overwhelmed by the ideology of McCarthyism in the 1950s, and voting patterns there were disrupted during the decade, although in general the more Norwegian and German parts of the state have showed stronger Democratic trends since the 1950s than the more Polish parts of the state.[2]

Within the northern tier of the entire United States, relatively few counties have trended Republican. In New England, only the most French-Canadian areas have become more Republican since the 1950s, especially in New Hampshire. Between New Hampshire and portions of northwestern Minnesota and the Great Plains States, the only counties to grow more Republican are in Michigan, in the predominantly Dutch areas along Lake Michigan, discussed in Chapter 6, and in the Detroit suburbs.

North of Detroit lie the heavily populated suburban counties of Macomb and Oakland, the latter once being the home and base of Father Charles Coughlin, the popular conservative anti-Semitic radio priest of the 1930s. These two counties, which include large populations of voters of Polish and Southern United States ancestry, made Michigan one of only three Northern states east of the Rocky Mountains to vote slightly more Republican for Reagan and Bush in 1984 and 1988 than for Eisenhower in the 1950s (the other states being New Hampshire and Indiana). Polish areas in Upstate New York and Wisconsin, and almost all Southern white areas, have been among those most likely in the nation to be trending Republican in the last forty years, so an ethnic explanation for Oakland and Macomb counties' political trends seems plausible.

But the particular politics of Detroit have probably strengthened the trends. Of all the urban riots of the late 1960s, many have called the 1967 Detroit riot "the most disastrous riot of all" with forty-three deaths, thousands of arrests, and millions in property damage.[3] By the 1970s, Detroit was majority African American, poorer than ever, and known nationally as the murder capital of the nation. Racial tensions remained

2. See Rogin, The Intellectuals and McCarthy, 59–103, for a discussion of McCarthy's impact on Wisconsin politics. One source with a solid discussion of the union of the Farmer-Labor and Democratic parties in Minnesota is Fenton, Midwest Politics, 75–113.

3. Martha Mitchell Bigelow, "Michigan," in Madison, ed., Heartland, 53.

strong. "Racism/white flight/irrationally rapid dispersion of population afflicted Detroit perhaps more severely than any other American city. . . . Part of this can be attributed to suburban . . . prejudice, but part too, to the implied racism of pronouncements by [former black Detroit Mayor] Coleman Young and his colleagues."[4] In 1968, suburban Detroit was the area farthest north in states east of the Rocky Mountains where George Wallace received more than 10 percent of the vote, and in 1972, Wallace won a majority of the Democratic primary vote in Oakland County's largest city, Pontiac, which has a large population of Southern white ancestry.[5]

In most of the Northern U.S. areas that have trended Democratic, racial issues have been fairly unimportant to most voters, partly because of the absence of any significant African American populations. This is one reason that national Republican appeals to Southern views on racial issues have been something of a turnoff for traditionally Republican Northerners. But in suburban Detroit, where race has been as politically polarizing as in the South, Democratic liberalism on civil rights has lost votes, causing conservative Democrats to turn to Wallace in 1968, and then to Republicans in presidential elections ever since (including 1976), surpassing trends found in ethnically similar areas of the North.[6]

Between the northern tier of states and the Southern border states lies a broad area, including central Pennsylvania, southern and western Ohio, most of Indiana, and central Illinois, that has remained largely stable in its partisan preferences in the last forty years, although some counties in the region are trending Republican. These areas contain the principal routes of Scotch-Irish westward migration from Pennsylvania and Southern border state migration into the Midwest that Kevin Phillips noted in *The Emerging Republican Majority*, and which in Oregon have also become more Republican.[7] Traditionally, most of these portions of Pennsylvania, Ohio, Indiana, and Illinois have favored conservative Republicanism and

4. Peirce and Hagstrom, *Book of America*, 262–263.
5. Duncan, *Politics in America 1992*, 737.
6. Racial antagonisms obviously play a role politically in many other Northern metropolitan areas. It is therefore the combination of racial issues and the unique ethnic components of Detroit's suburban counties, including Southerners who used to be strongly Democratic, that has probably caused Republican trends to be stronger here than in other suburbs of the North. Clinton did manage to win these counties north of Detroit in 1996, although not in 1992. Whether this will be a new pattern of voting behavior in the area remains to be seen.
7. Phillips, *Emerging Republican Majority*, 300–301.

supported less of the Progressive or liberal Republicanism that has often been so popular in the Democratic-trending areas of the North.[8]

This Republican-trending region between central Pennsylvania and central Illinois is broken up, though, by western Pennsylvania and eastern Ohio, where the trend in presidential elections over the last forty years has been Democratic. Down the Appalachian Mountain chain from Pennsylvania and Ohio through western West Virginia, eastern Kentucky, southwestern Virginia, and northeastern Tennessee lie a large string of counties that have trended Democratic, surrounded on the east and the west by counties trending Republican. Some of these counties, mostly in the Southern part of the chain, went from voting 80 percent Republican in the 1950s to "only" 60 to 70 percent Republican in the 1980s, but others switched their preferences from majority Republican to majority Democratic, or went from slightly Democratic to overwhelmingly Democratic in presidential elections.

These areas do not have higher-than-average educational levels, and their ethnic compositions are not at all similar to New England or the Upper Midwest. They therefore make up a separate Democratic-realigning region in the United States not directly related to the Northern states' pattern. What these Appalachian areas do have in common are a recent or current economic dependence on steel, in western Pennsylvania, or coal, in the other parts. In this frequently economically depressed region, unionization remains high, and Democratic presidential candidates have seemed friendlier to union interests and local economic concerns. Unlike voters in the Northern states, which have been attracted to the Democratic party more for its liberalism on noneconomic issues,

---

8. Unlike the German portions of the Upper Midwest, German areas in South Central Pennsylvania and western Ohio have remained as staunchly Republican as ever in the last forty years. There are a couple of possible reasons for this difference. First, more of the ancestors of Upper Midwest Germans came to the United States after the Civil War. Throughout the United States, the war had a key influence on many political patterns found among voters in the following years. Later German immigrants may have been less influenced by Civil War divisions and more influenced by European politics of the late 1800s, and may have had differing backgrounds and motivations for immigrating than the Germans who preceded them. Second, Upper Midwest Germans are surrounded physically by the Yankee and Scandinavian populations that have frequently favored progressive and liberal Republicanism, while Ohio and Pennsylvania Germans are largely surrounded by those of Scotch-Irish and Southern ancestry, who have had more conservative political traditions. The resulting political cultures have undoubtedly had some influence on those who live with them. (Many Germans in western Ohio are descendants of Pennsylvania Germans, known as "the Pennsylvania Dutch," who emigrated westward along with Scotch-Irish Pennsylvanians before the Civil War.)

the Appalachian region has been drawn more to the party's New Deal past of government assistance or concern for those in need.

At the same time that the Democrats gained voters who were attracted to New Deal–type policies in this relatively small portion of the nation, though, the Republicans took over totally in presidential elections, in what used to be the largest part of the Democrats' New Deal coalition, the South. The vast majority of all counties[9] across the eleven states of the old confederacy and the border states of Delaware, Maryland, Kentucky, Missouri, and Oklahoma have switched their allegiances and turned the formerly Democratic "Solid South" into the biggest source of electoral votes for Republican presidential candidates. Although regional favorite Jimmy Carter was able to bring back temporarily to the Democrats many Southern whites in 1976, by 1992 even fellow Southerner Bill Clinton had little appeal in many states in the region, and the South seemed to be the only part of the nation where Republican Bush was very popular.

Republican trends have been strongest since the 1950s in the four Deep South states of Alabama, Mississippi, Georgia, and South Carolina.[10] South Carolina, where the Civil War began, perhaps best epitomized the Old South. Since the Civil War, South Carolina has ranked second only to Mississippi in percentage of state residents who were black. In his study of Southern politics, V. O. Key commented that the Southern states with the highest percentage of black residents seemed to produce the most racist political demagogues:

> South Carolina's preoccupation with the Negro stifles political conflict. . . . In part, issues are deliberately repressed, for, at least in the long run, concern with genuine issues would bring an end to the consensus by which the Negro is kept out of politics. . . . In part, the race issue provides in itself a tool for the diversion of attention from issues. . . . Perhaps South Carolina's record, since it is an extreme case, illuminates the real effects of race over the entire South.[11]

9. All references to Southern "counties" in this chapter include the parishes of Louisiana.

10. Several other Southern states had traditionally had higher Republican votes before the 1960s, and Eisenhower was able to win Florida, Tennessee, Texas, and Virginia in both 1952 and 1956. These were the same four states of the old Confederacy, along with North Carolina, that Republican Herbert Hoover won in 1928 in a reaction against Catholic Democratic nominee Al Smith.

11. Key, *Southern Politics*, 131.

Table 7.1. Multiple regression of several variables and Republican gains in presidential voting in 46 South Carolina counties, 1950s–1980s (insignificant variables not included)

$R^2 = 75.7\%$ R^2 (adjusted) $= 72.7\%$
$s = 6.783$ with $46 - 6 = 40$ degrees of freedom

Source	Sum of Squares	df	Mean Square	F-ratio
Regression	5743.30	5	1149	25.0
Residual	1840.45	40	46.0114	

Variable	Coefficient	s.e. of Coeff	t-ratio
Constant	− 9.462320	18.7900	− 0.504
Income	0.009417	0.0032	2.90**
College grad	− 1.219280	0.5990	− 2.04*
Black	− 0.278737	0.1273	− 2.19*
Episcopal	− 1.413270	0.5861	− 2.41*
Southern Baptist	0.170522	0.0831	2.05*

SOURCES: 1980 per capita income, % college graduates, and % black residents in a county from *1980 Census of Population: General Social and Economic Characteristics*. % county residents in Episcopal Church and Southern Baptist Convention from *Churches and Church Membership in the United States 1980*. Voting statistics from *America Votes*.

*Significant at the .05 level.
**Significant at the .01 level.

Since Key made those comments, the politics of the South have changed enormously in many ways (see Table 7.1), including the demise of the region's Democratic party traditions in national elections. But in one way, the politics of South Carolina have stayed the same: the state's politics remain divided racially.[12]

One difference between South Carolina and the Northern states studied is the strong role that higher-income areas played in the Southern state's Republican trend. Suburban areas in South Carolina have been particularly likely to become overwhelmingly Republican. In the North, and especially in Oregon, of the states closely studied, higher-income areas have tended to become more Democratic, although this tendency seemed everywhere to be a function of higher educational levels, which are related to high incomes rather than to the incomes themselves. Another feature unique to the South is the high Southern Baptist Convention membership. This church organization, a Southern remnant of Civil

12. For a good description of changes both in South Carolina politics and in politics in other individual Southern states during the 1960s, 1970s, and early 1980s, see Lamis, *The Two-Party South*.

War divisions that has come to be increasingly dominated by fundamentalists in recent years, has its highest concentration of South Carolina members in the state's western Piedmont section, an area settled originally by poor Scotch-Irish farmers who have traditionally been in political opposition to the former slaveowning areas of coastal South Carolina.

But perhaps the most important distinction between the Northern states studied in earlier chapters and South Carolina is the presence of large numbers of African Americans in the latter. Northern New England, Rhode Island, Upstate New York, Iowa, and Oregon have relatively few black residents, and racial issues have historically never been very divisive. In South Carolina, where the opposite is true, the contrast in voting between majority black counties and predominantly white counties is stark. Majority black Jasper County is alone in South Carolina in voting less Republican in 1980s presidential elections than in the 1950s. The counties in South Carolina's Piedmont, suburban, and Myrtle Beach resort areas have relatively few African American residents and have shown the strongest Republican trends in the state. Some might speculate that white residents of heavily black areas might be the most likely to have become more Republican. It is impossible to prove or disprove such a point without looking at very local precinct-level voting data, but it is clear that even the most exclusively white areas of South Carolina have shifted much more Republican.

The Southern strategies of Republican presidential candidates to emphasize their conservative stance on civil rights, religious, and patriotic issues compared with the liberalism of the national Democrats has had the frequently unnoticed effect of losing many traditional Northern Republican voters. But the strategy has certainly had success among its intended audience. White Southerners are now one of the most Republican groups in the nation in presidential elections.

Even in South Carolina, however, the conservative Republican strategy seems to have had somewhat less success among the same types of groups that have been less supportive in the North. Once other factors are taken into account, counties with high numbers of college graduates are showing smaller Republican gains than the counties around them. And although Episcopal Church membership is not that high anywhere in the state, the counties with the highest number of Episcopalians along coastal South Carolina show weaker Republican trends than would be expected based on other factors. The original plantation-owning elites of South Carolina were members of the Church of England, which later became the Episcopal Church in the United States. Their descendants in the state's coastal regions, like the descendants of English Yankees in the North, are apparently somewhat less enamored of the national Republicans' cultural conservatism than are the Southern Baptist sections of the state.[13]

Despite possible differences in enthusiasm among areas trending Republican, though, almost the entire South has been abandoning Democratic presidential candidates in droves. No county in South Carolina or Arkansas, and only one county in Georgia, saw a Democratic gain of more than 1 or 2 percent between the 1950s and the 1980s. The other Southern states do contain scattered counties that have gone against the regional trend by shifting Democratic. All these increased Democratic areas in the South fit into one of five simple categories. The first is the previously discussed Southern Appalachian mining-oriented area, where many counties are less overwhelmingly Republican than they used to be. In the second category are the few college-oriented counties where academic communities have outweighed the more conservative views of local residents. These include Orange County in North Carolina (University of North Carolina) and Alachua County in Florida (University of Florida).

Unique to the state of Florida in the region is a third group of counties with very large Democratic gains since the 1950s, and all these counties contain high populations of elderly migrants from the North and include Palm Beach (West Palm Beach), Broward (Fort Lauderdale), and Pinellas (St. Petersburg) counties. In 1996, these counties were key to changing Florida's overwhelmingly Republican presidential voting patterns in recent years to make Florida one of only two states that voted against Clinton in 1992, but for him in his reelection effort.[14]

The final two groups of counties in the South that have trended Demo-

13. Southeastern South Carolina, which includes the city of Charleston, was even represented by an oddity in the U.S. House of Representatives between 1987 and 1994: a Southern Republican moderate. Arthur Ravenel, a descendant of French Huguenot settlers (who with the Episcopalians formed the old elite), established an environmentalist reputation in the House and was initially denied a House committee position in 1989 because of his moderate politics. Ravenel threatened to switch to the Democratic party—the opposite path from other congressional party-switchers in the South in the last thirty years—but Republican National Committee Chairman Lee Atwater intervened to get Ravenel his desired position and to save the party from embarrassment. Barone and Ujifusa, *Almanac of American Politics 1992*, 1120–1121. Ravenel ran as a moderate alternative to conservative David Beasley in the 1994 South Carolina Republican gubernatorial primary. Beasley won the primary and the general election.

14. The other state was Arizona, with a similarly significant migrant elderly population.

cratic in presidential elections contain racial minorities as majorities of the population—either African Americans or, in southwestern Texas, Hispanic Americans. Counties in the Deep South that are mostly African American have shifted Democratic largely because the voting power of newly enfranchised and strongly Democratic black residents outweighed that of the Republican-trending minority white populations in the counties after national laws were passed to end discriminatory voter registration procedures. In southwestern Texas, several heavily Hispanic counties have increased their Democratic votes during the same period.

Despite these scattered Democratic increases in the South, the overwhelming trend of the region in the last forty years has been Republican, as stated previously. Between the 1952–1956 period and the 1984–1988 period, fifteen of the sixteen largest Republican state trends in presidential elections were in Southern or border states (the eleven states of the old Confederacy, Oklahoma, Missouri, Kentucky, and Delaware). Utah had the seventh-largest Republican trend, and Wyoming, Idaho, Arizona, and Nevada ranked seventeenth through twentieth.[15] Therefore, in the last forty years, the Rocky Mountain States region is second only to the South in its Republican shift.

Unlike the South, where a region-wide aversion to Democratic presidential candidates has developed, the Western states are more divided. The five states listed above have had clear Republican trends, but Montana, Colorado, New Mexico, and the Pacific Coast states of Washington and California shifted slightly Democratic during the period. Since 1960, only Oregon and Hawaii among the Western states had clear Democratic gains. The divisions between the Republican- and the Democratic-trending states have frequently been distinct since 1964. The five states with Republican gains (Utah, Idaho, Wyoming, Arizona, and Nevada) were Goldwater's best in the West in 1964, Nixon's best in 1972, and Reagan's best in 1980 and 1984 in the region, not including Alaska. Four of these five made up Wallace's best Western states in 1968. (Mormon Utah, with a history of religious intolerance against it in its early years, found the Wallace message less appealing and was one of his worst states nationwide.)

In 1976, when the presidential election was less of a clear choice between Republican conservatism and Democratic liberalism, the pattern

---

15. New Hampshire, Indiana, Michigan, and West Virginia also had small Republican gains less than the states listed. See Table 2.2 for full details.

of distinctions between these two groups of Western states disappeared. But by 1988 the pattern was strong enough for Bush to win with 59 percent or more of the vote in the Republican-trending states, and to either lose or to win with 53 percent or less of the vote in the Democratic-trending states of the West. In 1992, Clinton won all the Democratic-trending states in the region, breaking the supposed "lock" of the Republicans in the West with the best Democratic performance in the region since 1948. Bush, meanwhile, won all the Republican-trending states except Nevada, where a high Perot vote allowed Clinton to win with just 37 percent of the vote. By 1996, statewide distinctions in the Rocky Mountain region again became unclear when Clinton won previously Republican-trending Arizona, which he had lost in 1992, and Clinton lost previously Democratic-trending Montana and Colorado, which he had won in 1992. It is therefore easier to analyze Western voting trends at the county level.

As in the South, the vast majority of counties in the Western United States have trended Republican in the last forty years. And except in the Pacific Coast states, the exceptions to the Republican trend generally fit into the same five categories of exceptions found in the South, except that African American Democrats are replaced by a different racial minority: Native Americans. The most significant difference between the South and the West is that in the South, with the exceptions of black-majority New Orleans and the Florida counties containing elderly Northerners, all the Democratic-gaining areas are not major population centers and are far outweighed in statewide voting by major metropolitan areas trending Republican. In the West, almost all the counties in the heavily populated Pacific Coast areas have trended Democratic, as have the counties containing the large inland cities of Denver, Albuquerque, and Tucson.

So while every Southern state shifted strongly Republican in presidential elections between the 1950s and the 1980s, only five states in the West did the same: Arizona and lightly populated Idaho, Nevada, Utah, and Wyoming. In the other Western states, including population behemoth California, the Democratic trends of several population centers and certain other areas canceled out the Republican trends in the majority of counties, to register either a small statewide Democratic gain or, in the case of Oregon, a large gain in presidential elections since the 1950s.[16]

16. Alaska and Hawaii are excluded from this analysis, for they were not yet states during

Of all the Western counties showing Democratic gains since the 1950s, the heaviest population concentrations occur along the Pacific Coast. Every county that borders on the Pacific Ocean in Washington, Oregon, and California trended at least slightly Democratic in presidential elections between 1952 and 1988, with just two exceptions: suburban Ventura and Orange counties in California, which are directly to the north and to the south of Los Angeles County. The largest Democratic gains have occurred in the area with the West's second highest concentration of population: northern California. Democratic presidential candidates averaged at least 10 percent better in the 1980s than Adlai Stevenson in the 1950s in San Francisco County, the four coastal counties to its north (including wealthy Marin County), and the two coastal counties to its south. In San Francisco, Marin, and Santa Cruz counties, the Democrats of the 1980s averaged more than 20 percent higher than in the 1950s. Strongly liberal on cultural and environmental issues, these areas in the past frequently favored liberal Republicans who may have been more conservative on economic issues.[17] Voters in northern coastal California are apparently much less enthusiastic about Goldwater, Nixon, Reagan, and Bush Republicanism.[18]

Also showing significant Democratic shifts in California have been the heavily populated counties containing the cities of Oakland, San Jose, Santa Barbara, and Los Angeles. But keeping the statewide trend from being significantly Democratic have been the Los Angeles suburbs and the Central Valley agricultural region, which have become much more Republican.

The other areas of the West trending Democratic fit into the similar patterns found in the South, except that counties with Democratic gains in the inland West are more numerous and include more population than those in the South. First, a few counties dependent on mining economies

---

the 1952 and 1956 elections. Since statehood in 1959, Alaska, with its strong streak of libertarianism, has trended Republican for similar reasons to the non-Mormon Republican-trending sections of the Rocky Mountain states. Hawaii, meanwhile, with its "majority minority" population of Asian Americans and Native Hawaiians, and its liberal politics in general, has trended Democratic.

17. The area south of San Francisco includes an area once represented by liberal Republican Pete McCloskey in the U.S. House of Representatives. An opponent of the Vietnam War, McCloskey ran against President Nixon in some of the Republican primaries in 1972.

18. Like the Democratic-trending areas of Oregon, Marin County's favorite Republican presidential candidate in the last thirty-five years was Gerald Ford in 1976, when he ran against Jimmy Carter.

have shown strong Democratic trends similar to those in the Appalachian mining areas. Two of the four largest Democratic shifts in Montana (each more than 10 percent) have been in Silver Bow and Deer Lodge counties, where the old mining cities of Anaconda and Butte are located.

Second, counties in the West containing large academic communities have seen unusually large Democratic trends, especially because many of them are surrounded by areas that are shifting heavily Republican. Whitman County, Washington (Washington State University); Latah County, Idaho (University of Idaho); Missoula County, Montana (University of Montana); and Boulder and Larimer Counties, Colorado (University of Colorado and Colorado State University) all stand out as having had Democratic trends that are unusual or unusually high for their regions.

Related to the Democratic trends in relatively highly educated and culturally and environmentally liberal academic communities and Pacific Coast communities are the strong Democratic gains in lightly populated, tourist resort areas. The counties around Lake Tahoe in Nevada and California have seen large population growth, as has Teton County, Wyoming (Jackson Hole), which has had the largest Democratic shift in its state. In addition, most of the ski resort areas in Colorado have trended Democratic, especially Pitkin (Aspen) and San Miguel (Telluride) counties.[19] These Colorado ski resort counties were among John Anderson's best nationwide in 1980, and along with Denver and the university counties made Colorado the only state between New England and the Pacific Coast where Anderson received at least 10 percent of the vote that year.

Finally, counties of predominantly racial minority populations are trending Democratic in the West, as in the South. Hispanic counties in northern New Mexico and southern Colorado, like those in Southwest Texas, have been voting in increasing numbers for Democratic presidential candidates in the last forty years. Any Democratic trend among Hispanic voters in Southern California, however, is apparently being equaled or surpassed by Republican trends among non-Hispanic voters within the counties, except in Los Angeles.

And throughout the Rocky Mountain States, and in the neighboring states of North and South Dakota as well, counties containing large Indian reservations have become much more Democratic in recent years.

19. Eagle County, which includes Vail, is an exception here and has become more Republican. Vail in recent years has tended to attract an older and more conservative population as residents and tourists than Aspen or Telluride.

Shannon County, South Dakota, which contains the Pine Ridge Reservation and the town of Wounded Knee, and Sioux County, North Dakota, which contains part of the Standing Rock Reservation and the burial site of Sitting Bull, had the two highest Democratic shifts in the Midwest and the third and fifth highest in the entire United States between the 1950s and the 1980s. Apache County, Arizona, which includes part of the large Navajo Reservation, had the strongest Democratic trend in the Rocky Mountain States. (The other counties in the reservation also had Democratic gains.) The two counties with the largest Democratic shifts in Montana are also on reservations. Following the large spurt of growth among American Indian Rights movements in the 1960s, Native Americans on reservations began voting in larger numbers than in the past (for several decades of the twentieth century, they were not legally allowed to vote in many states), and perceived the Democrats as more hospitable than the Republicans, for the same reasons other relatively poor racial minority groups, such as African and Hispanic Americans, did.

Despite Democratic gains in many counties of the West inland from the Pacific Coast, though, the vast majority of counties in the region have trended Republican. Four explanations of the area's Republican gains seem strong, each applicable to a different part of the region, although in many parts of the West, more then one explanation likely applies.

Simplest to explain are the high Republican shifts in the counties of southeastern New Mexico. The area, nicknamed "Little Texas" and settled by Texans early in the twentieth century, has always been politically similar to neighboring parts of Texas and has been following the political trends of its namesake over the last forty years.[20] The Republican gains in southeastern New Mexico have canceled out statewide the strong Democratic gains in Hispanic and Native American northern New Mexico since the 1950s.

A similar phenomenon of Republican gains canceling out Democratic gains statewide has occurred in Colorado and Washington. Despite their often observed similarity to Oregon in cultural and environmental liberalism, and despite being two of the four Western states (along with Oregon and Hawaii) where Independent John Anderson won at least 10 percent of the vote in 1980, Washington and Colorado have not had the

20. Duncan, *Politics in America 1992*, 978.

same, strong statewide Democratic trend as Oregon.[21] One key reason for the difference in Washington and Colorado seems to be the presence of large numbers of military installations or naval shipyards in the states. El Paso County, which contains Colorado's second largest city of Colorado Springs, also contains the U.S. Air Force Academy, the army's large Fort Carson, and North American Air Defense Command (NORAD) head-quarters, and had the second highest Republican trend in the state.[22] The counties surrounding Seattle on Puget Sound contain several naval installations and have shifted Republican, as have the counties in south central Washington, which include Hanford Nuclear Reservation. Even in Hawaii, where Dukakis in 1988 bested Kennedy's percentage of the vote in 1960 in all of the state's counties, the lowest gain occurred in Oahu County, site of Honolulu, Pearl Harbor, and all the state's military bases. In Oregon, however, defense contractors and military installations are a fairly insignificant part of the economy.[23]

Most of the highest Republican gains among counties in the West have occurred in Utah, southeast Idaho, and a few neighboring counties in Nevada and Wyoming. As in eastern Oregon, the Mormon religion is predominant throughout this region, and this presents an anomaly for those who study political culture.

Many writers on regional and state political culture have noted the contributions of Daniel J. Elazar to their studies. Elazar has created a typology of three political subcultures in the United States that origi-nated in the colonial era and expanded geographically with the migra-tions of settlers across the nation. Designed for comparing local forms of government and policymaking processes, Elazar's typology has also been used to explain regional partisan preferences. The traditionalistic subcul-ture, rooted in the South, is centered on the preservation of existing social orders and in the past traditionally favored the Democratic party. The individualistic subculture, rooted in the Middle Atlantic States, is based on a politics of professional politicians and the pursuit of self-inter-

21. These four Western states and the six New England states were the only ten nationwide where Anderson received 10 percent or more.

22. Colorado Springs is also home to a growing fundamentalist Christian community.

23. Malone and Etulain, *American West*, 225. The lack of defense dollars in the state proba-bly resulted in part from Oregon always sending Republican delegations to Congress during the golden years of military buildup and pork barrel under Democratic presidents and Demo-cratically controlled Congresses between the 1930s and the 1960s. Oregon's first non-Republi-can senator of the period, Wayne Morse, is best known for being one of two in Congress to vote against the Gulf of Tonkin resolution.

ests and has mixed party loyalties. And the moralistic subculture, rooted in New England, includes a combination of entrepreneurial economics and community-based politics aimed at social and individual moral improvement and traditionally supported Republicans.[24]

Elazar's typology likely remains useful for the study of local politics. And at first glance, he seems to have captured almost perfectly a reason for the national partisan changes over the last forty years (although that was not the focus of his research). The areas settled by Southerners that he labels as traditionalistic have almost uniformly become more Republican, and the Northern areas settled by New England Yankees and Scandinavians that he labels moralistic have almost uniformly become more Democratic. However, Elazar's political cultures do not by themselves serve as a simple explanation for realignment, because not all groups within each assigned subculture have been politically changing in the same way as the rest of their subculture. The "traditionalistic" Hispanics of the Southwest have engaged in political patterns that are very different from those of Southern whites. The "moralistic" Dutch Reformed have not joined the other moralistic areas in trending Democratic. And, most conspicuous, the Western followers of a religion founded by New England Yankees in Upstate New York during a period of religious revivalism, the Mormons, have been shifting in the extreme opposite partisan direction from their fellow Yankee descendants.

The influence of the Mormon Church on Utah elections in this 70 percent Mormon state has long been debated by students of the state's politics. Frank Jonas has noted that the Mormon Church leaders' strong preference for Republicans, including open endorsements, was ignored by Utah voters in the 1930s and 1940s, who elected Democrats to Congress and chose Roosevelt for president by wide margins in every election.[25] Before that time, Utah voters had also generally shown Democratic party preferences, probably due to a sense of intolerance from the Northeastern and Midwestern Republicans who dominated the national government.

If Mormon voters do not always listen to their church's leaders, then perhaps in recent years they have been influenced by Utah media sources, many of which are owned by the Mormon Church organization. That

24. The most extensive explanation of Elazar's typology is Daniel J. Elazar, *Cities of the Prairie* (New York: Basic Books, 1970). A good summarized version is found in Elazar's *American Federalism: A View from the States*.

25. Frank H. Jonas, "Utah: The Different State," in Frank H. Jonas, ed., *Politics in the American West* (Salt Lake City: University of Utah Press, 1969), 332–333.

seems likely, but it would not explain the similar Republican trends of the Mormon sections of other Western states. What seems to be the best explanation for the realignment of Mormon voters toward the Republicans is the cultural conservatism preached by the church, which the national Republican party has promoted to gain Southern white voters and which seems increasingly out of step with the views of national Democratic party leaders.

Although not all church members follow their religious obligations closely, the Mormon social practices of abstinence from tobacco, alcohol, and caffeine, encouragement of large families and hard work, and respect for ancestral traditions are likely to have a strong impact on many or most people in an area where such values are promoted and accepted to such an extent.[26] These conservative social values are especially prominent in Utah County, which includes the city of Provo, the Singing Osmond Family home, and the large Brigham Young University campus. Utah County, with the second largest population in the state, has also had the highest Republican shift of any county in the state. Unlike other academic communities in the West, Brigham Young's influence is strongly Republican.

Along with Southern settlers, military installations, and Mormonism, a fourth likely source of Republican gains in the West was the Sagebrush Rebellion, which affected politics in all the Rocky Mountain states, but probably had its strongest impact in lightly populated ranching and grazing areas that have added to the Republican statewide trends of Nevada and Wyoming and the Republican trends in sections of Colorado and Montana. In 1979, the Nevada state government passed a law that claimed ownership of 49 million acres of federally owned land in the state without the national government's approval. Several other Western states followed suit. The 1980 Republican presidential candidate, Ronald Reagan, announced his support for the rebellion on the campaign trail, telling crowds to "count me in as a rebel."[27] The federal government at the time owned a majority of territory in Nevada, Wyoming, Idaho, Utah, and Alaska.

In previous years, Western Democratic politicians had gained popularity by bringing to their home states a good deal of federal money for

26. Barone and Ujifusa, *Almanac of American Politics 1992*, 1241–1242.
27. Richard H. Foster, "The Federal Government and the West," in Clive S. Thomas, ed., *Politics and Public Policy in the Contemporary American West* (Albuquerque: University of New Mexico Press, 1991), 79.

various economic development projects, including water diversion, while the rest of the nation paid little attention. By the late 1970s, however, a movement had begun among Democrats from outside the area to prevent the perceived further environmental destruction of Western lands and to promote the spread of native wildlife—angering local ranchers and others who used the land for economic purposes. The administration of Democratic President Carter did not help its party's situation in the region when it attempted to cut federal spending on local water projects and to place MX missiles under the desert of Utah and Nevada.[28] After President Reagan was elected and appointed a number of people hostile to the environmental movement to key positions that dealt with Western land issues, the rebellion temporarily seemed to dissipate.[29] But the perception of the national Democratic party as a party whose views were antagonistic to those who use Western lands for economic purposes did not disappear, and many rural Western areas have become much more Republican.

A combination of all the factors given so far for increased Republicanism in the West seems to be present in the most heavily populated Republican-trending sections of the West: Arizona and California's Central Valley agricultural region and Los Angeles suburbs. Settled in large numbers by Southerners earlier in the twentieth century, many of them "Okies" fleeing the Dust Bowl farm conditions of Oklahoma and Texas in the 1930s, Arizona and Southern California are also home to a huge number of defense contractors and military installations.[30] Touched somewhat by the Sagebrush Rebellion like the rest of the West, the areas also contain higher-than-average numbers of Mormons, although not in similar proportions to Utah or Idaho. The Republican trends in the areas may also have been reinforced by large numbers of conservative whites moving in who were either attached to military projects and bases or who were taking their families and fleeing the less wholesome social atmospheres of California's big cities.

28. Ibid.

29. Another Democratic president, Bill Clinton, may have served to revive the movement, whose most extreme elements have committed terroristic acts, such as the bombing of the federal building in Oklahoma City.

30. Suburban Orange County, known for its sometimes extreme conservatism, is among the Los Angeles area counties that have large numbers of residents descended from Dust Bowl refugees. In a previous Congress, Orange County was represented in the House of Representatives by John Schmitz, who was chosen as the 1972 presidential candidate of the organization that remained from George Wallace's presidential bid in 1968, and who was later dismissed from the executive council of the John Birch Society for extremism. Duncan, *Politics in America 1992*, 218.

Despite the differing explanations for Republican gains in various parts of the West, almost all the Republican-trending areas had one political factor in common: since at least World War II and into the 1960s, they had tended to favor moderate Democrats over other types of politicians. Just as the South for years elected conservative Democrats and is now voting Republican in presidential elections, and many Northern areas for years elected moderate and liberal Republicans and are now voting more Democratic in presidential elections, voters in most inland parts of the West have sensed a divergence in the ideology of the local Democrats they usually supported and the national Democratic party.

Realignment toward the Republicans in much of the inland West has in general covered political offices at all levels. The region has not only increased its percentage of the vote for Republican presidential candidates, but is also electing more Republicans to Congress, state legislatures, and state offices than it did forty years ago. For that reason, a 1987 volume edited by Utah political scientists Peter Galderisi, Michael Lyons, Randy Simmons, and John Francis, which is one of the best recent books on regional realignment, asserted that, despite mixed evidence of realignment in the rest of the nation, "in the Mountain West . . . the case for a Republican realignment is almost irrefutable."[31] Although, as shown earlier, the Republican realignment does not cover all parts of the region, and although the realignment has been more of a gradual nature than the result of a "critical" election, Mountain West realignment would seem to meet the standard realignment theory criterion espoused by some political scientists, that changes in partisan voting behavior must occur at all office levels for a true realignment to have occurred. But despite increased Republican voting for most offices, one important government position remained outside the trend for years.

Table 7.2 compares the average Republican percentages of the vote for president and for governor in the two decades of the 1950s and the 1980s in the eight Mountain West states. The table shows again the division among the states in presidential elections—five trending Republican and three trending slightly Democratic. However the states are united (with the possible exception of New Mexico) on trends for another office—in governor's races all the states voted less Republican in the 1980s than in

---

31. Peter F. Galderisi and Michael S. Lyons, "Realignment Past and Present," in Galderisi et al., *Politics of Realignment*, 3.

Table 7.2. Average Republican vote for president and governor in eight western states, 1950s and 1980s (percentage)

State	President 1950s	President 1980s	Governor 1950s	Governor 1980s
Utah	62	71	52	47
Idaho	63	67	53	49
Wyoming	61	65	51	42
Arizona	60	62	51	36
Nevada	60	63	50	37
New Mexico	57	56	50	50
Montana	58	56	51	41
Colorado	60	57	49	39

SOURCES: 1950s from *Congressional Quarterly's Guide to U.S. Elections*; 1980s from *The Almanac of American Politics* (Washington, D.C.: National Journal, 1984–1992).

NOTE: 1980s averages include the 1980 presidential election and therefore differ from other figures in this and other chapters, which include only the 1984 and 1988 presidential elections.

the 1950s, usually switching from majority Republican to majority Democratic.[32]

In the Galderisi volume, two political scientists dismissed the Democratic performance in gubernatorial elections as a "fluke" but offered no persuasive reasons for the disparity with elections for other offices.[33] If they had considered the concept of a federalized realignment rather than the traditional idea that realignments must occur at all office levels, they may have come up with a solid explanation.

As stated earlier, just as most politicians elected in many Northern areas were moderate and liberal Republicans in earlier years, most popular politicians in much of the Mountain West used to be moderate Democrats.[34] In Congress, many Western Democrats more liberal than those in

32. In two states, third-party efforts played an important role in 1980s gubernatorial elections. In Utah, Republican candidates still averaged a higher share of the vote than Democrats in the 1980s, but the Democrats' share went up to 46 percent from 39 percent in the 1950s. In Arizona, a third-party effort by a Democrat in 1986 kept the official party's candidates' average down to 48 percent in the 1980s, compared with 49 percent in the 1950s, while Republican candidates dropped to 36 percent in the 1980s from 51 percent in the 1950s. In all the other states, the Republican decline has been matched by corresponding Democratic gains.

33. Eric R. A. N. Smith and Peverill Squire, "State and National Politics in the Mountain West," in Galderisi et al., *Politics of Realignment*, 48.

34. Mountain West Democrats in Congress usually averaged somewhere between 50 and 75 for liberalism in the ratings by the Americans for Democratic Action group. See ibid., 43, for some of these ratings averages.

the South but more conservative than those in other parts of the nation served for dozens of years, some of the best known being Arizona's Carl Hayden, Idaho's Frank Church, Nevada's Howard Cannon, Utah's Frank Moss, and Wyoming's Gale McGee, all U.S. senators for long periods from states currently trending Republican. The latter four all lost reelection during the height of the Sagebrush Rebellion between 1976 and 1982. Hayden, who had the longest congressional service in American history between 1912 and 1969, spent much of his time in the Senate acquiring federal money for Arizona water and road projects, as did other Mountain West Democrats for their states.[35]

One of the newer Democrats in Congress was Representative Bill Orton, first elected in 1990, who represented eastern sections of Utah in a district that contains Brigham Young University and in which Bush beat Dukakis in 1988 by 69 percent to 29 percent and Reagan won 77 percent in both 1980 and 1984.[36] Orton, a Mormon, promoted himself as a conservative Democrat, voted that way during his first term in Congress, won easily in 1990, and won reelection easily in 1992 and 1994 before losing in 1996.

While a few other Democrats have also been able to win congressional elections in the Mountain States in recent years, despite Republican presidential majorities, Democratic gubernatorial candidates in the region were so successful in the 1980s that they won more often than not and on the average gained increasing margins over Republican opponents. Many of these Democratic governors were fairly liberal, but like congressional Western Democrats of the past, the governors portrayed themselves as defenders of the state against outside interests and maintained images as typical Westerners, unlike the urban or suburban liberal image of many national Democrats.

In 1994, the Mountain West had five Democratic governors. Idaho Governor Cecil Andrus, a former secretary of the interior under President Carter, refused to allow further federal shipments of nuclear energy waste into the state or to allow Idaho water to be diverted to California. Andrus also used his reputation as a lifelong hunter to oppose the National Rifle Association's opposition to a ban on armor-piercing bullets. Wyoming Governor Mike Sullivan wore a trademark Stetson while campaigning, and New Mexico Governor Bruce King, a rancher, spoke with a thick

---

35. Peirce and Hagstrom, *Book of America*, 732.
36. Duncan, *Politics in America 1992*, 1507–1508.

Texas or Southwest-style accent.[37] All five of the Mountain West Democratic governors, including Nevada's Bob Miller and Colorado's Roy
Romer, emphasized their pragmatic approaches to government with a
focus on local economic development and improved public education,
rather than any ideological stances. This emphasis on pragmatism is common in modern governors across the nation, but in the Mountain States,
before 1994, Democrats campaigning as typical Westerners against frequently more ideological Republicans were unusually successful, considering the Republican trends in other types of elections in the region.

Colorado, Wyoming, and Idaho had Democratic governors for the entire 1980s decade, and all eight Rocky Mountain states, including the
three headed by Republicans in 1994, had Democratic governors during
at least half of the 1980s.[38] Some might call this a fluke and attribute it
just to the individual personal popularity of various Democratic governors, but flukes are generally not part of consistent long-term patterns.
Between the 1950s and the 1980s, all the Mountain States became more
Democratic in their choices for governor, even while most of the states
trended Republican for other offices.[39]

Instead of some dealignment phenomenon in which voters show no
consistent voting habits, the Mountain West pattern might better be described as a federalized realignment. In this federalized realignment, the
old moderate Democratic preferences of many voters have turned into
Republican votes for offices at the federal level, where modern Democrats
are often perceived as too urban or too liberal for Western tastes, but
grew even more Democratic in governors' races, where the Democrats
consistently upheld images that were different from those of their national party.

Between 1952 and 1988, most Northern states realigned toward the
Democrats in presidential elections while Republican gains were espe-

37. *The Almanac of American Politics* volumes contain brief political descriptions of all governors, including the information used here.

38. Arizona would also have had a Democratic governor for the entire decade, except that
in 1986 Republican Evan Meacham was elected with only 40 percent of the vote against two
Democrats, one running as an independent. Meacham was impeached and removed from office
in 1988 and replaced by a Democrat.

39. In the 1994 national Republican landslide, Andrus and Sullivan retired and were replaced by Republicans, while King lost reelection. Miller and Romer won reelection and in
1998 are the only two Democratic governors of the Mountain West. At this writing, it is too
early to tell whether 1994 was just a fluke or whether gubernatorial elections of the future will
begin to align more closely with Mountain West voting in federal elections.

cially strong in the South and in many parts of the West. In all states and regions, the form of the realignment was frequently different from the form in neighboring areas. Then, in 1992, a Texas multibillionaire named Ross Perot entered the presidential race as an independent, scrambling at least temporarily the voting patterns of previous elections. His impact and role in voting trends will be examined in Chapter 8.

Chapter Eight

The National Elections of 1992–1996

The Northern realignment in presidential elections that has occurred since 1952 became most apparent in 1992 and 1996, when the Democratic presidential candidate won every state in the Northeast, a majority of Midwestern states, and all the Pacific Coast states (except Alaska). The Republican presidential candidates in those years were left with victories in most Southern states, several lightly populated Rocky Mountain states, four lightly populated Great Plains states, and Indiana. One hundred years earlier, in 1896, the electoral map in presidential elections looked almost exactly the opposite, and many of the best Democratic states of forty to fifty years ago are now among the most Republican states, while formerly solid Republican states like Vermont, Iowa, and Oregon are among the most Democratic.

Also in 1992 and 1996, the purported Republican lock on the electoral college, in which many believed that a solidly Republican South and West would make it nearly impossible for Democrats to win presidential elections, proved to be a less than formidable barrier. Some saw the 1992 Democratic victory as resulting mainly from the independent candidacy of Ross Perot and the perceived weak economic conditions of the nation, and not as evidence of any permanent realignment. Indeed, evidence from the 1994 congressional elections seemed to indicate, if anything, a possible strong realignment all in favor of the Republicans.

Perot's candidacy and Bush's unpopularity may indeed have been the key to Democratic victory in 1992, especially because Clinton himself was not an overwhelmingly popular candidate in many Democratic-trending areas.[1] Yet 1992 may have also symbolized the potential for an alternative lock on the electoral college, in which Northern Democratic candidates could expect to win most of the Northeast, Midwest, and Pacific Coast states in the future. This new electoral college advantage for Democrats held together in 1996.

While many at first attributed Clinton's victory in 1992 solely to temporary phenomena, such as Perot and the economy, the decline in the Republican presidential vote in the North has been an ongoing trend that became visible to many only in the 1992 election, and economic conditions probably only temporarily exaggerated that trend, as they always do in every election. But while Perot's candidacy and Bush's unpopularity did not play a role in which states were Clinton's best, Perot's performance did disrupt some of the distinctive Republican and Democratic trends of the last forty years either temporarily or permanently, and Clinton was greatly helped by displeasure with Bush; voters' similar lack of enthusiasm for Clinton allowed him to win with 3 percent less of the vote than Dukakis received four years earlier.

Although during his first year as president Clinton converted himself somewhat to a deficit-cutting advocate and was forced by the Republican takeover of Congress in 1995 to support the idea of a balanced budget, he campaigned in 1992 with old-style Democratic economic populist messages that had little appeal in many of the old Republican areas that had trended Democratic, some of which voted for Clinton's opponents Paul Tsongas and Jerry Brown in primary elections. Clinton was saved in many of these formerly Republican areas that were crucial to his November victory by his stances to the left of Bush on cultural and environmental issues and by the overwhelming unpopularity of Bush in the areas. However, the Perot factor should not be ignored, for the Perot vote cut heavily into specific groups and parts of the nation, some of which had been drifting from Republican to Democratic in recent years, and some of which had been drifting in the opposite direction.

Third parties in American history have long been seen as playing crucial roles in political realignments, either as waystations for voters switching parties or for pushing established parties to adopt new policies that

1. Clinton in 1992 did better than Dukakis in 1988 in only thirteen states, including ten of the eleven states of the old Confederacy (all but Texas) and the two Southern border states of Maryland and Kentucky. Dukakis did better than Clinton in all the non-Southern states except New Hampshire. The two did about the same in Delaware and New Jersey. Of course, it is unknown how well Clinton would have performed without Perot on the ballot.

change their social bases. Some of the most significant such parties of the past included the antislavery parties before the Civil War, the Populists of the 1890s, and the La Follette Progressives of the 1920s. Since 1952, four third-party presidential candidacies have attracted significant shares of the national vote: Wallace in 1968, Anderson in 1980, and Perot in 1992 and 1996.

As discussed in earlier chapters, the Wallace and Anderson votes fit neatly into realignments that have occurred throughout the nation, although each represents an opposite pattern. Wallace's highest vote shares came in the South, and his two best states outside the South and its border region were Idaho and Nevada. These two states and the entire South have trended Republican since 1952, and Wallace can be seen as a representative of disgruntled conservative Southern and Western former Democrats. Wallace's worst performances were in New England, the Upper Midwest, and the Pacific Coast region, and those were the areas where Anderson did best while doing his poorest throughout the entire South. Anderson should be seen as a representative of disgruntled liberal and moderate former Republicans in the parts of the nation where he did well, as all these areas have trended Democratic since 1952. Data from earlier chapters confirmed these interpretations of the Wallace and Anderson votes.

Perot, on the other hand, did not fit into such a neat partisan or ideological pattern in 1992. Perot finished with 22 percent or more of the vote that year in all six New England states, with 19 percent or more of the vote in every Midwestern state except Illinois, and with at least 21 percent of the vote in every Western state except New Mexico. Meanwhile, in the eleven states of the old Southern Confederacy, Perot managed to climb above 14 percent only in Florida and in his home state of Texas. Perot's support may therefore seem much more similar to that of the Anderson Democratic-trending areas than to that of the Wallace Republican-trending areas, but a closer look at the voting data will indicate that is not so. Perot's popularity was much more widespread across the nation than that of either Wallace or Anderson, and Perot's areas of greatest strength in 1992 cut across the realignment of the last forty years and combine certain Democratic trending areas and certain Republican trending areas, as Table 8.1 shows.

The key to understanding the Perot phenomenon in the 1992 voting results is to avoid attributing his popularity to one single issue or characteristic and to realize that the source of his appeal varied by region. While

Table 8.1. Relationship of many variables to the Ross Perot for President vote in 1992 in counties in four states

Variable	Upstate New York	Iowa	Oregon	South Carolina
Democratic gains, 1952–88***	−.02	−.16	−.51**	−.74**
Anderson '80	−.37**	−.15	−.44**	n.c.
Wallace in '68	.25	.12	.16	n.c.
English	.29*	−.12	−.15	.52**
Irish	−.38**	−.06	.40*	.68**
German	.39**	.32**	.26	.31*
Dutch	−.12	−.36**	n.c.	n.c.
Norwegian	n.c.	.11	.01	n.c.
African American	n.c.	n.c.	n.c.	−.78**
Catholic	−.15	.10	−.56**	.07
Episcopal	.00	n.c.	.03	.07
Church of Christ	.32*	.09	.12	n.c.
Mormon	n.c.	n.c.	.26	n.c.
Southern Baptist	n.c.	n.c.	.18	.35*
College grad	−.54**	−.31**	−.58**	.18
High school grad	−.31*	−.26**	−.39*	.32*
Per capital income	−.31*	−.32**	−.25	.67**
Population	−.10	−.37**	−.60**	.16
Farm Area	n.c.	.42**	n.c.	n.c.

SOURCE: See source notes for Tables in Chapters 6 and 7. 1992 election data is from *The World Almanac and Book of Facts 1993* (New York: Pharos Books, 1992).

EXPLANATIONS OF VARIABLES: See tables in Chapters 6 and 7.

NOTE: "n.c." indicates that figures were not calculated for that state.

  *Significant at the .05 level.
  **Significant at the .01 level.
***Negative correlations in Oregon and South Carolina indicate high Perot vote in areas with highest Republican gains in the period. Democratic gains of 1960–1988 tabulated for Upstate New York.

Perot did very well for an independent candidate in most counties in the nation, he did especially well in certain types of counties. Some of these counties did have similar traits in all regions of the nation. Although Perot did his worst in the South—Wallace's best region of the nation in 1968 and Anderson's worst in 1980—within individual states Perot's popularity seemed opposite to Anderson's and to have more in common with Wallace's. Perot also did better in areas with lower levels of educational achievement than in well-educated areas across the nation. (In South Carolina, high educational levels become significantly negatively related to a high Perot vote once other factors were taken into account.) Therefore, Perot is clearly not associated with the county characteristics of high educational levels, which have been strongly related to a high Anderson vote and strong Democratic gains in every state studied in the last forty years.

However, educational levels have not been the only factors in realignment in recent years, and it is with other factors that Perot cuts across both Democratic and Republican trends. In 1992, Perot presented at least three sets of political images, which were interrelated but separate enough to gain different types of emphasis in voter decisions among national regions. First, Perot cast himself as the one candidate willing to tell the American public the truth about the budget deficit and proclaimed that balancing the budget would be his highest priority (although he sometimes named other "highest" priorities as well). Second, Perot cultivated an image as a plain-speaking, truth-telling populist who took pragmatic positions on all issues and would not talk in doublespeak like typical politicians and Eastern Establishment types do (including Clinton and Bush, he implied). And third, Perot sold himself as the candidate least likely to spend a lot of time in office worrying about foreign affairs. Besides his campaign emphasis on fixing domestic problems once in office, a tactic similar to the Clinton campaign, Perot opposed the Persian Gulf War and the North American Free Trade Agreement, both of which Bush had supported wholeheartedly and Clinton had supported with somewhat less enthusiasm.

These three political images of Perot each played an at least partially independent role in Perot's success in different regions. Perot received 22 percent or more of the vote in every New England state, including Maine, his best state in the nation, where he beat Bush to finish second (in the state that Bush usually used as a second home while in the White House). In Upstate New York, Perot received more than 20 percent of the vote in all but five counties.[2] Once all factors in Upstate New York are taken into account, only three shown above remain significantly related to a high Perot vote: low educational levels, high percentages of English ancestry, and high percentages of German ancestry. Democratic gains in Upstate New York (and in Vermont) were related to high educational levels and

2. Excluded from this analysis for reasons stated in Chapter 6 are upstate Tompkins County, dominated by the Cornell University and Ithaca College academic communities, and the downstate counties in the New York City area, where Perot did considerably worse than upstate, dragging his statewide percentage down to only 14 percent.

high English ancestry, so the Perot vote cuts across the Democratic re-alignment of the upstate region.[3]

Perot did poorly in all highly educated areas across the nation, but his strong performance in English counties in New York merits special attention. By the mid-1800s, Upstate New York was dominated by New England Yankee populations that had moved west, and many or most of the area's current English ancestry residents are descendants of those settlers. New England Yankees have a reputation for frugality, derived both from their personal behavior and from their political opposition to the perceived free-spending habits of national Democrats during the 1930s. While promises to cut spending and raise taxes to balance the budget are not usually popular anywhere in the nation, such proposals probably find their most enthusiastic audience among New England Yan-kees (outside of New Hampshire), who have long supported Republicans who supported balanced budgets but were liberal on other issues. These voters apparently found appealing Perot's economic pragmatism mixed with his usually moderate views on other issues. After the 1992 election, two former New England U.S. senators, Republican Warren Rudman of New Hampshire and Democrat Paul Tsongas of Massachusetts, formed a new political group (the Concord Coalition) aimed at focusing public attention on the budget deficit problem.

While the German areas of Upstate New York, like the German areas of Pennsylvania and Ohio, have not been a source of Democratic gains over the last forty years, these upstate areas did go strongly for Perot. In the upper Midwest, however, where Germans from different backgrounds generally immigrated to the United States later than those in the East, German areas not only gave Perot some of his highest vote percentages as in New York, but in Iowa these areas had also trended heavily Demo-cratic in the previous two decades.

Several authors have noted the tendency of Midwest Germans to show isolationist views when voting in reaction to the two world wars and the Korean War (see Chapter 6). Opposition to interventionist foreign poli-cies is probably one key reason for the declining Republican vote in mainly German counties in Iowa during the 1970s and 1980s. Once all factors are taken into account in Iowa, high levels of German ancestry,

---

3. A cursory glance at voting data for the small number of counties in Vermont and Maine reveals that Perot seemed to do best in the more rural, less educated parts of these states, including the English and French areas.

high dependence on agriculture, and low levels of Dutch ancestry and low income or educational levels are all related to a high Perot vote. As in Upstate New York, the Perot vote cut across Iowa's Democratic realignment, which has included German areas and well-educated areas.

Iowa's most Dutch counties remained loyally Republican, and Perot had a minimal impact in them. Perot's best performances came in rural, agriculturally oriented German counties, where his image as the candidate least likely to get involved in overseas obligations apparently helped him steal previously Democratic voters from Clinton. In Minnesota, Perot also did particularly well in the state's most German counties. A *Congressional Quarterly Weekly Report* following the 1992 election noted that the decline in Clinton's vote from Dukakis's vote four years earlier was especially severe in the upper Midwest and claimed there were signs of a Republican countertrend (although Bush did much worse too than he had four years earlier).[4]

The article cited a *Des Moines Register* reporter as attributing the Clinton falloff in Iowa to the state's stronger economy in 1992, to Clinton's lack of campaigning in the state due to the uncontested Iowa caucuses, and to 1988 being an aberration when Iowa seemed more Democratic than it really was.[5] The reporter also mentioned Perot as a possible factor, although not as a more important one than the others he listed, but he may have been wrong in calling 1988 an aberration, considering the state's trend over the previous twenty years. The data above seem to indicate that Perot's somewhat isolationist views may have been the key factor in Clinton's falloff in the state and in much of the Upper Midwest, a region where Germans are the most numerous ethnic group. To label this a Republican countertrend in 1992 was an error, as Bush also did worse in 1992 in the region and was certainly not gaining votes among those who thought the United States should be less involved in world affairs.[6]

In Upstate New York and Iowa, Perot support cut across the Democratic realignment by being especially high in some areas that had trended Democratic and some that had not, but in Oregon the Perot vote is

---

4. *Congressional Quarterly Weekly Report*, December 12, 1992, 3813.

5. Ibid.

6. In the 1994 congressional elections, Republicans picked up many seats in the Midwest. It is possible that the end of the Cold War and the resurgence of isolationist views within the Republican party will end or turn back the Republican losses of the previous forty years in the future, but the Democrats again did well in the Great Lakes part of the region in 1996.

clearly negatively related to the Democratic gains of the last forty years and is instead positively related to the Republican realignment of the eastern part of the state. Perot did very well throughout Oregon, winning at least 20 percent of the vote in every county and at least 25 percent of the vote in all the state's counties outside its northwestern portion. But once all factors are taken into account, Perot did less well in the more populated, highly educated areas that have been trending Democratic, but did especially well in the rural, less-educated areas of Oregon that have generally been trending Republican. Ethnic and religious factors did not seem to play a key role in Oregon's Perot vote.

A high Perot vote is not related to recent Republican trends every-where in the West, for in the Rocky Mountain States, some of the catego-ries of counties, such as lightly populated resort areas and depressed mining areas, where Democrats have been gaining, also supported Perot in relatively high numbers. But for the most part, Perot did best in the parts of the West that have been shifting toward the Republicans in presi-dential elections. Perot's vote was lower in coastal California than in inland California, for example. And Utah, with the strongest Republican trends in the West, was also the one state in the nation where Perot beat Clinton, who finished third.

The strong Perot performance in every state in the West, given the political histories of the states, would seem to be clearly related to his somewhat stereotypical Western image as a no-nonsense problem-solving self-made man, not to his balanced-budget promises or isolationist tend-encies. Most of the Mountain West's popular recent Democratic gover-nors projected the same image. Perot may have appealed to Western antagonism toward Eastern Establishment types and shifty politicians in the same way that Populists won over the same areas a one hundred years earlier.

In South Carolina, a relatively high Perot vote was also likely in the counties that have most trended Republican. White suburban and small-city areas with lower educational levels typified the best Perot counties. However, in no county did Perot receive more than 17 percent of the vote, which is even worse than he did in all the Democratic-trending counties of Oregon. Perot, a native Texan, seemed to portray more of a Western image than a Southern image, and Bush, the transplanted Texan, and Clinton, the native Arkansan, shut out Perot in the South more than in any other region. In addition, Perot's mostly libertarian stance on social issues probably played much better in the West than in the South.

Following the 1992 presidential election, political movements and speeches critical of the national government seemed to grow exponentially. Many reasons can be offered for this phenomenon. A president had just been elected who won only 43 percent of the national vote, who broke longtime hegemony by the Republicans in the office, and who did not seem to inspire trust or respect for the office due to certain alleged past personal behavior. The Perot candidacy had apparently brought to light some questionable government accounting methods, showing that people had been promised constantly expanded spending programs when there was not enough revenue to pay for them. The Democratic party had controlled Congress for forty years and its leadership had seemed to grow complacent there with the perks of office and a tedious and complicated lawmaking process. And perhaps most important, but not often given enough credit, is that a group of Republicans in Congress, often led by Newt Gingrich of Georgia, had decided that the best opportunity for Republican takeover of the institution lay in direct attacks on the institution itself as well as the whole federal government.

Assisted by talk radio personalities like Rush Limbaugh, Republican leaders and activists around the nation attacked Congress as consumed with power, unresponsive to the true needs of the public, and completely ineffective. Within Congress, Republicans made sure their public claims were exposed or came true through speeches on the floor of the House of Representatives to the C-Span audience, where various scandals and bills bottled up by House leaders were discussed, or through Senate filibusters, where almost all major bills supported by the Democratic majority were killed by the Republican minority led by Bob Dole in 1994.

Combined with the usual midterm effect, where a president's party always loses seats in Congress halfway through the presidential term, President Clinton's perceived ineffectiveness his first two years in office, and other factors mentioned above, the Republican antigovernment, anti-Congress campaign succeeded spectacularly in the 1994 congressional elections; there were huge gains for the party in both chambers of Congress, and a Republican takeover of that branch of government. The 1994 election was a national sweep for the Republicans; they gained House seats in every region of the nation except New England, where there was no overall partisan change in the delegation.[7]

7. The only state in the nation where Democrats actually gained seats in the U.S. House in 1994 was Rhode Island, where Patrick Kennedy, son of Massachusetts Senator Ted Kennedy, won the seat vacated by Ronald Machtley in his unsuccessful run for governor in the primary against Lincoln Almond.

Table 8.2. Regional partisan gains in 1996 U.S. House elections

New England	+4D	South	+4R
Mid-Atlantic	+2D	Great Plains	+1R
Great Lakes Midwest	+5D	Rocky Mountain West	+2R
Pacific Coast	+5D		
	+16D		+7R

NOTE:

Mid-Atlantic = New York, New Jersey, Pennsylvania, Delaware, Maryland, West Virginia.

Great Lakes Midwest = all Midwest states on the Great Lakes and Iowa and Missouri.

South = Eleven states that formed the Confederacy, plus Kentucky and Oklahoma.

Great Plains = North Dakota, South Dakota, Nebraska, Kansas.

Rocky Mountain West = Idaho, Montana, Wyoming, Nevada, Utah, Colorado, Arizona, New Mexico.

But in the aftermath of the Republican takeover, as an entirely Southern leadership took over, as the Republicans began to follow some of the same practices they had previously criticized under the Democrats, as the Republican Speaker of the House became enmeshed in his own scandals, and as the antigovernment rhetoric died down now that many of the people who led it were running the Congress, the public returned to the voting habits it had established in the previous forty years of realignment. This was apparent in 1996 (see Table 8.2).

In the regional coalitions that voted Republican for president in 1896 and Democratic for president in 1996, there were major Democratic gains for the House of Representatives. But these were partially offset by the regional coalition that voted for losing candidates Bryan in 1896 and Dole in 1996, where Republicans had gains in the House in 1996. A regional partisan breakdown of House membership in August 1997 presents similar evidence of regional division in U.S. politics (see Table 8.3).

Democrats have a solid majority of House seats in the Northern states; the Republican majority is created by the Southern coalition with Mountain and Plains states. This is a first in U.S. history. Until the 1970s, longtime Democratic control of Congress was possible only through the

Table 8.3. Regional partisan membership in the U.S. House, August 1997

New England	4R-19D*	South	82R-55D
Mid-Atlantic	35R-42D	Great Plains	8R-1D
Great Lakes Midwest	47R-49D	Rocky Mountain West	21R-3D
Pacific Coast	31R-38D		
	117R-148D		111R-59D

*Vermont Independent Bernard Sanders is counted with the Democrats.

Table 8.4. Regional partisan membership in the U.S. Senate, 1987 and 1997

	1987	1997		1987	1997
New England	6R-6D	6R-6D	South	8R-18D	18R-8D
Mid-Atlantic	4R-8D	4R-8D	Great Plains	3R-5D	3R-5D
Great Lakes			Rocky Mountain		
Midwest	8R-8D	8R-8D	West	10R-6D	12R-4D
Pacific Coast	6R-4D	4R-6D			
	24R-26D	22R-28D		21R-29D	33R-17D

overwhelming support for the party in the South. Throughout all but four years of the 1940s, 1950s, and 1960s, Republicans held a majority of non-Southern seats in the House. Now the situation is reversed—instead of creating the Democratic majority in the House, the South allows for Republican dominance.

The situation is similar in the U.S. Senate. In 1987, Democrats held a 55–45 majority in that chamber. In 1997, the Republicans held a 55–45 majority. Table 8.4 demonstrates the cause of that change. Between 1987 and 1997, there was a shift of ten seats toward the Republicans in the Senate. During that same period, that same number of Senate seats switched from Democrat to Republican in the South. There has been no national trend toward the Republicans in the Senate in the last ten years; there has been a regional Southern trend toward the Republicans. In 1997 the Democrats still had a majority of Senate seats from the Northern coalition of states, and two more seats than they did ten years earlier.

The 1994 congressional elections created great gains for the Republicans, but the 1996 elections and the composition of the following Congress indicate that the real gains are regional and that many parts of the nation are becoming more Democratic in congressional elections, as they are in presidential elections. The 1996 presidential election also demonstrated the persistence of the regional realignments, especially with the decline in the vote for Ross Perot. Contrary to the assertions of many Republicans in 1992 that Perot took most of his votes away from Bush, Perot won over a wide variety of voters that year, including in areas where former Republicans had grown disenchanted with their party and started voting Democratic for president long before 1992.

The 1996 presidential election results bear this out. With the decline of the Perot vote in 1996, Clinton's margin of victory over the Republican candidate grew significantly in every New England state and in the Upper Midwest. Dole improved the Republican share of the two-party

Table 8.5. Gain in partisan vote in presidential elections, by state, 1992–1996 (percentage)

State	Democrat	Republican	State	Democrat	Republican
Maine	+13	+1	Montana	+3	+9
New Hampshire	+10	+1	Idaho	+6	+10
Vermont	+7	+1	Wyoming	+3	+10
Massachusetts	+14	−1	Nevada	+7	+8
Rhode Island	+13	−2	Utah	+8	+11
Connecticut	+11	−1	Colorado	+4	+10
New York	+10	−3	New Mexico	+3	+5
New Jersey	+11	−5	Arizona	+10	+5
Pennsylvania	+4	+4	North Dakota	+8	+3
Delaware	+8	+2	South Dakota	+6	+6
Maryland	+4	+2	Nebraska	+6	+7
West Virginia	+4	+2	Kansas	+2	+15
Ohio	+7	+3	Virginia	+4	+2
Illinois	+5	+3	North Carolina	+1	+6
Indiana	+5	+4	South Carolina	+4	+2
Wisconsin	+8	+2	Georgia	+2	+4
Michigan	+8	+3	Florida	+9	+1
Minnesota	+7	+3	Alabama	+2	+2
Iowa	+7	+3	Mississippi	+3	−1
Missouri	+4	+7	Louisiana	+6	−1
Alaska	+3	+11	Texas	+7	+8
Washington	+7	+5	Arkansas	+1	+1
Oregon	+4	+6	Tennessee	+1	+4
California	+5	+5	Kentucky	+1	+4
Hawaii	+9	−5	Oklahoma	+6	+5

SOURCE: 1996 election figures from *Congressional Quarterly Weekly Report*, January 18, 1997, 188.

NOTE: Figures are rounded to the nearest whole number.

vote in seven of the eight Rocky Mountain states. Once Perot was less of a factor, most Rocky Mountain Perot voters in 1992 went Republican for president in 1996, while most Northeast and Midwest Perot voters in 1992 went Democrat. The Perot voters of 1992 split more evenly else-where in the nation in 1996, including the Pacific Coast states, which contain coastal regions that have trended Democratic in recent years and inland regions that have trended Republican. (See Table 8.5.)

Following the 1994 congressional elections, it seemed that a national trend toward the Republicans might be under way. But by Election Day 1996, Republicans had elected an entirely Southern congressional leader-ship and had provided increased visibility for Southern Republican politicians and traditional Southern conservatism in politics. The North seemed to react by electing more Democrats and creating large Democratic majorities from the North in both houses of Congress.

Increased support for Democrats in the North was also clear in the presidential election, where Clinton increased his margin of victory over that of 1992 in every one of the Northeastern states and in all the Midwest states bordering on the Great Lakes. Clinton increased his percent of the vote by 10 percent or more in eight states between 1992 and 1996, including five of the New England states, New York, New Jersey, and also in Arizona. Dole actually did worse than Bush in eight states, including Connecticut, Massachusetts, Rhode Island, New York, New Jersey, Hawaii, Mississippi, and Louisiana. His drop-off in the latter two states may be due to increased African American participation in favor of Clinton.

Some might wonder how there can be a Northern regional trend toward the Democrats when Republicans control the governor's seat in the three Southern New England states as well as every state bordering the Great Lakes except one.[8] The answer is that the United States is a federal system and that a federalized form of realignment has been taking place for the last forty years. While the national Republican party increasingly projects an image that is more popular in the South than in the North, Northern Republicans are free to set their own agendas at the state level, where they rarely emphasize cultural conservatism or patriotism. Instead they have focused on cutting back certain spending programs and opposition to perceived corruption and incompetence in Democratic urban areas, the same kinds of issues that historically formed the basis of Northern Republican support. It is perfectly rational for an electorate to vote Republican at the state level while rejecting that party at the national level.

While the congressional elections of 1994 seemed to indicate a national Republican victory, the results of 1996 again showed the true regional nature of recent Republican success. The Republican failure to create a permanent North-South coalition for the party will be examined in further detail in Chapter 9, as will the implications and future possibilities of regional coalitions within both parties.

8. In mid-1997, Indiana was the only state bordering on the Great Lakes with a Democratic governor. Oddly, Indiana is also the only state bordering on the Great Lakes that voted Republican in the 1992 and 1996 presidential elections.

Chapter 9

—————

Realignment in the 1990s

Some might continue to discount any sort of regional realignment toward the Democrats in national politics over the last forty years, especially by pointing out the 1994 Republican takeover in Congress. But the Republican majorities in Congress have been largely created by the South and the Rocky Mountain West. Among the Northeastern, Great Lakes Midwestern, and Pacific Coast States, a solid majority of House members and senators remain Democrats—unlike forty years ago, when more of these areas were represented by Republicans. This is not to ignore the significance that Republican gains in the South and in the Rocky Mountain States had in establishing Republican congressional dominance in 1995, but merely to state that important Democratic gains have also been made in many Northern states.

In some states, the realignment has been federalized in nature. Upstate New York has trended strongly Democratic in presidential elections—but Republican in state legislative elections, where issues different from those at the national level dominate. Many local Republican parties in the North retain a moderate or liberal flavor and therefore retain support in state and local elections while losing it in presidential elections. This explains the popularity of Republican senators, such as Jeffords of Vermont, Chafee of Rhode Island, and Snowe of Maine, and the widespread popularity of a number of Republican governors in the states around the Great Lakes in the 1990s.[1]

---

1. Just as partisan preferences between the national and state levels can differ depending on the images national and state party politicians project, there can also be a difference in partisan preferences between the state and local levels. Elections for state legislature, for instance, take

Finally, the Northern realignment of 1952–1988 was caused in large part by disaffection with the increased conservatism and increased role of the South in the Republican party, and possibly less by any great attraction to Democratic policies and presidential candidates. For that reason, many voters in traditionally moderate and liberal Republican areas may be voting regularly for Democratic presidential candidates without feeling any strong attachments to the party. This may explain why Ross Perot did so well in New England, the Upper Midwest, and all the Western states in 1992.

The congressional election results of 1994 therefore did not negate the previous forty-year realigning trends, and the 1996 elections demonstrated the continuing gains the Democrats were making in the Northern United States. Such dramatic changes in partisan voting behavior should rightfully be labeled an electoral realignment.

Many realignment theorists have assumed that true realignments must be critical in nature, characterized by quick re-formation of electoral coalitions that had been torn apart by major crises affecting the nation. Such critical realignments create new national partisan majorities in which groups of voters in an area consistently choose the same party in voting for all office levels. Evidence such as increased split-ticket voting, lack of any clear critical election or major crisis that tore old coalitions apart, and a decline in partisan identification in national public opinion surveys have convinced many of these realignment theorists that the United States has been in a long period of dealignment, or decline of party significance for voters.

However, a revised approach to realignment, which does not try to cram recent voting trends into some pattern that was somehow automatic over one hundred years of American elections, shows that the political changes of the last forty years are significant and consistent and continue to revolve around the two major parties. Some recent challenges to the theory of realignment have disputed the supposedly critical nature of some electoral shifts of the past.[2] Such challenges should not imply,

---

place in fairly small constituencies where personal ties and traditional voting habits often continue to play a much stronger role than any ideological or issue-oriented concerns, which become more significant in statewide and national elections. Therefore, many Southern and urban Northeastern states continued to have lopsided Democratic state legislative majorities in the 1990s, while many Great Plains and Rocky Mountain states continued to elect solid Republican state legislatures, with all these local election preferences not necessarily connected to any recent changes in partisan preferences in national or statewide elections.

2. See Shafer, ed., *The End of Realignment?*

though, that the concept of realignment is useless as a tool for political analysis; rather, the demise of critical realignment theory should allow political analysts to focus instead on the much more common secular trends that have occurred in American history, especially in the last forty years. Although in Vermont and in other Northern states, certain election years, such as 1964, 1972, and 1980, have played an especially strong role in reshaping partisan choices among voters, no one election stands out, and a continuing shift in many areas has persisted with every election over the last forty years.

The overuse of public opinion surveys to analyze electoral behavior has also led to an undervaluation of recent political trends. Good surveys have the potential to provide the best measurements of individual political opinions. Yet reliance on surveys limits other types of analysis, which often provide fuller, if not better, explanations for changes in voter behavior. Examining the roles of political parties and historical voting trends places recent electoral changes in their proper context—a context that is missing from typical survey analysis, which can lead to an inability to recognize the type of realignment that has occurred since 1950.

If survey data contradict voting data in measuring electoral behavior, it seems odd to dismiss the voting data, which come from actual choices for political leaders, in favor of survey data results, which only measure hypothetical choices. If more voters in the 1990s say they are independent than in the 1950s, and fewer now identify with a party in a poll, so what? It is what voters do on Election Day that has any significance; if individual voters are consistently choosing a party in elections, even if they tell a pollster that they belong to another party or are independent, then the voter's electoral choice is what should be analyzed to determine the extent of realignment.

One reason many voters may claim to be independent is that they favor one party in presidential elections and another in state or local elections. According to classical realignment theory, such people are in a state of political confusion or are losing any partisan preferences. But if a voter in Vermont likes balanced budgets and environmental protection, that voter may oppose Republican presidential candidates who promise tax cuts, increased defense spending, and weaker government regulations, but still support local Republicans whose views are closer to those of the voter. And a voter in South Carolina may oppose national Democrats who seem to hold values very different from the voter, but support local Democrats who share the values of the local culture. Are these voters in a state of confusion? Are partisan labels meaningless to these voters? The answer to both questions is no; these voters have undergone a federalized realignment, a form of partisan change that is not recognized by theorists of historical realignments during periods when voters were not easily able to split ballots, had less education, were more frequently illiterate, and had no access to a national media.

In addition, those who look for realignments only on a national or a large regional basis miss the rich variety of trends occurring among and within the states. Vermont has become much more Democratic, while New Hampshire has become much more Republican. Western Oregon has shifted strongly Democratic; eastern Oregon has done the opposite. Such trends do not appear in national public opinion surveys.

Because no crisis has occurred to tear apart old coalitions, completely reshape one or both parties, and create a new majority party, some would still deny the existence of a realignment in the last forty years. However, the key components of realignment have taken place, even if not as dramatically as in previous times. The Republican and Democratic coalitions of the 1930s, the last accepted period of critical realignment, have been torn apart since then, over such issues as civil rights, defense policy, crime, cultural values, and environmentalism. Only those who believe mistakenly that all politics has an economic basis could have missed this. The national Republicans have reshaped themselves to attract Southern and Western conservatives; the national Democrats now appeal more to Northern liberals and to the better educated. Republicans between 1968 and 1988 became the new majority party in presidential elections and since 1994 have been the congressional majority.

The case that realignment no longer exists in the modern era and that dealignment of partisan preferences has taken over fails to persuade, once recent political trends are understood under a modern set of circumstances rather than forced to fit in with types of voting behavior from one hundred years ago. In most Northern states over the last forty years, well-educated areas, Yankee and Norwegian areas, and German sections of the Upper Midwest have all become increasingly Democratic, while neighboring less-educated areas, French Canadian, Scotch-Irish, and Mormon areas and Dutch sections of the Midwest, have maintained or increased their Republican preferences in presidential elections. The North in general is more Democratic; the South is much more Republican.

The implications for policymaking of these electoral changes may not be as great as in realignment at all electoral levels, since continuing, although diminishing, support for moderate Republicans in the North and for moderate and conservative Democrats in the South is expressed in congressional and gubernatorial elections. But in presidential elections and policymaking, the implications may be significant. A Democratic party controlled by Northerners in which Southern and rural Western conservatives and moderates have had declining influence has led to dramatic policy changes in such areas as civil rights for African Americans, other racial minorities, and women, a decline in the postwar consensus of promoting American interests abroad through military might or covert operations, and stronger promotion of environmental causes over economic development. A Republican party in which Southern views play an increasingly important role has lent voice to those concerned with a decline in moral values among the American public, added increased feelings of American nationalism and patriotism to public discourse, and helped to diminish support for government welfare programs for those who cannot or will not work for a living.

Even on economic matters, changes in each party's social base have helped to affect policy positions. The Republicans lost some of their balanced-budget reputation in the 1980s not only by advocating tax cuts, which were popular in New Hampshire and many suburban areas, but also by advocating greatly increased defense spending, most of it distributed to contractors and military bases in the South and in the West. The Democrats—which to Northern Yankees no longer stood out as the party of fiscal irresponsibility compared with the Republicans—called for balanced budgets and for spending cuts more frequently than they did during the heyday of Keynesian economics.

In its first months in office, the Clinton administration overturned Republican presidents' policies on abortion, family-related leaves from jobs, gay rights, and environmental protection of Northwestern forests. And after Clinton's attempt to appeal to 1930s and 1960s Democratic constituencies with a "jobs stimulus" package failed to pass Congress with little concern shown among previously Republican constituencies, the president switched to promotion of deficit-cutting economics and decried the allegedly irresponsible Republican economics of the previous twelve years. By 1997, a Democratic president and a Republican-dominated Congress were working together to trumpet their compromise agreement to create the first balanced budget since 1969.[3]

---

3. The political claims and cheers by political leaders were probably not adequately scruti-

Critical elections, if they ever existed, are probably a phenomenon of the past when less-educated voters unexposed to a national media went to the polls, chose a party, and went home. Most of these voters of the past chose their party in response to local political pressures or issues of the moment that swept the nation, or to register their affiliation with some sort of cultural grouping, either local, regional, ethnic, or religious, that was opposed to some other cultural grouping. While critical realignments have not endured, some of the old motivations behind long-term voting behavior have. During the last forty years of secular realignment, cultural groupings in historic political opposition seem to have shifted in opposite partisan directions, almost as if in direct reaction to each other.

Between the Civil War and 1976, all Democratic victories in presidential elections included a Solid South electoral base that usually provided the margin of victory. This history led most purveyors of political wisdom since the 1950s to repeat adages like "The Democrats have never won a presidential election without Texas." Such wisdom led Democratic presidential candidate Michael Dukakis to choose conservative Texas Democratic Senator Lloyd Bentsen as his running mate in 1988, in a futile attempt to win Southern states in the election. Dukakis squandered valuable campaign time in Southern states he had no chance of winning, while announcing he planned to win the region, and Bentsen gave speeches telling Southern voters he had been chosen specifically as a symbol of the importance of the region to Dukakis.[4]

In 1992, before that year's election, Earl and Merle Black published a book that contended that a presidential candidate had to win in the South to be victorious. They asserted: "Today one looks at the South and sees America. There is abundant reason to pay close attention to future political developments in the South, for it now shapes the trends and sets the pace of national political outcomes and processes. Above all, this is the portrait of a *vital* South, a region once again at the center of struggles to define winners and losers in American politics."[5]

In November 1992, the Democrats won the presidency while losing Texas. Far from being an integral part of the Democratic victory, the

---

nized by the press. Most of the credit for any future balanced budgets belongs to the expanding economy, which expands revenue collections, and the tax cuts and spending increases contained in the "balanced budget" agreement of 1997 actually prolong the period before which a balanced budget may actually occur.

4. Lamis, *The Two-Party South*, 305–306.
5. Black and Black, *The Vital South*, 366.

South positioned itself as the most supportive region of losing Republican candidate Bush. Clinton did win five states in the region: his home state of Arkansas, Al Gore's home state of Tennessee, neighboring Louisiana and Kentucky, and by a tiny margin, Georgia, where Perot won enough white voters to take away a Bush victory.[6] But Bush won all other states in the South, including the region's three largest: Texas, Florida, and North Carolina. Clinton could easily have won nationally without winning any Southern states.[7] The electoral college map in 1996 looked similar in the South, with Clinton winning the same states he won in 1992, with the exceptions of Florida, which he won only in his second presidential election, and Georgia, which he lost in his second run.

For years, national Democratic leaders and political analysts seemed reluctant to give up the idea that Democratic presidential victories depend on the South based on the party's history. Yet they never ventured to look at the political history of that other major party since the Civil War—the Republicans, who won almost all presidential elections between 1860 and 1928 while losing Texas and the South. If the Democrats were to begin winning in all the old traditionally Republican areas, they could obviously win presidential elections even while losing traditionally Democratic areas to the Republicans.

Just as a New Deal Democratic coalition that contained both blacks and Southern whites was doomed to disintegrate, a Republican strategy to add Southern whites to the party while keeping a Northern Yankee base was not viable. Although some have tried to describe historical American politics as economically class-based, using theories derived from studies of European politics, most studies of American elections have more accurately noted that long-term voting behavior in the United States has usually revolved around cultural and social differences, partly because of the types of issues politicians have often emphasized in their campaigns. When the Republicans began to gain votes among Southern white voters, the Democrats gained in reaction many votes among the historical political opponents of the South, Northern Yankees. When the Democrats increased their support among highly educated voters, the

6. Clinton also won West Virginia, which is sometimes classified as a Southern state, but Dukakis won there also, and the state has long voted differently from other Southern states.

7. Of course, even though the South was not vital to presidential victories in 1992 and 1996, the region was vital to the Republican takeover of Congress in 1994. Therefore, Black and Black were partially right about the region defining the winners and losers of American politics.

Republicans gained support among less-educated voters.[8] The United States remains a nation where electoral realignments are based on cultural and social differences.

Parties must recognize that attempts to expand a party coalition through appeals to new cultural, regional, or social groupings may at the same time put in jeopardy the party's support among opposite groupings in the party's traditional base. In 1896, Democrats took a gamble by adopting many of the themes of the smaller Populist party. They lost the gamble, winning for one year some small Western and Midwestern states where Populism was popular, but losing important support in much larger Northeastern and Midwestern states. For the next thirty years, only the South voted consistently Democratic, while the rest of the nation almost always solidly backed Republican presidential candidates.

In the 1930s, the Democrats under Roosevelt gambled and won. The party attracted many Northerners back to the party while holding on to the South, at least temporarily, allowing the party to win a series of presidential elections. Yet trying to add liberal Northerners and African Americans to a coalition previously based on Southern cultural conservatism proved to be an impossible combination to maintain, as the newcomers to the party eventually crowded out the views of the Democrats' oldest group of supporters in the South.

The Republicans took advantage of the inevitable breakup of the Democratic coalition by putting together their own presidential electoral majority in which white Southerners were added to the party's traditional base of Yankees and other Protestants living in suburbs, small cities, small towns, and rural areas throughout the Northeast, the Midwest, and the Pacific Coast states. For twenty years between 1968 and 1988, this new Republican coalition was strong enough to win five presidential elections. But as with the Democratic coalition of the 1930s, the ideas and values of the newcomers to the party eventually crowded out or turned away many in the party's longtime traditional base of support, and by 1992, enough moderate and liberal Republicans were abandoning the party to hand Bush the first defeat for an incumbent Republican president since 1928.

When parties reach out to expand their coalitions by emphasizing new

8. Although educational levels are related to the economic factor of income levels, they are distinct enough variables that most statistical analysis in previous chapters showed that recent realignments have been based much more on the social differences in educational levels than on strictly class-based income levels.

messages, ideas, or values, they inevitably do damage to the old portions of their coalition. Sometimes, as in the 1930s, the gains to the party outweigh any losses, and sometimes the losses overwhelm the gains, as with the Democrats in the 1890s. This persistent aspect of partisan realignments may seem a bit obvious, but its importance to the study of political parties and elections in the United States has so far been underemphasized by those who study these topics.

One hundred years ago, despite the slogan, Maine always voted Republican whether the rest of the nation did or not. Almost sixty years ago, Roosevelt campaign manager James Farley joked about Vermont joining trend-setting Maine in giving Alf Landon his eight electoral votes in the 1936 presidential election. Since then, others have discounted the political significance of these small Northern New England states and looked to the South as the source of key national political trends of the future.[9]

But in 1996, Vermont returned to a position of political prominence in national voting trends, giving Democrat Clinton his fifth largest margin of victory in the nation and his largest margin of victory outside the more urban Democratic states of Massachusetts, Rhode Island, New York, and Hawaii. The state with the unmatched record of voting Democratic for president only once (in 1964) since the Republican party's formation in the 1850s emerged as one of Republican Bush's four worst states in 1992 and Dole's worst five states in 1996.

And the regional divisions and trends at the national level were also clear in 1996. In 1936, the Republicans nominated Kansan Alf Landon for president. On the day of the election, his best states, and the only two he won, were Maine and Vermont. His worse two states were South Carolina and Mississippi. In 1996, the Republicans nominated Kansan Bob Dole for president. On the day of the election, South Carolina and Mississippi were among Dole's best nine states; Maine and Vermont were among his five worst.

In 1996 as in 1936, as Maine went so went Vermont. The difference is that this time both went for the Democrats—and this time, as Maine and Vermont went so went the nation. And in this 1996 election as well as in 1992, the gradual Northern realignment toward the Democrats became even more apparent when it overwhelmed the much more trumpeted realignment of the South toward the Republicans that had helped cause the realignment of the North toward the Democrats in the first place.

9. See Black and Black, *The Vital South,* or Phillips, *The Emerging Republican Majority,* as examples.

Bibliography

For the convenience of the reader, the Bibliography is divided into seven sections: Books and Articles on American National Politics; Books and Articles on American Regional and State Politics; Newspapers and Political Periodicals; Local Newspapers Located in Newsbank; Sources of Election Statistics; Sources of Demographic Statistics; and Other Works Cited.

Books and Articles on American National Politics

Abramson, Paul A.; Aldrich, John H.; and Rohde, David W. *Change and Continuity in the 1988 Elections.* Washington, D.C.: Congressional Quarterly, 1991.

Benson, Lee. *The Concept of Jacksonian Democracy.* Princeton: Princeton University Press, 1961.

Burnham, Walter Dean. *Critical Elections and the Mainsprings of American Politics.* New York: W. W. Norton & Company, 1970.

Campbell, Angus; Converse, Philip E.; Miller, Warren E.; and Stokes, Donald E. *The American Voter.* New York: John Wiley & Sons, 1960.

Carlin, David R., Jr. "Facing the Canons." *Commonweal*, January 27, 1984, 38.

Elazar, Daniel J. *American Federalism: A View from the States.* New York: Harper & Row, 1984.

Faber, Harold, ed. *The Road to the White House.* New York: New York Times, 1965.

Fiorina, Morris P. *Congress: Keystone of the Washington Establishment.* New Haven: Yale University Press, 1989.

Fischer, David Hackett. *Albion's Seed.* Oxford, Eng.: Oxford University Press, 1989.

Gastil, Raymond D. *Cultural Regions of the United States.* Seattle: University of Washington Press, 1975.

Ginsberg, Benjamin, and Shefter, Martin. "A Critical Realignment? The New Politics, the Reconstituted Right, and the 1984 Election." In Nelson, Michael, ed., *The Elections of 1984.* Washington, D.C.: Congressional Quarterly, 1985.

Jacobson, Gary C. *The Politics of Congressional Elections.* Boston: Little, Brown & Company, 1987.

Kelley, Robert. *The Cultural Pattern in American Politics: The First Century.* Washington, D.C.: University Press of America, 1979.

Kessel, John H. *The Goldwater Coalition.* Indianapolis: Bobbs-Merrill Company, 1968.

Key, V. O., Jr. *American State Politics: An Introduction.* New York: Alfred A. Knopf, 1956.

————. "Secular Realignment and the Party System." *Journal of Politics* 21 (1959), 198–210.

————. "A Theory of Critical Elections." *Journal of Politics* 17 (1955), 3–18.

Ladd, Everett Carll, Jr., and Hadley, Charles D. *Transformations of the American Party System*. New York: W. W. Norton & Company, 1978.

Lipset, Seymour Martin, ed. *Party Coalitions in the 1980s*. San Francisco: Institute for Contemporary Studies, 1981.

McCormick, Richard P. *The Second American Party System*. Chapel Hill: University of North Carolina Press, 1966.

Nie, Norman H.; Verba, Sidney; and Petrocik, John R. *The Changing American Voter*. Cambridge, Mass.: Harvard University Press, 1979.

Peirce, Neal R., and Hagstrom, Jerry. *The Book of America*. New York: W. W. Norton & Company, 1983.

Petrocik, John R. *Party Coalitions*. Chicago: University of Chicago Press, 1981.

Phillips, Kevin P. *Boiling Point*. New York: Random House, 1993.

————. *The Emerging Republican Majority*. New Rochelle, N.Y.: Arlington House, 1969.

————. *Mediacracy*. Garden City, N.Y.: Doubleday & Company, 1975.

————. *The Politics of Rich and Poor*. New York: Random House, 1990.

————. *Post-Conservative America*. New York: Random House, 1982.

Piven, Frances Fox, and Cloward, Richard A. *Poor People's Movements*. New York: Vintage Books, 1979.

Pomper, Gerald M., ed. *The Election of 1988*. Chatham, N.J.: Chatham House Publishers, 1989.

Rae, Nicol C. *The Decline and Fall of the Liberal Republicans from 1952 to the Present*. New York: Oxford University Press, 1989.

Schattschneider, E. E. *The Semi-Sovereign People*. New York: Holt, Rinehart & Winston, 1960.

Shafer, Byron E., ed. *The End of Realignment?* Madison: University of Wisconsin Press, 1991.

Shefter, Martin. *Political Crisis / Fiscal Crisis*. New York: Basic Books, 1987.

————. "Regional Receptivity to Reform: The Legacy of the Progressive Era." *Political Science Quarterly* 98 (1983), 459–483.

Silbey, Joel H.; Bogue, Allan G.; and Flanigan, William H., eds. *The History of American Electoral Behavior*. Princeton: Princeton University Press, 1978.

Silbey, Joel H., and McSeveney, Samuel T., eds. *Voters, Parties, and Elections*. Lexington, Mass.: Xerox College Publishing, 1972.

Smallwood, Frank. *The Other Candidates*. Hanover, N.H.: University Press of New England, 1983.

Sundquist, James L. *Dynamics of the Party System*. Washington, D.C.: The Brookings Institution, 1983.

Swierenga, Robert P., ed. *The Dutch in America*. New Brunswick, N.J.: Rutgers University Press, 1985.

White, Theodore H. *The Making of the President 1964*. New York: Atheneum Publishers, 1965.

Books and Articles on American Regional and State Politics

Benjamin, Gerald, and Brecher, Charles, eds. *The Two New Yorks*. New York: Russell Sage Foundation, 1988.

Black, Earl, and Black, Merle. *The Vital South*. Cambridge, Mass.: Harvard University Press, 1992.

Burton, Robert E. *Democrats of Oregon: The Pattern of Minority Politics 1900–1956*. Eugene: University of Oregon Books, 1970.

Bryan, Frank M. *Yankee Politics in Rural Vermont*. Hanover, N.H.: University Press of New England, 1974.

Bryan, Frank M., and McClaughry, John. *The Vermont Papers*. Post Mills, Vt.: Chelsea Green Publishing, 1989.

Colby, Peter W., and White, John K., eds. *New York State Today*. Albany: State University of New York Press, 1989.

Doyle, William. *The Vermont Political Tradition and Those Who Helped Make It*. Barre, Vt.: Northlight Studio Press, 1984.

Elazar, Daniel J. *Cities of the Prairie*. New York: Basic Books, 1970.

Ellis, David Maldwyn. *New York: State and City*. Ithaca, N.Y.: Cornell University Press, 1979.

Fenton, John H. *Midwest Politics*. New York: Holt, Rinehart & Winston, 1966.

Gabriel, Richard A. *The Political Machine in Rhode Island*. Kingston, R.I.: Bureau of Government Research, University of Rhode Island, 1970.

Galderisi, Peter F.; Lyons, Michael S.; Simmons, Randy T.; and Francis, John G. *The Politics of Realignment: Party Change in the Mountain West*. Boulder, Colo.: Westview Press, 1987.

Hill, Ralph Nading. *Yankee Kingdom: Vermont and New Hampshire*. New York: Harper & Row, 1973.

Johansen, Dorothy O. *Empire of the Columbia*. New York: Harper & Row, 1967.

Jonas, Frank H., ed. *Politics in the American West*. Salt Lake City: University of Utah Press, 1969.

Key, V. O., Jr. *Southern Politics*. New York: Alfred A. Knopf, 1949.

Lamis, Alexander P. *The Two-Party South*. New York: Oxford University Press, 1984.

Lockard, Duane. *New England State Politics*. Princeton: Princeton University Press, 1959.

Madison, James H., ed. *Heartland*. Bloomington: Indiana University Press, 1988.

Malone, Michael P., and Etulain, Richard W. *The American West*. Lincoln: University of Nebraska Press, 1989.

Margulies, Herbert F. *The Decline of the Progressive Movement in Wisconsin*. Madison, Wis.: State Historical Society of Wisconsin, 1968.

McLoughlin, William G. *Rhode Island: A History*. New York: W. W. Norton & Company, 1986.

Meeks, Harold A. *Time and Change in Vermont: A Human Geography*. Chester, Conn.: The Globe Pequot Press, 1986.

Milburn, Josephine F., and Doyle, William. *New England Political Parties*. Cambridge, Mass.: Schenkman Publishing Company, 1983.

Morrissey, Charles T. *Vermont*. New York: W. W. Norton & Company, 1981.

Peirce, Neal R. *The New England States*. New York: W. W. Norton & Company, 1976.

Reed, John Shelton. *The Enduring South*. Chapel Hill: University of North Carolina Press, 1986.

———. *Southerners*. Chapel Hill: University of North Carolina Press, 1983.

Rogin, Michael Paul. *The Intellectuals and McCarthy: The Radical Specter*. Cambridge, Mass.: M.I.T. Press, 1967.

Rosenthal, Alan, and Moakley, Maureen, eds., *The Political Life of the American States*. New York: Praeger, 1984.

Thomas, Clive S., ed. *Politics and Public Policy in the Contemporary American West*. Albuquerque: University of New Mexico Press, 1991.

Veblen, Eric P. *The Manchester Union Leader in New Hampshire Elections*. Hanover, N.H.: University Press of New England, 1975.

Wall, Joseph Frazier. *Iowa*. New York: W. W. Norton & Company, 1978.

White, John Kenneth. *The Fractured Electorate: Political Parties and Social Change in Southern New England*. Hanover, N.H.: University Press of New England, 1983.

Winters, Richard. "Political Choice and Expenditure Change in New Hampshire and Vermont." *Polity* 12 (1980), 598–621.

Newspapers and Political Periodicals

Barone, Michael, and Ujifusa, Grant. *The Almanac of American Politics*. Washington, D.C.: National Journal.

Congressional Quarterly's Politics in America. Washington, D.C.: Congressional Quarterly.

Congressional Quarterly Weekly Report.

The East Greenwich (R.I.) Pendulum.

The New Republic.

Newsweek.

The New York Times.

The Wall Street Journal.

The Washington Post National Weekly Edition.

Local Newspapers Located in Newsbank

Barre (Vt.) Times-Argus.

Boston Globe.

Burlington (Vt.) Free Press.

Hartford (Conn.) Courant.

Providence (R.I.) Journal.

Rutland (Vt.) Daily Herald.

White River Junction (Vt.) Valley News.

Sources of Election Statistics

America Votes. Washington, D.C.: Congressional Quarterly Elections Research Center, 1956–1992.

Burnham, Walter Dean. *Presidential Ballots 1836–1892*. Baltimore: Johns Hopkins University Press, 1955.

Congressional Quarterly's Guide to U.S. Elections. Washington, D.C.: Congressional Quarterly, 1985.

Cox, Edward Franklin. *State + National Voting in Federal Elections 1910–1970*. Hamden, Conn.: Archon Books, 1972.

The Journal-Bulletin Rhode Island Almanac. Providence, R.I.: Providence Journal-Bulletin.

Manual for the General Court of Massachusetts. Boston: Causeway Print.

Manual for the Use of the Legislature of the State of New York. Albany: New York Department of State.

New Hampshire Manual for the General Court. Office of the Secretary of State of New Hampshire.

Official Count of the Ballots Cast. Rhode Island Board of Elections.

Primary and General Elections: Vermont. Office of the Secretary of State of Vermont.

The Rhode Island Manual. Office of the Secretary of State of Rhode Island.

Vermont Legislative Directory and State Manual. Office of the Secretary of State of Vermont.

The World Almanac and Book of Facts. New York: World Almanac Publications, 1983–1993.

Sources of Demographic Statistics

Allen, James Paul. *We the People: An Atlas of America's Ethnic Diversity*. New York: Macmillan Company, 1988.

Almanac of the Fifty States. Palo Alto, Calif.: Information Publications, 1992.

Census of Iowa for the Year 1885. Des Moines: Iowa Secretary of State, 1885.

County and City Data Book 1988. Washington, D.C.: U.S. Department of Commerce, Bureau of the Census, Washington, D.C., 1988.

1980 Census of Population: General Social and Economic Characteristics. Washington, D.C.: U.S. Department of Commerce, Bureau of the Census, Washington, D.C., 1983.

1980 Census of Population and Housing: Summary Characteristics for Governmental Units and Standard Metropolitan Statistical Areas. Washington, D.C.: U.S. Department of Commerce, Bureau of the Census, Washington, D.C., 1982.

1980 Census of Population and Housing for Vermont: Summary Tape Files. U.S. Department of Commerce, Bureau of the Census, Washington, D.C.; printed by Vermont State Data Center: Burlington, Vt., 1982.

1987 Statistical Profile of Iowa. Iowa Department of Economic Development, Des Moines, 1987.

Quinn, Bernard, et al. *Churches and Church Membership in the United States 1980*. Atlanta, Ga.: Glenmary Research Center, 1982.

State + Metropolitan Area Data Book 1991. Washington, D.C.: U.S. Department of Commerce, Bureau of the Census, Washington, D.C., 1992.

Statistical Abstract of the United States: 1991. Washington, D.C.: U.S. Department of Commerce, Bureau of the Census, Washington, D.C., 1991.

Wright, Marion I., and Sullivan, Robert J. *The Rhode Island Atlas*. Providence: Rhode Island Publications Society, 1982.

Other Works Cited

Bartlett, John. *Familiar Quotations*. Edited by Emily Morison Beck. Boston: Little, Brown & Company, 1980.

Bohle, Bruce. *The Home Book of American Quotations*. New York: Dodd, Mead & Company, 1967.

Editor and Publisher International Year Book 1991. New York: Editor & Publisher Company, 1991.

Woods, Henry F. *American Sayings*. New York: Essential Books, 1945.

Index

About the Author

Robert W. Speel is Assistant Professor of Political Science at Penn State Erie—
The Behrend College.